Opera
Guide 36

Fanny Persiani who sang Rosina in 'The Barber of Seville' at Covent Garden in 1847 and 1848 (Opera Rara)

Preface

This series, published under the auspices of English National Opera and The Royal Opera, aims to prepare audiences to evaluate and enjoy opera performances. Each book contains the complete text, set out in the original language together with a current performing translation. The accompanying essays have been commissioned as general introductions to aspects of interest in each work. As many illustrations and musical examples as possible have been included because the sound and spectacle of opera are clearly central to any sympathetic appreciation of it. We hope that, as companions to the opera should be, they are well-informed, witty and attractive.

Nicholas John
Series Editor

36

The Barber of Seville / Moses
Il Barbiere di Siviglia / Moïse et Pharaon

Gioachino Rossini

Opera Guide Series Editor: Nicholas John

Published in association with
English National Opera and The Royal Opera
assisted by a generous donation from The Baring Foundation

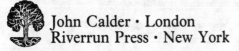

John Calder · London
Riverrun Press · New York

First published in Great Britain, 1985 by   First published in the U.S.A., 1985 by
John Calder (Publishers) Ltd.,   Riverrun Press Inc.,
18 Brewer Street,   1170 Broadway,
London, W1R 4AS   New York, NY 10001

BRITISH LIBRARY CATALOGUING IN PUBLICATION DATA

Rossini, Gioacchino
   The barber of Seville = il barbiere di Siviglia; Moses = Moïse et Pharaon — (Opera
   guide; 36)
   I. Operas — Librettos
   I. Title   II. Rossini, Gioacchino. Moïse et Pharaon   III. Sterbini, Cesare
   IV. Dent, Edward J.
   V. Moody, John   VI. Moody, Nell   VII. Balochi, G.L.   VIII. Jouy, V.J.
   Etienne de   IX. English National Opera   X. Royal Opera   XI. Il barbiere
   di Siviglia *English and Italian*   XII. Series
   782.1'2   ML50.P.835

ISBN 0-7145-4080-3

AMERICAN LIBRARY OF CONGRESS CATALOG NUMBER 85-52162

Typeset in Plantin by Margaret Spooner Typesetting, Bridport, Dorset
Printed by Camelot Press Ltd, Southampton

Contents

List of Illustrations

Contributors

Philip Gossett is Professor of Music at the University of Chicago. He is the general editor of the new critical edition of Verdi, editor of the Rossini edition, and a director of the Fondazione Rossini in Pesaro.

John Rosselli is Reader in History at the University of Sussex, and the author of *The Opera Industry in Italy from Cimarosa to Verdi*.

Marco Spada is a graduate in the history of music at the University of Rome. He is currently working with the University of Chicago Press and the Fondazione Rossini in Pesaro.

Pierluigi Petrobelli is director of the Istituto di Studi Verdiani, Parma and Professor of Music at the University 'La sapienza' of Rome.

Richard Bernas is a conductor and musician actively involved in contemporary music. This has not prevented him from sustaining a lifelong interest in the works of Verdi, Rossini and opera in general.

Rossini: the Serious and the Comic

Philip Gossett

Whether or not Beethoven told Rossini that Italians were unsuited to serious opera and that he should 'make more *Barbers*', as the oft-repeated and probably fictitious anecdote would have it, the twentieth century, until recently, has viewed the composer almost entirely from the vantage point of the great comic operas: *The Italian Girl in Algiers, Cinderella* and, most significantly, *The Barber of Seville*. That there were many more serious operas among Rossini's works than comic ones encouraged the view that the former were somehow indistinguishable from one another. The ten Neapolitan operas written between 1815 and 1822, while Rossini was music director of the Teatro San Carlo, nine of which were serious, became an undifferentiated list of names, when they were mentioned at all. The three serious operas for the French stage were rarely produced (a fate they shared with most compositions prepared for the Opéra during the nineteenth century). When they did turn up, they were frequently rewritten to suit the needs of an improperly-cast prima donna.

Yet the remarkable differences in tone among the great comic operas, despite important stylistic similarities, should have given us pause. If Rossini's muse was so unsuited to serious subjects, why did he continue choosing them? There was a question of prestige, to be sure — the composition of *opera seria* was considered a more dignified and worthy task in the early nineteenth century — but by the time Rossini had reached the age of thirty in 1822, he was the undisputed reigning master of operatic stages throughout Europe. He was as free to compose precisely what he wanted as any other musician in the century, and from 1817 until the end of his active career as a composer for the stage he chose to concentrate his attention almost exclusively on serious opera.

Italian composers of the early nineteenth century lived in a chaotic, yet vital, theatrical world, surrounded by imperious prima donnas jealous of their prerogatives, harried impresarios responsible to both political authorities and the public, and able (though rarely masterful) librettists frantically seeking to ply their craft under severe constraints of time.[1] They produced works which have, rightly or wrongly, been characterised by those who enjoy this repertory as 'bel canto opera' and by those whose feelings are more ambivalent as 'canary opera'.[2] The sheer number of compositions for the stage by Rossini (some 40) or Donizetti (upwards of 70) can too easily encourage facile generalisations about the speed with which they composed, their supposed flippant or pliant attitudes, and the stylistic uniformity of their music. These critical commonplaces are neatly summarised in a facetious anecdote about Rossini's method of composition. He was composing in bed, the story begins, when a sudden gust of wind blew away a sheet of music paper he had practically filled. Rather than get up, the indolent composer took a new sheet and began again. That succinctly was supposed to sum up Rossini's laziness, endless invention, and meagre artistic conscience.

1 See Rosselli: *The Opera Industry in Italy from Cimarosa to Verdi: The Role of the Impresario* (Cambridge, 1984)
2 See reviews of the ROH 1985 revival of Rossini's *The Lady of the Lake*.

Cultural contexts, stylistic generalisations, anecdotes: all combine to encourage certain attitudes towards Rossini's operas. How we think about a work, after all, is crucial to how we perform it, listen to it, and criticize it. If Rossini's serious operas, in particular, are primarily vehicles for 'canaries', what matters is the quality of the birds paraded on stage, not the realisation of the work as a whole or the sensitivity of the conductor or director. Failure to give primary emphasis to the whole, or a poorly conducted and misdirected performance lead, circularly, to a continuing belief in the triviality of a work, and attempts to penetrate these surfaces emerge as 'special pleading'.

Rossini's serious operas need no special pleading, any more than do his comic ones, but they do need to be approached without prejudices and stereotyped views. Their sole *raison d'être* is *not* the glorification of the singer; they were *not* all written in less than a month (though even those that were can hardly be evaluated by presuming their worth to be proportional to their period of gestation); they do *not* use florid writing as external decoration alone but seek to integrate it into the drama. Most of all, Rossini was a composer of the highest seriousness about his art, and failure to recognise this inevitably compromises our understanding of that art.

This is not to suggest that we accept Rossini's style uncritically or fail to recognise its weaknesses and limitations. The intimate, personal drama of characters created, motivated and humanised by the power of music which we treasure in the greatest operas of Mozart and Verdi is not the central element of Rossini's art.[3] Nor was he immune to external theatrical pressures emerging from the frenetic schedules with which operas were prepared and produced. In most of his works with *secco* recitative, he allowed this music to be prepared by other hands, even though his own *secco* recitative (in *Tancredi* for example) is far superior to the music prepared by others (as in *The Barber of Seville*, where none of the recitative is by Rossini). Even in major Neapolitan operas such as *Moses in Egypt* or *The Lady of the Lake*, he called on inferior composers to write entire musical numbers, so-called 'arie di sorbetti'.[4]

There are specific musical problems that cannot be swept away. Rossini resorted to self-borrowing on many occasions, and the same piece or fragment is known to reappear in three or four different compositions. He defended this practice later in his life by asserting that he borrowed only from failed works, which would not have been expected to circulate further, a partial truth at best. Many passages in the operas are overly generic, even mechanical. At its most exciting a Rossini crescendo can be exhilarating, but its recurrence in similar places in opera after opera grows wearisome. Cadential passages inevitably have the same repetitive structure and only rarely does he find a musical gesture that raises them above banality. The great largos within his finales are almost always imaginative and novel; the final strettas are too often imitations of one another. The most dramatic ensemble will conclude with a passage that could exist almost without change in a comic opera, and no matter how one adjusts the performance to give such a passage increased weight the defect is palpable. Rossini was a composer of his time, and his operas suffer from the merits and the problems generated by the social system

3 See Robinson: *Opera & Ideas: From Mozart to Strauss* (New York, 1985), although I am not convinced that the history of ideas is a sufficient explanation for differences in character between *The Marriage of Figaro* and *The Barber of Seville* that stem largely from the extraordinarily diverse genres of comedy to which they belong.

4 Numbers in which the audience paid less attention and ate ices ('sorbetti').

within which he worked and the stylistic norms on which he built the edifice of his music.

He was also a genius. His music transcends the limits of its genre just as Chopin's piano music transcends the limits of the salon genre of which it is an unabashed example. Not all operas by Rossini are completely successful, but even those which are not (with few exceptions) are seriously considered and beautifully-executed compositions. This statement depends on internal examination of both the works and the manuscripts, as well as external documentation. More and more evidence is emerging to suggest that the time of gestation of Rossini's mature operas was significantly longer than the cases of *The Italian Girl in Algiers* or *The Barber of Seville* would lead us to believe. Correspondence between Rossini and the librettist Felice Romani demonstrates that in one case (*Bianca and Falliero*) the composer was given an opportunity to examine and approve the subject of a libretto months before he began its composition. In another, he chose a subject and then tried to convince a librettist with whom he had earlier worked to prepare the text (*Torvaldo and Dorliska*). In still another, we watch the birth of an opera over many months through the correspondence of Rossini's librettist, Gaetano Rossi (*Semiramide*).[5]

The increasing care and precision with which Rossini prepared his autograph manuscripts during the course of his operatic career is remarkable, and it corresponds to a significant slowing down of his rate of production. By 1818 he was essentially writing no more than two operas a year; by 1820 only one. And the tragedy of his creative life was that his most innovative, consistent, and dramatically intense operas, works such as *Ermione* and *Maometto II*, were so far beyond the capacities of his audiences that he ultimately compromised their integrity or abandoned them altogether. The equivocal reception of *William Tell* by the French public only intensified his sense of creative isolation. We cannot fully understand the psychological bases of Rossini's renunciation of the operatic stage unless we recognise in this isolation some of the roots that fed his notorious cynicism in retirement. But we must not equate the cynicism of the bitter older man with the attitude of the younger artist; whatever else one may say about him, Rossini was not a cynical composer.

He is often accused of cobbling together several of his scores. In fact, the role of 'pastiche' operas, such as *Eduardo and Cristina*, in Rossini's career is miniscule. Even the music of *Elizabeth, Queen of England* and *The Gazette*, with which he began his Neapolitan career in 1815, though heavily indebted to earlier operas, is entirely rethought and reorchestrated for the new settings. When faced with fresh responsibilities, in Naples and later in Paris, Rossini served up music from older works while trying to gauge the responses of his new audiences. After his first two Neapolitan operas, there is precious little self-borrowing in further works for that city, just as the completely novel and enormously inventive *William Tell* follows several adaptations of earlier operas for the French stage.

Moses is one of these Parisian adaptations. First performed at the Teatro San Carlo of Naples in 1818 as *Moses in Egypt*, it was revised and improved for the same theatre in 1819. For this second version, the one normally performed throughout the early nineteenth century and today, Rossini eliminated a piece borrowed intact from an earlier opera and altered the final

5 Documentation will be included in Vol I of the Rossini *Epistolario* (through 1830), ed. B. Cagli, to be published by the Fondazione Rossini in 1987/88.

act, introducing the famous Prayer before the Red Sea. The French version is Rossini's second work for Paris, first performed on March 26, 1927.

Moses in Egypt is the first opera by Rossini in which the chorus is a principal protagonist, both in the quantity of choral music and, more important, its quality and significance. The opera begins with the 'Chorus of Darkness', shifted to the beginning of the second act in *Moses*. The first act of *Moses in Egypt* closes with a plague of fire for the full ensemble, essentially the same music used at the end of the first act in *Moses*, a chromatic, largely unison stretta, unique in his operas. The famous ensemble 'Prayer' in the last act, of course, was the hit of the show since its insertion in 1819. In *Moses in Egypt*, Rossini paid little attention to solo numbers, with the exception of the impressive aria for Elcia with ensemble that concludes the second act. For Paris, he further abbreviated the solo numbers, preserving only this one aria from *Moses in Egypt* (transferred from the Hebrew lover, Elcia, to the Egyptian mother, Sinaïde) and writing also a superb scene for Anaï in the last act, 'Quelle horrible destinée'. Otherwise, his additions reinforce the choral and spectacular side of the opera.

It is possible to argue that the Italian version of 1819 strikes a better balance between the focus on the Egyptian and Hebrew peoples and the emotions of the principal characters. The tautness of its structure (with some dead spots only in the middle of the second act) is certainly compelling, and there are few opening numbers in nineteenth-century Italian opera as gripping as the 'Chorus of Darkness', with its sinuous orchestral melody and pleading solo and ensemble voices emerging from the gloom.

Something is certainly lost when the work is adapted to the larger Parisian stage, with the composer striving further to expand the role of the chorus and the use of dance. In the process he writes some superlative music and, as Pierluigi Petrobelli has pointed out, the scene that opens the new first act is the direct model for Verdi's similar scene in *Nabucco*.[6] It is an honest adaptation, made to precise theatrical circumstances, neither superior nor inferior to the original. The Italian version is more florid because the language of passion in Rossini's Italian works is a language of vocal exuberance; simplifying the lines for France does not make them better, just different. But in neither version does Rossini lose sight of the tone that makes this work unique: the function of the chorus, the declamatory force associated with Moses himself, the conflict between two peoples.

All Rossini's major serious operas, just as his major comic operas, have this quality of individuality, however much we can identify common elements. *The Barber of Seville* has supported many mediocre, routine performances in our century. It is plagued by the worst kind of 'tradition': the kind invented long after the composer's death, then memorised and passed down mindlessly from one generation to another, without being reinterpreted either to correspond to what the composer might have wanted or adapted to the style of new performers. Whether because of silly and repetitive slapstick routines, the curse of over-familiarity, or vocal ornamentation repeated so often that it is no longer ornamental, the unique qualities of *The Barber of Seville* are often submerged.

It is perhaps Rossini's most self-reflexive work (matched only by *The Journey to Rheims*). It lacks the sentimentality of *Cinderella* or the patriotic qualities and character traits that raise Isabella to the quasi-heroic in *The Italian Girl in Algiers*. Instead, its roots are deeply in the commedia dell'arte

6 See Petrobelli, 'Nabucco', *Conferenze 1966-67: Associazione Amici della Scala*.

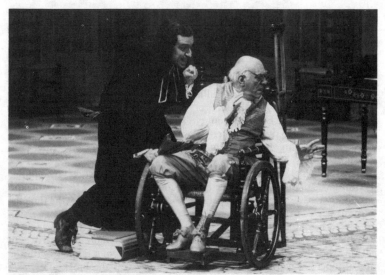

Ruggero Raimondi as Don Basilio and Gabriel Bacquier as Doctor Bartolo in the 1983 production of 'The Barber of Seville' by Alain Marcel, designed by Carlos Cyrtrynowski and Michel Dussarrat in Geneva (photo: Grand Théâtre de Genève)

tradition, the theatre of improvised comedy. Rossini pokes fun at his characters, his own music, himself, by using his musical formal structures as dramatic metaphors: the 'crescendo' becomes the growth of rumour in Basilio's aria; the 'cabaletta', with its standard repetition, becomes the device that assures the failure of the lovers' plan to escape 'by the balcony ladder'; a 'sonata form' design makes Bartolo, the pedant, even more ridiculous. Formal arias embedded within longer musical numbers (such as the Count's 'Introduction') or free passages of non-formal dialogue within what ostensibly pretends to be a formal aria (the 'Lesson scene') are both devices which distance the characters themselves and us from the action. A conscious artist knows his material; he can use it to create remarkable effects and he can also stand back and parody it for comic effect. His ability both to be engaged and to observe makes Rossini's comic and serious operas two sides of the same coin.

What is ultimately most striking about Rossini's art is the extent to which sensitive readings of his finest operas, both serious and comic, cannot fail but to emphasise their uniqueness. Just as the major comic operas are different in character from one another[7], the major serious operas, especially those written for Naples or adapted from these Neapolitan operas, *Moses in Egypt* and *Moses, Armida, Maometto II* and *The Siege of Corinth, Ermione, Otello,* etc., are as different from one another, fundamentally, as are the operas of the famous Verdi trilogy from the early 1850s. If that seems a provocative statement, it is meant to be so. Even the positive term used to describe these works, 'bel canto', is a smoke-screen that hides as much as it reveals. Only when we cease to see these operas as 'vehicles' for singers and turn our primary attention as performers, listeners, and critics to the works themselves will we begin better to appreciate Rossini's artistry, an artistry as vital in his serious operas as in his comic ones.

7 How could the original audience have imagined, for instance, that *The Turk*, a dark and even disturbing comedy, resembles *The Italian Girl*?

The Composer at Work

John Rosselli

A journalist rushing to meet a deadline; a television scriptwriter struggling to keep up with the instalments of a situation comedy; Rodgers and Hammerstein at the Boston tryout of *Oklahoma!*, cutting and revising to get the first-act curtain right and avert a flop — all these stand closer to the young Gioachino Rossini, Italian opera confectioner, than does any twentieth-century 'serious' composer.

Rossini was 18 when a minor Venetian theatre first gave a public performance of one of his operas; he was not quite 24 when a leading theatre in Rome gave his seventeenth opera — *The Barber of Seville*; by the time the biggest theatre in Europe put on his twenty-fourth opera, the Italian version of *Moses*, he had just turned 26; his fortieth and last opera, *Guillaume Tell*, was first performed when he was 37 and had almost 40 more years to live. In all this the only thing that would have surprised anyone familiar with the Italian operatic world of the eighteenth century was the break after *Tell*: composers famous in their day, such as Leo, Hasse, and Jommelli, had each written between 50 and 90 operas; as a rule each of their works was commissioned for a particular group of singers in a particular theatre at a particular season, and could afterwards be dismantled and the best numbers recycled elsewhere — a practice which Rossini time and again resorted to in his own operatic career.

Here, as in much else, Rossini was an enigmatic Janus-figure, at once the last of the eighteenth-century craftsmen and the first of the nineteenth-century experimenters. The reasons for his long silence as opera composer were complex; one of them was the strenuous creative effort needed to set the mould of nineteenth-century grand opera, as Rossini did with the Paris versions of *Maometto II* (*Le Siège de Corinthe*, 1826) and of *Mosè in Egitto* (*Moïse et Pharaon*, 1827), and *Guillaume Tell* (1829). The old journalistic methods might linger on in Italy, where in the 1860s Rossini's disciple Giovanni Pacini was still grinding out the last of his 70 or so operas in the face of public indifference; but in the Paris of the 1830s, the self-conscious capital of intelligence in the heyday of the Romantic movement, only grand, ever more startling masterpieces would do.

How the old Italian operatic world got through its business is illustrated by a few months in Rossini's career, from October 1815 to February 1816. On October 4 the Teatro San Carlo at Naples gave the first performance of *Elisabetta Regina d'Inghilterra*, the first of a number of serious operas which Rossini had contracted to write at the rate of two a year, while also acting as musical director of the royal theatres. The contract, however, allowed him to compose for other theatres as well, and so he managed to fit two less demanding works into the carnival season of 1815–16, both for theatres in Rome.

Carnival, generally the busiest and most fashionable season in the theatrical year, began as a rule on Boxing Night and went on till Shrove Tuesday; in Lent most of the old governments of pre-unification Italy allowed at best only the performance of a 'sacred drama', that is, an opera on a Biblical theme, such as *Moses* was to be in Lent 1818. While a theatre was preparing a new work for December 26 it might well be getting through the tail end of the autumn season, up to about November 30.

With *Elisabetta* out of the way, Rossini spent the late autumn of 1815 in Rome, supervising the production at the Teatro Valle of his *Il Turco in Italia* (a work composed for Milan over a year earlier) and writing a new work for the opening of the carnival season in the same theatre; the Valle, a relatively small house, specialised in comic and sentimental ('semi-serious') opera, so *Torvaldo e Dorliska* was labelled a *dramma semiserio*. Not at all unusually for the time, Rossini had agreed to compose a second new opera to be given later in the same carnival season but at another Rome theatre, the Argentina. This was a larger house, of more exalted standing: in the carnival season it would normally have given *opera seria*, the most prestigious form, for which prices were supposed to be jacked up, star singers engaged, sets and costumes new and lavish, and audiences at their most aristocratic.

As it happened, the owner and virtual impresario of the Argentina, Duke Sforza-Cesarini, was having to cut costs: the Papal Government, restored in the previous year, had withdrawn the subsidy previously paid by the defeated Napoleonic authorities, and the only way the Duke could find of making ends meet was to fall back on a cheaper comic opera season. He still had more trouble than was normal even in the early nineteenth-century opera world with its incessant stream of new works. By early December the company for the coming season should have been assembled and the libretto and music partly composed, but by December 20, in spite of frantic correspondence with North Italian agents, the Duke still lacked a prima donna and a comic bass: it was, he wrote, 'enough to make a poor wretch like me spit blood'. He finally got his singers but, in order to open — late — on January 13, he had to 'put a knife to everyone's throat', and even then he feared that the singers would reach the first night unready and sung out. He chose to present Rossini's *L'Italiana in Algeri*, then two and a half years old; composer and singers rehearsed it shivering in rooms glacial as the unheated depths of Italian palazzi can be. At the same time, with the company laughing, talking and singing around him, the young composer was busy putting together his new composition. The libretto reached him in two parts, on January 25 and 29; *Almaviva o l'Inutile Precauzione*, the opera we now know as *The Barber of Seville*, opened on February 20. The title was changed only after Rossini's version of Beaumarchais' play had become established, since Paisiello's *opera buffa* (1782) was one of the cornerstones of the repertory.

Various people later — and on occasion Rossini himself — made much of the surprisingly short time it had taken him to compose *The Barber*. In fact, but for the accident of Duke Sforza-Cesarini's death two weeks before the first night, the timetable was nothing out of the way in the operatic world where Rossini had grown up. Only a few years earlier in the same theatre, the libretto of Zingarelli's *Baldovino* (1811) had been written in 12 days and the music in 14 — and that was a serious opera, which supposedly needed more time and thought. As a result of the trend both North and South of the Alps towards larger orchestras and more elaborate instrumentation, however, composers began to feel the need for four, five or more weeks from start to finish; and that was a development in which Rossini's Naples operas led the way, to the annoyance of deeply conservative Italian audiences.

There was, naturally, a price to pay for the high-speed methods of the old Italian lyric stage. Singers had to learn the second opera of the season while performing the first opera four or five times a week; often there was a single

*Luigi Alva as Count
Almaviva, Covent
Garden, 1960
(Houston Rogers,
Theatre Museum)*

understudy of either sex (and sometimes none); the dress rehearsal might be held on the very day of the first performance. Count Carlo Ritorni, an experienced man of the theatre, wrote in 1825:

> the singers tired and hoarse, the orchestra stumbling, the costumes held together with pins, the paint on the scenery still wet, the carpenters still hammering away amid the singers' roulades — all this makes for a babel and an ill-digested chaos that is left to settle down and mature as the performances go on.[1]

Unless — Ritorni might have added — the first night was such a disaster that the audience burst into storms of whistling (the Italian form of booing), helped out with blowing through keys and into seashells. The despotic governments of the old Italian states all forbade whistling, if necessary sending armed soldiers into the theatre to arrest the more unruly members of the audience; in an extreme case the impresario himself might be sent to jail for a few days to pacify an enraged public. But hostile demonstrations could not always be contained: when that happened, the opera that had flopped was hurriedly taken off and a fall-back opera substituted after even more hurried rehearsal — generally a recent work, known to the leading singers and pieced out with their favourite 'suitcase arias' (the numbers they carried with them for this purpose).

Such audience behaviour was not just bad manners. The two operas given in a season would, if reasonably successful, each have 20 or 25 performances; many in the audience were regulars, local residents for whom the opera season was the centre of social life. What with the opera, and the ballet usually performed between the acts, they expected to spend in the theatre some five hours a night, four or five nights a week, eight to twelve weeks on end. There they ate, drank, played cards, visited each other, and chatted; the noise of an Italian audience struck foreign visitors even at a time when no European audience kept silence. All the same, they did listen to the more striking

1 *Consigli sull'arte di dirigere gli spettacoli* (Bologna, 1825)

numbers, and if they were moved they uttered brief cries of approval at particular phrases, of a kind now to be heard (in my experience) only in India at sitar recitals and the like, where the audience still has the sense of sharing with the performer in creating the music. If an Italian audience wanted to avoid putting up with what it judged to be a tedious opera or a bad singer for twenty nights in a row, it had to make its feelings plain.

In these conditions even an ultimately successful work could make an awkward start. What happened at the first night of Rossini's *Barber* is beyond disentangling; there may or may not have been a cabal by supporters of Paisiello's older *Barber* (though it was common for a number of composers to set the same story or even the same libretto). The likeliest explanation is that the company were tired out, things went wrong on stage, and the audience whistled or laughed in the wrong places. The same hazard — an exhausted cast singing below their best — was to make for a cool reception at the first night of Bellini's *Norma* at La Scala some 16 years later. In each case the second performance picked up and the work rapidly became a success.

When Rossini wrote *The Barber* no one expected it to stand out as the most successful comic opera of the century. Comic opera was, anyhow, less popular in the Restoration period: a few years later, in 1823, an experienced agent and impresario described *opera buffa* as the genre 'which used to amuse all classes, did not need to be mounted lavishly, and incurred nothing like the present excessive costs of production' — but, he added, it was 'almost proscribed by modern taste'.[2] The reasons are fairly clear. Governments made wary by the experience of revolution looked askance at a genre that had always had about it a touch of subversiveness; though comic librettists and singers knew that nothing remotely like political satire would ever get past the censor, even a take-off of a local notable could seem threatening. Then, even in Italy with its conservative, classicising habit of mind, Romantic sensibility was beginning to spread, and with it a delight in extreme emotions and outlandish settings. Because of this, Rossini would probably have taken to writing fewer strictly comic operas without the terms and circumstances of his Neapolitan engagement which obliged and encouraged him to do so. After *The Barber* he wrote only two more comic operas for Italian theatres, *La Gazzetta* (Naples, 1816), a failure, and *La Cenerentola* (Rome, 1817); but his other eight Naples operas and his last work for Italy, *Semiramide* (Venice, 1823), set Italian opera on the road that led to Verdi's central works — a development which Rossini, himself a classicist to the last, looked upon with ironic reserve.

Naples in 1815 presented him with a special opportunity. Until 1812–13 he had alternated between writing one-act 'farces' for a minor Venetian theatre that specialised in this modest genre, and longer operas (one serious, one comic) for second-rank theatres elsewhere. The breakthrough came with operas written for two leading theatres: La Scala, Milan (*La Pietra del paragone*, 1812, comic) and La Fenice, Venice (*Tancredi*, 1813, serious). Rossini was now the dominant Italian composer, as no one had been since the heyday of Cimarosa and Paisiello in the 1790s. It was natural that a contract with the Naples royal theatres should spur him to his most ambitious efforts.

Naples was then the biggest city in Italy, the capital of the largest of the Italian states; its Bourbon monarchs had set out to have the biggest of everything — the biggest royal palace (later familiar to the Eighth Army as GHQ Caserta), the biggest poorhouse, the biggest opera house. In 1815 the San Carlo enjoyed the biggest subsidy granted to any theatre in Italy, on top of

2 G. Valle, *Cenni teorici-pratici sulle aziende teatrali* (Milan, 1823)

15

a lucrative gambling monopoly held by its impresario, Domenico Barbaja — something which had been suppressed elsewhere in Italy at the fall of the Napoleonic regime in the previous year; Barbaja paid Rossini a cut of the gambling profits, and when it became clear that this unpopular gambling concession was not going to be renewed — it had been suppressed in Naples during the short-lived 1820 revolution — the news probably contributed to Rossini's decision to leave Naples in 1822.

To begin with, however, the management of the royal theatres in Naples could outdo all other Italian theatres in its artistic and material resources. It was unusual in giving opera all the year round, with short breaks for religious festivals, rather than at set seasons. Again unusually, it engaged artists by the year, or at least for several months, rather than by the season, and it could count on more singers of the first rank at any one time than any other Italian theatre. Where an ordinary management generally had as its leading singers one or two sopranos, a contralto (often, at that time, singing breeches parts), perhaps a tenor, and a bass, the San Carlo in Rossini's day could often field three leading tenors, all capable of the most demanding coloratura singing (Andrea Nozzari and Giovanni David, joined at various times by Giuseppe Ciccimarra): hence such oddities as the three leading tenor parts in Rossini's *Otello* (1816) or the trio for three tenors in *Armida* (1817), which help to make these works so difficult to revive today. The Naples management could, besides, call upon a famous orchestra, elaborate scenery, and many extras — recruited, if need be, from the Bourbon infantry and cavalry.

In charge of it all was Barbaja, a semi-literate former café waiter and billiard player from Milan, who had made a fortune by introducing the newly invented roulette wheel into the foyer of La Scala and had then, in favourable wartime conditions, built up an official gambling monopoly over large parts of Napoleonic Italy. Since the Italian upper classes were used to gambling in the spacious foyers of their opera houses (that was why the foyers were so spacious), Barbaja and his fellow gambling concessionaires doubled as opera impresarios. The skills needed in the two lines of work were much alike. The gambling monopoly had its shady, bullying side but — like the Mafia in later times — it traded on its punctuality and its ability to organise and control large numbers of people: the Barbaja syndicate was liked by the governments it dealt with because it paid on the nail. Barbaja was also an employer of labour on a large scale; as an Army and then as a building contractor.

He liked lavish spectacle: it is not surprising that *Armida* should have run to flying machines and transformation scenes – stagings that looked back one way to the seventeenth century, forward the other way to mid-nineteenth-century Parisian Grand Opera. What is more surprising is that Naples, many of whose operagoers prided themselves on the city's standing as the fount of Italian melody entrusted to the solo voice, should have played a leading part in introducing to Italy the operas of Mozart and Spontini; neither was much liked, but Spontini's striving after grandeur through declamation and choral singing had some influence on Rossini.

Rossini's output in 1816–22, after *The Barber* and *La Gazzetta*, consisted of eight *opere serie* for Naples, all of them ambitious and in various ways experimental, interspersed with seven works for other cities, involving more haste and less commitment. He did not take much trouble about the text. Eighteenth-century composers had often set the libretti of Metastasio, masterpieces of Italian poetic diction and, some of them, subtly worked out dramas. Bellini and then Verdi were to make stringent demands on their

16

librettists for words that would carry dramatic conviction. Rossini, in his Naples period, however, seems to have been content with the output of journeymen like Andrea Leone Tottola and Giovanni Schmidt; he could fit the same tune (as in the Naples and Paris versions of *Moses*) to words expressive of either rage or joy, and used recurrent melodies (as in *Semiramide*) to establish musical patterns regardless of the words they accompanied.

Rossini's wordsmiths have been generally disparaged. Hardly any were distinguished poets, though some were decent craftsmen, like Giacomo Ferretti (*La Cenerentola*) and even the much maligned Tottola; Cesare Sterbini (*The Barber*) was a competent amateur. Some librettists acted as stage managers, but it is not clear how much any of these had to do with the production of Rossini's operas, a job which at that time might be done by the composer or the chief repetiteur or the impresario; the producer as such was unknown. The business of a Tottola or a Schmidt was to turn plays or stories into operas much as Hollywood scriptwriters would do a 'treatment' of a

John Rawnsley as Figaro and Maria Ewing as Rosina in 'The Barber of Seville' at Glyndebourne in 1981; producer, John Cox; designer, William Dudley (photo: Guy Gravett)

recent best-seller. Metastasio had regarded his texts as independent works of art. Rossini was one of a generation of composers who demanded a libretto which laid out occasions for different musical structures, typically the double aria (slow, then fast) with a sudden dramatic reversal as its hinge, and the elaborate act finale with all the principals and chorus. With these new priorities, he and others pared away much of the recitative on which Metastasio's librettos had depended to move along the dramatic action. Tottola's original *Moses* libretto is repetitive because its ultimate source is repetitive (first one plague of Egypt, then another); but it is clear, its language decorous. It seems classical beside the 1827 French adaptation by Victor de Jouy and Louis Balochy (Luigi Balocchi) with its still more repetitive plot and its crashing pyramid that erupts into glowing lava streams. The Paris Opéra, on the eve of the bourgeois revolution of 1830, already felt the need to catch the middle-class public with extravagant spectacle. It was typical of Rossini's professionalism that in the revised *Moses* he managed to stretch himself to meet these new demands while still containing the spectacle within dignified and well-proportioned musical forms.

The Roots of a Masterpiece

Marco Spada

From the morning after the celebrated first night disaster in 1816, *The Barber of Seville*, Rossini's tenth *opera buffa* and his penultimate work in this genre (if we except the incomplete *Adina*, 1818, and *Count Ory*, 1828, which belongs to a wholly un-Italian theatrical tradition), has generated much mythology. Cultural fashion, and the prejudice of Romantic idealism against early 19th-century opera, involved the almost total disappearance of Rossini's works from the repertory, reducing a catalogue of some 39 operas to two or three. Apart from occasional performances of *The Italian Girl in Algiers*, it has thus fallen to *The Barber* alone to represent Rossini to the world — and even then in versions cut and mutilated by performance practice — nourishing the myth that he only composed comic operas. *The Barber*, isolated in its miraculous perfection, seemed to be born from nowhere, the unique and mysterious offspring of a composer of genius. Today, however, a different cultural climate and intense musicological research have brought life back to a large part of the Rossini repertory (both comic and serious), which demonstrates the quite exceptional nature of his artistic development and the extraordinary modernity of his message. We can again approach *The Barber* with a different attitude, over and above our veneration for it as a 'masterpiece', to identify its musical and dramaturgical roots and to ascertain its real originality — and thus the reasons for its eternal fascination.

It has often been said, and this is supported by a closer acquaintance with his youthful works, that Rossini belongs to that rare category of geniuses with no 'prehistory', whose creative apprenticeship remains a secret. Indeed, his first *opera seria*, *Demetrio e Polibio*, written in 1806, is already a 'Rossini' opera in its perfect architectonic conception, the novelty of its rhythmic and melodic forms, its orchestration and its generally 'sublime' colouring (all elements which were to remain constant in varying proportions right up to *Semiramide*); and in the area of comic opera there are also any number of instances where the four masterpieces, and *The Barber* especially, are anticipated, in the *farse* written for the San Moisè in Venice: *La cambiale di matrimonio* (1810), *L'inganno felice* (1812), *La scala di seta* (1812), *L'occasione fa il ladro* (1812) and *Il Signor Bruschino* (1813). With these Rossini had a means of trying himself as an architect of musical form. Even within the smaller framework of a one-act *farsa* he would identify the strong points of the drama in order to create a musical discourse which reached a definite climax *before* the denouement. The *farsa* was divided into two imaginary parts by including an ensemble (a terzetto or quartetto) in the centre of the action, and this anticipates Rossini's preference for a two act arrangement for larger works. But there were other characteristics, established then, once and for ever, such as the compositional structure of the introduction (for instance, the Duettino — Cavatina — Stretta in *Cambiale* or the Cavatina — Duettino — Duet in *Bruschino*) and the bipartite structure of the *cavatina*. In addition, he clearly set out his ways of treating words and, above all, the style of his vocal writing. These follow two basic patterns: the syllabic patter song which is sung while the orchestra carries the actual 'theme', to which he resorted in passages of major comic agitation, in his 'little finales' and comic cavatinas: and, secondly, where the theme is entrusted to

18

an elaborate wordless melisma, below which the orchestra plays a neutral accompaniment (*pizzicato* or *arpeggio*). As a rule, this latter type of writing was to be used to introduce lovers but also, on the other hand, comic characters whose pretentiousness he wished to emphasise. Except in *L'inganno felice* (which has a 'semi-serious' subject), Rossini devised infinite variations in the *farse* on the theme of the cunning female pupil, the jealous lover, and the tutor in his dotage, and he was constantly looking for ways to give these more or less identical theatrical types characteristics to differentiate them. These realistic subjects contain a mild element of good-humoured social satire; the theme of money (which was to be fundamental in *The Barber*) is also present here as the explanation of social relationships. The girls who are to be brides are, in effect, defined as 'capital' and the inevitable wedding, apparently opposed throughout the opera, satisfies everyone's interests. It should also be mentioned that two of the most successful *farse*, *La scala di seta* and *Il Signor Bruschino*, are based on French plays, in which the taste for repartee and intrigue involves witty remarks and urbanity; what remains of commedia dell'arte is now combined with new features from bourgeois theatre.

The next step Rossini took in this direction was *La pietra del paragone* (1812), his first large scale masterpiece in the comic vein. Here, alongside traditional aristocratic characters, left over from Goldonian comedy, appear new figures whose professions belong to the up-and-coming bourgeoisie, like the journalist Macrobio. And, once again, the themes of friendship for self-interest and money furnish the basic co-ordinates of the story. Rossini's musical language is still closely tied to the 'naturalistic' style of the *farsa* where characterisation is built into the vocal disposition, that is, by identifying each voice register with a role. Splitting up the syllables again achieves a comic effect just by the utterance of the last parts of words, as in Pacuvio's famous 'Ombretta sdegnosa del Missipipi pipi . . . pipi', a fore-runner of Bruschino's 'Son pentito, tito-tito'. Rossini's sense of the comic still aimed, at this stage, to provoke spontaneous laughter rather than any more serious effect of alienation.

With *L'Italiana in Algeri* (1813), however, which is generally considered to be a happy anticipation of the comedic sense of *The Barber*, Rossini changed his conception of the comic genre. The narrative structure of the fable, with its subjects deriving from Greek theatre (the shipwreck with the happy ending)[1] and an implicit moral content, led Rossini to rethink the structure and to emphasise the element of pure convention. *Il Turco in Italia* (1814) and *La Cenerentola* (1817) were both conceived in the same way, but more radically: the former through the 'meta-theatrical' device of the 'Poet', who is writing the action on stage into his own farce, and the latter through the archetype of Perrault's fairy tale. To be sure, as to their outward appearance, the styles and formulas remain as before, but now they are handled in a detached way, no longer to construct characters and situations of a directly imitative type but to present them as 'rhetorical' portraits. It is impossible to compare, for instance, the apparent ingenuousness of the arias of Fanny (*Cambiale*), Sofia (*Bruschino*) or Berenice (*L'occasione*) in the *farse* with the *cavatine* of Isabella (*Italiana*), Fiorilla (*Turco*) and Angelina (*Cenerentola*). The aim in the latter is to present characters tied to a certain destiny and not to some logical and consequential train of events: hence the necessity for pushing musical characters to extremes. In other words, where Donna Fulvia

1 Cesare Questa, *Il ratto del serraglio: da Euripide a Rossini*, Bologna 1979.

really laments in *Pietra* that Conte Asdrubale does not love her, Angelina acts the part of the persecuted girl, and where Slook in *Cambiale is* a conceited suitor, Dandini consciously adopts his role.

What is now the effect of the coloratura if not the depiction of these double personalities? It is enough to note the experienced and gradual use which Rossini makes of it in *Cenerentola* to portray the two facets of the title role — first kitchen maid and then princess. Thus when he now tackles the *concertato 'di stupore'*, he consciously eliminates all realism, splitting the words to make pure 'nonsense' — what Stendhal called 'folie organisée et complète.'

So how does *The Barber* fit into the development of Rossini's comic theatre? By 1816 Rossini was already absolute master of the musical form and the appropriate dramaturgical language of comic opera. He had definitively shown, with *L'Italiana* and *Turco*, that he could handle comedy in music by sublimating the stock mechanism of responses. But he had also produced a masterpiece in the serious genre, *Tancredi* (1813), and, when he tackled *Elisabetta regina d'Inghilterra* (1815), his first opera for Naples, he entirely rethought his own approach with a view to unhinging from within the delicate symmetries which governed its closed form. Indeed, the novelty of the subject of *Elisabetta* suggested to him, in treating the dramatic recitative and arioso, the need to adhere to the inner meaning of the text, considered for its psychological values and not just metrically. Rossini put the importance of this experience to good use in *The Barber* when, once again returning to a farcical subject, he hit upon a libretto as rich in social content and psychological subtleties as that of Beaumarchais. In fact the characters in *Le Barbier de Seville* (1775) retain only the shell of their origins in the masks of the traditional burlesques[3], and are charged internally with new values, the products of a new age. In the first place there is Figaro, heir to the old Harlequin family who represents a new and active bourgeoisie, conscious of its rights; but there is also Don Bartolo, his antagonist, who has nothing of the foolish tutor as conventionally defined. He places many obstacles in the way of the barber's attempts, pursued for the promise of payment, to bring the Count and Rosina together. If, in the end, he succumbs to the requirements of a happy ending, it is not a victory of astuteness over stupidity, but of a new, more materialistic but less hypocritical, way of understanding how the world works, one no longer based on the pretence of class distinction (in which Don Basilio and his slanderous accusations may be included). As is well known, Beaumarchais' *Barbier* (the first comedy of a trilogy completed by *Le mariage de Figaro* (1784) and *La mère coupable* (1792)) enjoyed much success in the musical theatre; before Rossini, Giovanni Paisiello's version of 1782 had made it famous. But that libretto, concocted by Giuseppe Petrosellini for the Imperial Theatre in St Petersburg, eliminated every revolutionary element, in particular from the character of Figaro, by reducing the social satire to zero, and the plot to its essence of farce. Nonetheless the opera prospered and, even in 1816, when he was no longer active, the composer was surrounded by a halo of glory. But young Rossini, proposing the Beaumarchais subject again 34 years later, could certainly not accept Petrosellini's sugary version. Instead he referred back to the original and, in the 'Notice to the Public' in his own libretto by Cesare Sterbini, having rendered diplomatic homage to Paisiello, he gauged the distance between them by letting Sterbini specify that there

2 See also Bruno Cagli, *Il comico rossiniano come sfida ala società moderna*, Teatro Lirico Sperimentale di Spoleto 'Adriano Belli', settembre/ottobre 1979.

3 Popular theatrical entertainments in France in the 18th and 19th centuries.

were 'quite a lot of new situations for musical numbers which were claimed by modern theatrical taste . . . so much have times changed since the renowned Paisiello wrote his score.' A quick comparison between the librettos of Paisiello and Rossini allows us to understand how much the latter guided Sterbini's hand when making his final choice in modifying scenes and characters: we may think of the invention of the knowing Berta, or the first Finale, where instead of the Rosina-Bartolo dialogue (Beaumarchais II-5) he introduces the arrival of the militia. From the splendid foundation of French comedy, Rossini thus had a means of regenerating the naturalistic *farsa* with realistic characters and situations. This he achieved by fusing it with his more mature, 'meta-theatrical' conception of comic opera, as tested in *L'Italiana* and *Turco*, which was based on the sublimation of the theatrical *topos*.

The final reason for the fascination of *The Barber* is the dimension of time, different from that in any other opera: miraculously, real time is continuously changing into theatrical time and vice versa. If here the conventions are exposed to the unexpected (who would really be surprised if Rosina married Bartolo because the Count had an accident on his way to the assignation?), this unexpected is always calculated; the charade of anxieties and fears is thus always acted out by the characters, who are perfectly aware from the start that the story will end in the only possible way, in spite of all 'useless precautions'.

The Music

The brief space of time in which it was written certainly contributes to the legends surrounding *The Barber*. In less than 15 days, Rossini wrote 600 pages of music in full score, as usual leaving the writing out of the passages of *recitativo secco* to a collaborator in the theatre. After the fiasco of the first night — which was, according to a tradition as picturesque as it is unreliable, provoked by the supporters of old Paisiello — the opera enjoyed a sweeping success, partly due to a cast which included Manuel Garcia the elder (Almaviva), Gertrude Righetti-Giorgi (Rosina) and Luigi Zamboni (Figaro).

Because of the rush Rossini, who had a habit of borrowing from himself, introduced into *The Barber* themes and musical pieces extracted from his lesser known and less successful previous works, such as *Aureliano in Palmira* and *Sigismondo*, but also — and this was not by chance — from two *farse*, *La cambiale di matrimonio* and *Il Signor Bruschino*, and even two cantatas *Egle e Irene* and *Aurora*. Even if the re-use of themes in *The Barber* was minimal in comparison, for instance, with *Elisabetta*, where the self-borrowings directly account for 90% of the music, the process he used was the same. In both operas Rossini did not confine himself to adapting musical numbers *tout cour* to a new text but he sometimes saved only the original musical idea, taken out of its harmonic and lexical context, and the affecting element which justified transferring it to an analogous situation.

For the Sinfonia, given that the one 'on Spanish themes' which was performed at the première no longer exists, Rossini used that for *Aureliano* (already re-orchestrated to open *Elisabetta*), expanding in the new score the solo part for the bass. This famous number is constructed according to Rossini's most classic archetype.[4] It begins with a slow 25 bar introduction in E major, which can be called tripartite: at the beginning and the end there are typical figures of hammering ascending and descending demi-semi-quavers, and in the centre, after a short interpolation from the oboe, a delicate 6 bar theme unwinds on flute and violins. A *fortissimo* chord on the dominant

4 Philip Gossett, *Le Sinfonie di Rossini*, 'Bollettino del Centro Rossiniano di Studi' 1979, nn. 1-3, Pesaro 1981.

prepares the attack on the *Allegro con brio*. The first theme in E minor [1], formed from the petulant interpolation of three (and then two) quavers on violins and violas accompanied by the other strings, is repeated twice before the development (bridge) section which precedes the attack on the second theme. This [2] in G major is given, as usual, to the oboe, flute and horn, and is more lyrical and expansive. It is thematically related to the short 8 bar *pre-crescendo* which prepares for the real *crescendo*; this is constructed on a balance of repeated phrases, increasing in dynamic intensity and with the participation of the whole orchestra, from the 4 bar theme [3]. The cadences and short modulations, which take us back to E minor, prepare the reprise of the whole section, this time without a bridge between the first and second themes (now in E major).

The Introduction (No. 1) has a three part structure which comprises the entrance of the musicians hired by the Count, led by Fiorello (a character who does not appear in Beaumarchais), the Cavatina for Almaviva and the final *Vivace*. The initial musical idea, set to 'Piano, pianissimo' ('Softly now, softly there') in G major is derived from *Sigismondo*. It depicts the night-time tranquillity of the place, while the comic triplets (taken up by Fiorello at the words 'venite qua' ('follow me') imitate the musicians' furtive arrival. The Count's sudden appearance, on two bars of recitative, 'Fiorello . . . Olà', stops the music for a moment. When it starts again the *motum perpetuum* of the strings underlines the comic effect of the clandestine meeting. Almaviva's Cavatina in C major is, despite its apparent simplicity, furnished with a very refined orchestration that includes guitars and a sistrum, and is a masterpiece of amorous rhetoric. The 'pathetic' clarinet theme, borrowed from *Aureliano*, expresses the lover's anxiety, only lightly satirised by the very rapid sextuplets of the other wind instruments. In the song [4] the broad and expansive melody is suitably embellished on the words 'cielo' and 'speme'. In the *cabaletta*, the atmosphere changes suddenly and both the fast patter of the vocal line and the bouncing rhythm in the accompaniment (with piccolos) denote his certainty of success in the enterprise. Since Rosina still does not appear, the Count dismisses the musicians, paying them generously. In the 6/8 G major *Vivace*, there is the first explosion of Rossini's sense of the comic absurd.

Figaro's entrance is carefully prepared to make the biggest effect. The call of his song is actually heard in the distance before the Cavatina (No. 2) bursts onto the stage. In this very long number in C major, Rossini closely follows the unusual structure of the text, inventing three themes from the single principal idea [5], which throw themselves forward and develop, creating an unstoppable musical continuum. The rhythmic scansion of the song closely follows the number of accents in the text, which comprises five-syllable lines, ending alternately in truncated words and dactyls, creating an effect of great variety and tension. Rossini freely introduces passages of almost *Sprechgesang*, at the words 'V'è la risorsa / poi del mestiere' ('And I may tell you, I can be useful') and at the very rapid repetitions of 'Figaro'.

Even the Count's Canzone (No. 3) which follows, in A minor/C major [6], contains an element of rhythmic tension which conveys his desire to see her. Rossini 'opens' the form of the closed number by inserting, after the first exposition, an unaccompanied repeat of the *ritornello* for Rosina behind the shutters. Then there are two short bars of recitative, a complete reprise of the song and another reply, which is brusquely interrupted by Bartolo's arrival. The structural symmetry here creates an unprecedentedly lively effect on stage. In the G major Duet (No. 4) (Count-Figaro), the picture of the 'factotum' is drawn. The effect of gold is demonstrated in the vocal theme with which it opens [7], built upon wide intervals with a very marked rhythm above unison strings playing rapidly ascending and descending scales. To the *Vivace* 'Un vulcano è la mia mente', ('Then my brain begins to boil like Mount Vesuvius') [8], the Count replies repeating the theme for flute and violins [9]. Above this, a true leitmotif, Rossini leaves the vocal declamation free. A third theme [10] completes the first part of the duet, in which there is also an *Andante* 6/8 episode in B minor, when Figaro realistically imitates the behaviour of a drunk. In the concluding *Allegro*, the *cabaletta* of the duet, a gay theme is introduced for Figaro to describe the location of his shop to the Count, articulating the text for 27 bars on the single note of D; the theme is taken up again by the Count [11] with the inevitable *bel canto* variations.

Rosina's Cavatina (No. 15) is placed at the centre of the act. The calculated delay in her appearance was, according to Righetti-Giorgi, one of the causes of the fiasco of the première, but, on the contrary, it stimulates our curiosity in the object of the love which has already cost the Count two serenades and a purse of gold. Many of Rossini's contemporaries, used to Paisiello's more languid heroine, and to decades of tearful and persecuted stage maidens, were struck by this girl's lively character. But Beaumarchais wanted her thus, resolute and very resourceful. In the play, indeed, he gave her a first line which encapsulates the character: 'Comme le grand air fait plaisir à respirer! Cette jalousie s'ouvre si rarement . . .'. If the critic of the *Journal de Bouillon* attacking the play defined Rosina as 'a badly brought up girl', so Stendhal was not without criticism of Rossini's version, and stated à propos the duet 'Dunque io son?': 'I will never believe that a girl's love, even in Rome, could be devoid of melancholy and, I dare to say it, of a certain bloom of delicacy and shyness . . .'. He likened Rosina to a 'lively widow' rather than an adolescent girl. Clearly, just like the arrogant and disrespectful Figaro, the 'messenger of love', Rosina had awakened sleeping fears and deep-rooted anxieties in so-called 'public opinion'. The rather sharp flavour of the E major *Andante* instrumental introduction (with its trills and runs), eliminates any misgivings about the naivety of this girl, who is a worthy sister to Isabella in *L'Italiana*. As always in Rossini's *cavatine* the theme of the first part is stated by the voice and is developed with an increasing display of coloratura [12]; however, a theme entrusted to the orchestra and taken up by the voice is *Moderato* [13, 14]. Rossini took it from *Aureliano* and in a second version re-used it in *Elisabetta*. The few modifications which Rossini adopted here are enough to transform its character which, instead of Elisabetta's palpitating heart, now depicts the 'viper' Rosina.

Her intention of coming to an agreement with Figaro is, of necessity, postponed by the arrival of the tutor with Don Basilio, the meddling old priest. In the famous 'slander' aria (No. 6) in D major, Rossini highlights the key words applying classic *buffo* declamation [15] above string semiquavers [16] which move from *pianissimo* to complete the *crescendo* on a modulation from E♭ to E major) at the words 'colpo di cannone' ('clap of thunder'). Finally Rosina succeeds in seeing Figaro secretly. In the Duet (No. 7), their mutual pretence is complete. Both are perfectly aware of the point of their meeting but they pretend to be astonished, the one that she is the Count's chosen one, the other to know that she knows. Rosina's timid anxiety is nevertheless well expressed in the questioning phrase which opens the *Allegro* 'Dunque io son?' ('Then it's me?') [17], notwithstanding her certainty in the rapid patter which immediately follows [18]. Figaro, using the same technique of mimicry as Mozart's *Don Giovanni*, imitates the verse, intervening to ask for a message. When Rosina presents him with one already written, his (pretended) surprise is expressed with a phrase of descending minims in unison with the orchestra. At the words 'Ah tu solo, amor tu sei' ('Ah, 'tis love, 'tis love, love only') Rosina attacks the theme of the final section [19], taken from the *Cambiale di matrimonio*, on which she performs variations of very fast roulades with a patter commentary from Figaro.

The sequence of solo arias in Act One concludes with Bartolo's aria 'A un dottor della mia sorte' ('I'm a lawyer of experience') (No. 8); because of the great difficulties it posed in terms of voice and interpretation, this was replaced, a few performances after the première, with the simpler 'Manca un foglio' by Pietro Romani. In the original two part aria (*Andante maestoso — Allegro vivace*) the vocal melody dominates, always supported and intensified by the orchestra. The first musical example [20] with slight variations is the dominant theme; it is heard again at the end, after the rapid section [21].

In the first Finale (No. 9) we watch the Count's first attempt, disguised as a soldier, to penetrate Bartolo's house. In the *Marziale* in C major, three *fortissimo* orchestral chords in unison announce the theme which characterises the Count's approach [22]. His interview with the suspicious Bartolo occurs instead over a serpentine musical thread in A minor [23]. These themes, in a spiral of different modulations, make up the leitmotifs on which their dialogue is built. A third theme, this time taken up by the voice, is articulated by the Count [24] and the duet section closes with the appearance of Rosina. Then all three leitmotifs return with the entry of Berta and Basilio; this first part closes with Figaro's arrival, trying to stop the Count from throwing himself at Bartolo with a drawn sword. The quick theme of the *Allegro* in E♭ is in hammering triplets [25]. The arrival of the militia, attracted by the brawl, makes way for a brief episode *a cappella*, that is for solo voices, in B♭ major, which slowly modulates into C major. In the *Vivace* Bartolo's G major vocal theme, [26], is repeated at successive entries by each singer, and initiates a first episode of 'nonsense' with the chattering caused by the words 'Si, signor'. But the confusion increases when Almaviva, taking advantage of his real identity, dismisses the Captain and the militia, leaving everyone stupefied. The theme of this A♭ major *Andante* is introduced by Rosina — during which increasing vocal decoration conveys their amazement — and is repeated by the Count and Basilio in the traditional way with a 'false canon'. Figaro replies with a motif of detached rhythm and mocking character [28]. In the C major stretta (*tutto sottovoce assai*) the characters separate for a moment, and come together to a theme with a strong rhythmic accent [29].

Act Two begins with Almaviva's renewed attempt to enter Bartolo's house, this time disguised as a music teacher. In the Almaviva-Bartolo Duet (No. 10) the honeyed approach of Don Basilio's pupil is expressed by the theme which repeatedly falls back on B♭ with malicious *acciaccaturas* [30], and the nasal timbre of a clarinet offers replies. The outburst towards a lyrical theme is attached to the thought of Rosina at the Count's words 'Ah mio ben fra pochi istanti / parterem in libertà' ('How to talk with fair Rosina / I shall shortly find a way'). When the girl, at first reluctant, recognises her suitor in Don Alonso, she graciously agrees to have a singing lesson. The theatrical, or rather 'meta-theatrical', effect of this number constitutes one of the strokes of genius in the opera. Rosina, focussing her gaze on Lindoro, addresses the message of the aria of 'The Guardian Outwitted' (literally 'The Useless Precaution') at the unwitting Don Bartolo, and executes a great tri-partite aria 'Contro un cor'

(No. 11) in D major where Rossini parodies himself [31]. The middle section is made up of the prayer, 'Caro, a te mi raccomando', whispered to Lindoro while Bartolo falls asleep; the third section, *Moderato*, is a sort of *cabaletta* [32] in which Rosina executes a delirious *crescendo* of vocal decorations. A theatrical tradition, which still exists today, has it that this aria of the 'Music Lesson' can often be replaced by a favourite piece chosen by the interpreter, a so-called 'suitcase aria', which shows off her virtuoso qualities. Adelaide Borghi-Mamo, for instance, performed 'Santa Lucia, arrangée en Rondo de Concert' with a Neapolitan text and innumerable vocal decorations. Today, Marilyn Horne often interpolates the Cavatina 'Di tanti palpiti' from Rossini's *Tancredi*. The effect of playing the scene for two audiences is continued into the following recitative, 'Bella voce, bravissima', and in Don Bartolo's *Arietta* (No. 12) which, as befits the defender of the music of the past, is a minuet in 6/8 in which Rossini politely satirises the 'pathetic' arias in the style of Paisiello [33]. The real theatrical action begins again when Figaro arrives, and Don Basilio puts in an unexpected appearance, thus creating another obstacle to Almaviva's plan. The Quintet (No. 13) begins with an *Andantino* in E♭, in which the exclamations of surprise are followed by a bassoon theme with a questioning character, that functions as a leitmotif. Thanks to a purse of gold, Basilio lets himself be persuaded to leave. His departure is accompanied by the *Moderato* in G major, 'Buona sera, mio signore' whose theme [34], sung in turn by each protagonist, develops into the agitated *Stretta* 'Maledetto seccatore' ('Plague upon the man'), constructed on the fast triplets of demi-semi-quavers in voices and orchestra. With Basilio's departure, the quintet becomes a quartet, interrupted by no *secco recitativo*. While Figaro shaves Bartolo, the lovers make an assignation for midnight. Rossini suggests the secrecy of the message by leaving the melody of the vocal line to a single repeated note above a buzzing of double basses while the other strings perform a descending pattern of connected scales. The deceit is, however, discovered and in the *Stretta* Bartolo turns Almaviva and Figaro out.

Berta's aria 'Il vecchiotto cerca moglie' ('Spite of sixty years to carry') (No. 14) in A major is the only closed number, forming no part of the action. This is a witty parody of an elderly spinster and the principal theme [35], in 2/4, does indeed suggest the laborious progress of ageing feet.

As he was also to do in *La Cenerentola*, Rossini inserted an orchestral Storm (No. 15) before the dénouement. This one was originally written for *La pietra del paragone*, and had then been incorporated into the Introduction of *L'occasione fa il ladro*. Yet this typical feature of Rossini's dramaturgy is in this case quite relevant to the action, and the expedient of bad weather was already present in Beaumarchais. The Rosina-Count-Figaro Terzetto (No. 16) is in four sections. In the E major *Andante* the girl's amazement is genuinely expressed by a theme which is extremely calm above a regular accompaniment [36], taken up by the Count and by Figaro. A section in which Almaviva asks Rosina to be his wife, precedes the 'Dolce nodo' ('Oh, what rapture') sequence, Rossini's tribute to the conventions of the lovers' sentimental duet. Here, however, Figaro undermines its sentimental value with the parody of *farsa* by echoing the decorations at the same pitch.

The conclusion of the terzetto, with the *Allegro* 'Zitti, zitti, piano, piano' ('If we all go very softly') [37], makes a paradox of the situation. Heedless of Bartolo's imminent arrival they take the opportunity to have a final little sing together and the purely rhetorical intention to 'be quiet' corresponds in the music to an infernal din. Thus Rossini makes clear his intention to exalt a melodramatic convention, and to parallel the analogous situation in the Introduction: they are the alpha and omega of a perfect architectonic structure.

Before the finale Rossini wrote another aria for the Count 'Cessa di più resistere' (Silence! Resist my will no more') preceded by a *Recitativo strumentato* (Nos. 17-18), in which Almaviva protests against Bartolo's obstinacy. This great tri-partite aria, which is extremely difficult for the singer, was composed to please the first Almaviva, but it is unnecessary for the purposes of the drama. It was cut almost immediately, but Rossini used the theme of the *cabaletta* for Angelina's final *Rondò* in *La Cenerentola*.

So while, in the structural plan of Rossini's works, the importance of the Introduction and the First Finale are underlined as numbers which build up with the entry of each character and which lengthen the dimension of theatrical time, the concluding finales are, on the contrary, very short, simply formal seals on recently concluded events. The performers shed their characters and come down stage to spell out the moral, winking at the audience to make them realise that all they have seen was merely a game: the spell is broken and everyday life begins again. In the *Finaletto II* of *The Barber* (No. 19) all can express their (sham) satisfaction, above a jolly polonaise rhythm (3/4, G major), led by Figaro [38]: Figaro and Don Basilio at the money they have earned; the one for services, the other for silence; Don Bartolo for having at least saved for himself his ward's dowry. And then Rosina and the Count, at last stepping out of their own characters, adopt the third person to join the general chorus and sing, perhaps with a rather fixed smile, 'Amore e fede eterna / si vegga in *voi* regnar.' — ' *Your* troubles now are ended, / *You*'re free from every care'.

A Note on the Fondazione Rossini

The Fondazione Rossini was established by the Commune di Pesaro after the composer's death to administer the bequest which he left to the town and to manage the music school which he wished to found in his birthplace. This was done by creating the Liceo Musicale 'G. Rossini' (now the Conservatorio), under the direction first of Carlo Pedrotti and then a succession of illustrious composers such as Mascagni, Zanella and Zandonai.

A new initiative came to the Fondazione with the appointment of Bruno Cagli as artistic director in 1971. In that year it was decided to make a critical edition of Rossini's works, with an editorial board of Cagli, Philip Gosset and Alberto Zedda, and with the collaboration of musicologists from all over the world. At present five volumes have appeared (*La gazza ladra*, *L'italiana in Algeri*, *Tancredi*, the collection of piano music *Quelques Riens pour Album*, and the incidental music for Sophocles' tragedy *Edipo Coloneo*) and another 15 are in the course of preparation; a total of about 80 volumes are anticipated for the whole project. The Fondazione publishes the *Bolletino del Centro Rossiniano di Studi* with the most progressive articles on Rossini studies and Italian opera of the early 19th century. Also in preparation are a monumental new edition of the letters and documents of Rossini, and a Thematic Catalogue of his music.

A Personal View of Rossini

Ubaldo Gardini

Maestro Gardini has coached singers and advised on performances at The Royal Opera House, Covent Garden, the Metropolitan Opera House, New York, the Juilliard School and the Tokyo National University. This is an edited transcript of a tape-recording he made in answer to various points put to him by the Editor.

Today singers perform every type of vocal music, most of the time forced to compete with the overwhelming sonority of the modern orchestra. How can they possibly do justice to the variety of styles which have arisen in the evolution of vocal art? In Rossini's time there were very celebrated established schools of singing. Their motto was: 'One is born a singer, but one becomes an artist by studying for the whole of one's life.' 'Cantare' meant singing *dolce, piano, espressivo, con sentimento*. Early 19th-century Italian opera was for the great heart of the people, not just for intellectuals.

Rossini and his colleagues knew the natural resources of the human voice. They were themselves singers, and their orchestras never dominated the dramatic action. Rapid and clear scenes infused with simple but human emotions were congenial to the Italian temperament. The orchestra was light, aiming in its own way at singing expressively and very rhythmically — one might say 'dancing'; not as square-cut and over-accentuated as today. The word was always of cardinal importance ('la parola musicata'), and this involved a concentration on the emotive expression of the singing voice and its marriage to the orchestral sound.

In a letter to Arrivabene, Verdi wrote: 'In *The Barber*, the phrase "Signor, giudizio, per carità" is neither melody nor harmony; it is the declaimed word, just true and essentially music.' In practically every phrase of *The Barber* we can see it was 'la parola' that gave birth spontaneously to the music. To take just one example, it is evidently the verbal line 'Pace e gioia sia con voi' which inspired the musical line, such is the naturalness of the Italian verbal expression, and the way it is accentuated in the music. It can also be seen in the dynamic variety of the recitatives. Rossini wrote as an Italian speaks, thinks and feels, full of warmth and enthusiasm, of joy and sorrow; he knew how to use the national idiom, and composed what Byron called 'musica favellata' — which is difficult to translate — 'spoken music', where the same delivery is given to musical phrases as to spoken words. Stendhal wrote: 'The Rossinian revolution has killed the originality of the singers. They are condemned to find everything already prepared for them.' So it seems that even Rossini may be given the accolade for a reform, or even a revolution! His enemies, and the mere virtuosi fanciers, said that 'with him the bel canto ceased to exist'. And later they were to say the same of Verdi — he was also supposed to ruin voices.

Monaldi has described a performance in Milan of Rossini's *Aureliano in Palmira* when the celebrated Velluti started to ornament his part with inimitable agility. Rossini, he said, did not find all this *fioritura* to his taste, but done in that impeccable way it produced an admirable effect. Yet in 1813 Rossini wrote to Cicognara, 'the sense of time, that essential part of the music, without which neither melody nor harmony can be understood . . . is violated

27

Della Jones as Rosina in the ENO production by Patrick Libby, designed by Frances Tempest and Steve Addison (photo: Donald Southern)

and ignored by singers. Their aim is to surprise instead of to move; and where, in the old days, the aim of the instrumental players was to sing like singers, with their instruments, now the singers studied to play with their voices like instrumentalists.' Knowing all the abuses of egocentric singers like La Marcolini, La Marchesi and La Colbran, Rossini thought he would embellish his melodies himself according to their particular abilities so as to prepare a uniform style for them and, in so doing, to ensure a unity in their performances.

Thus he was really responsible for restoring the melodic line to his scores — still in an adorned form, but capable of sincerity and meaning in performance. At the same time one cannot deny that the virtuosi of that period had an incomparable vocal dexterity, and superlative control of every aspect of the human voice. As a result any voice (whether soprano, contralto, tenor or bass) could tackle extremely difficult passages and sustain the same tessitura. Voices trained in that one, and only one, way (and in the way best suited to them, so as to exhibit what they considered their best features) could, for instance, equally well sing as what today we call a soprano (whether lyric or leggiero) or as a contralto.

Looking through Rossini's many operas, one cannot but be astonished at the extraordinary variety and versatility of his creative imagination. But one

28

thing stands out as the cornerstone of his temperament: the comic. The *opera buffa* belongs to the Italians, to the joy of their contagious laughter. And Rossini communicates this particular joy in that particular style of his time, more free and intense than that, for example, of Cimarosa, which is more restrained, more innocent, more tender and gracious. Rossini already belongs to a more modern time. He does not depict Beaumarchais' *Figaro*, but a typically Italian ambiance full of Roman intrigue and self-interested people whose lives bubble with comedy — and caustic irony too!

* * *

Let us now examine the requirements for peformance of Rossini's music. He wrote for voices with a considerable range and asked for exceptional flexibility rather than a mere display of virtuosity — for an expressive coloratura. This really means he wanted colours with which the voice could paint each note, independent of their velocity or intensity, treating each note as a *messa di voce*, like a 'pearl'. Never sing roughly; sing elegantly and aesthetically.

Regarding style: it is one of the hardest an artist can achieve, much more difficult than more advanced or complex compositions. It is based on the commedia dell'arte and requires the singer to be able to act with his voice and his whole body, with a voice both natural and free, and to avoid like the plague 'phoney' opera acting and singing. In Rossini's time all the straight actors of the *teatro di prosa* were encouraged to see and hear singers on the operatic stage. Much has been written about this; the best known text is by the Italian poet Gian Giulio Barrilli, but there is also the less-known though extraordinary book by Franceschini, *L'arte della parola*, 'On the art of the word'. He recommends actors to listen to the sublime interpretations of singers in Rossini's operas specifically in order to learn how to act and how to declaim effectively. The primary interest does not lie in quavers and semiquavers. *Ars longa vita brevis*, and it cannot be measured with a conductor's baton.

Regarding Rossini traditions (and not only his): one must always be very cautious. Under such pretexts one is so often forced to tolerate the most absurd oddities. Some are logical, and one can see why they have survived, but most of the time they are *illegal*. And so are 'cuts' — not that one always wants to do a work in its entirety, especially in Italian opera; just because cuts have always been made in a certain way, however, is not a sufficient reason for us to accept them. Italian opera must always be treated with a sense of interpretative freedom; by reading between the notes, music can be given life and spontaneity. A never-ending aim is to make it live, really live. Leonardo said 'simplicity is so difficult to achieve', and in that single statement one can sum up Italian opera in general. Its elements are just what are essentially necessary and sufficient, and in this apparent simplicity lie the great difficulties; success or failure rests on the shoulders of the artists alone. Italian music especially needs an interpreter, a true interpreter. This idea of 'freedom' to which I referred above, must not be misunderstood; the *tempo rubato* in the hands of someone who, however intellectually prepared, does not have an impeccable rhythmic sense is disastrous.

About the words: opera was born out of poetry. The poets were singers. We know from Caccini: 'Prima le parole, poi il ritmo, poi le note; e non per il contrario'. 'First the words, then the rhythm, then the notes, and not the other way around.' The words have always been of supreme importance for every Italian artist, even painters, architects, sculptors. Apart from the fact that the

Italian language has been universally recognised as the most beautiful for singing, and that 'parlate bene e cantate bene' ('speak beautifully and you will sing beautifully'), or 'si parla come si canta, o si canta come si parla' ('one speaks as one sings, and one sings as one speaks'), for us music without the voice, without the metaphysical power of the voice, never meant much at all. So pronunciation from that part of Italy where opera was born is the prime requisite for a modern singer. Italians too, not born in Tuscany, must learn, like any foreigner, that beauty of utterance. Manzoni, for example, studied for a long time in Florence, and, at the end, said, 'a peasant in Tuscany is a much greater poet than myself'. Furthermore, Italian poetry is very allusive, very ambiguous, with many second meanings, metaphors and allegories, which can only be understood if the lines are well rendered. Italian poetry is written to be read aloud. Italians call this art of speaking poetry, rhetoric; the emphasis on elocution, and the overstressed approach that one hears so persistently do not belong to our way of delivering poetry. Italian derives from Latin and it is a melodic, not a stressed, language. Generally, we aim to stress one important syllable, usually towards the end of a sentence, and so towards the end of a musical phrase. To perform Rossini, as for all Italian composers, you must be a master of speaking correctly: 'l'arte del dire' is everything. The pauses, also, must be full of interest and pulsating rhythm, and not merely stopping and resting places as we call pauses in English. Verdi said: 'Vivere le pause', 'Long live pauses!' — do not treat them as rests, but bridge them. If you take a rest, the public goes to sleep.

To *sing* with that beautiful and correct pronunciation is easy compared to rendering *recitativo secco* or *strumentato*. Here, the real artists truly emerge; the actor-singer here can excel, because everything depends on him alone. The drama, the colour, the speed, the pauses; music here is only a blueprint, schematically, conventionally written, and depends on the artist to make it alive and true. Everything which happens in the drama is said in the recitatives. So they are more difficult to perform than a concerto and must be studied as carefully! And when recitatives are followed by arias and ensembles etc., they must be integrated and joined in a logical, rhythmical way, that gives no sense of close to the ending of the recitative, but of continuity and inexorability to the unfolding of the lyric drama, which must be an entity from beginning to end.

We must finally turn to the Italians' much criticised habit of repeating themselves, especially in opera. When an Italian speaks, he generally repeats himself, and he elaborates and divagates; so in opera. Yes, it is one of our national characteristics. As soon as an Italian says something, he immediately thinks he has expressed it badly; in a word, that he has given a bad performance. And so he tries to do better by repeating it, until he has satisfied himself or, especially, he has his listener's approving consent. So please, whenever you have to repeat a phrase in Rossini's operas, aim always to improve the way you sing it; and, of course, you must also try to improve at every later performance. The saying 'Paganini non ripete', 'Paganini does not repeat', applies to all of us. You cannot expect Italian artists to be constant. Every night they try to do better, and they are different in every way, to the dismay of the conductor, directors — of everyone who is not Italian. So in this case we use the English saying, 'Variety is the spice of life'.

Thematic Guide

Many of the themes from this opera have been identified in the articles by numbers in square brackets, which refer to the themes set out on these pages. The themes are also identified by the numbers in square brackets at the corresponding points in the libretto, so that the words can be related to the musical themes.

[1]

Allegro con brio

[2]

Allegro

[3]

Allegro

[4]

Cavatina

Largo

Ec-co ri-den-te in cie - - lo spun-ta la bel-la au-ro - ra,
Far in the East-ern hea - - ven brigh-tly the dawn — is brea-king;

[5]

No. 2 Cavatina FIGARO

Allegro vivace

Lar - go al fac-to - tum del-la cit - tà, lar - go!
I ____ am the busi - est man in the town, I am.

[6]

No. 3 Canzone COUNT

Andante

mezza voce

Se il mio no - me sa - per voi bra - ma - - te,
Would you know who comes here to im - plore _____ you,

[7]

No. 4 Duet

Allegro maestoso

FIGARO All' i - dea di quel me - tal - lo
When I hear your lord - ship men-tion

31

[8]
Vivace

FIGARO Un vul‑ca‑ no, un vul‑ca‑no la mia men‑te
Then my brain be‑gins to boil likeMount Ve‑su‑vius

[9]
COUNT

p dolce
Su ve‑dia‑mo, su ve‑diam di quel me‑tal‑lo
Yes, I thought that the ef‑fect might be sur‑pris‑ing

You're a mar vel.
COUNT Che in ven zio ne.

[10]
Vivace

FIGARO Che in‑ven‑zio ‑ ne, che in‑ven‑zio‑ne pre‑li‑ba ‑ ta!
I'm a mar‑vel at in‑ven‑tion, at in‑ven ‑ tion.

[11]
Allegro

p
COUNT Ah, che d'a ‑ mo‑re la fiam‑ma io sen‑to,
Love burnd with ‑ in me, new joy in‑spir‑ing,

[12]
No. 5 Aria ROSINA
Andante

p
U‑na vo ‑ ce po‑co fa qui nel cor mi ri‑suo‑no!
Once a song at break of day in my heart did light a flame;

[13]
Moderato

p
ROSINA Io so ‑ no do‑ci ‑ le
I know my pro‑per place

[14]
Moderato

ROSINA Ma se mi toc ‑ ca‑no dov'è il mio de ‑ bo‑le
But if I may not do just what I want to do

[15]
No. 6 The 'Slander' Aria
Allegro

BASILIO La ca ‑ lun‑nia è un ven‑ti ‑ cel ‑ lo,
Start a slan‑der the mer‑est noth ‑ ing.

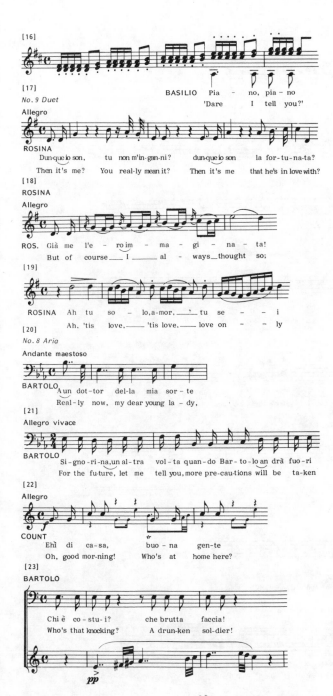

[16]

[17]

No. 9 Duet

Allegro

BASILIO Pia — no, pia — no
'Dare I tell you?'

ROSINA

Dun-que io son, tu non m'in-gan-ni? dun-que io son la for-tu-na-ta?
Then it's me? You real-ly mean it? Then it's me that he's in love with?

[18]

ROSINA

Allegro

ROS. Già me l'e — ro im — ma — gi — na — ta!
But of course___ I ___ al — ways___thought so;

[19]

ROSINA Ah tu so — lo, a-mor, ___ tu se — — i
Ah, 'tis love, ___ 'tis love, ___ love on — — ly

[20]

No. 8 Aria

Andante maestoso

BARTOLO A un dot-tor del-la mia sor-te
Real-ly now, my dear young la — dy,

[21]

Allegro vivace

BARTOLO Si-gno-ri-na, un al-tra vol-ta quan-do Bar-to-lo an drà fuo-ri
For the future, let me tell you, more pre-cau-tions will be ta-ken

[22]

Allegro

COUNT Ehi di ca-sa, buo — na gen-te
Oh, good mor-ning! Who's at home here?

[23]

BARTOLO

Chi è co — stu — i? che brutta faccia!
Who's that knocking? A drun-ken sol-dier!

pp

33

[24]

COUNT a tempo

Ah ve‑nis‑se il ca‑ro og‑get‑to,
Oh, if I could on‑ly find her.

[25]

Allegro

[26]

BARTOLO Vivace

Que‑sta be‑stia di sol‑da‑to, mio si‑gnor, m'ha mal‑trat‑ (...)
This in‑tox‑i‑cat‑ed sol‑dier is a dar‑ing des‑per‑ (...)

[27]

Andante

ROSINA Fred‑do ed im‑mo‑bi‑le co‑me u‑na sta‑tu‑a
I don't know what to think, 'tis in‑deed a mys‑te‑ry

[28]

Andante

FIGARO Guar‑da Don Bar‑to‑lo, guar‑da Don Bar‑to‑lo
Poor doc‑tor Bar‑to‑lo, does‑n't know what to do

[29]

Vivace sotto voce

ALL Mi par d'es‑ser col‑la te‑sta
All this noise and this com‑mo‑tion

[30]

No. 9 Duettino

Andante moderato

COUNT Pa‑ce e gio‑ia sia con vo‑i
Hea‑ven send you peace and glad‑ness

[31]

No. 13 Aria 'The Lesson Scene'

ROSINA Maestoso

Con‑tro un cor che ac‑ ‑ cen‑de a‑ ‑ mo‑re
When a heart by Cu‑ ‑ pid's ar‑ ‑ row

34

[32]

ROSINA

Moderato

Ca - ra im - ma - gi - ne ____ ri - den - te
Oh, ____ what ____ rap - ture to ____ find _ a lov - er

[33]

No. 14 Arietta BARTOLO

Andantino

Quan-do mi sei vi - ci - na, a - ma - bi - le Ro - si - na
Tell me if you have seen ____ her, my fair, my sweet Ro - si - na

[34]

Moderato

COUNT Buo - na se - ra, mio si - gno - re
Rev-'rend Fa - ther, must you leave ___ us?

[35]

No. 16 Arietta

Allegretto

BERTA Il vec-chiet-to cer - ca mo-glie, vuol ma - ri - to la ra - gaz - za
Spite of six-ty years to car - ry, our old doc-tor wants to mar - ry

[36]

No. 15 Terzetto ROSINA

Andante

Ah! Qual col - po, ah qual col - po in-a - spet - ta - to
Al - ma-vi - va, your ro-man - tic in - ti - ma - tion

[37]

Allegro

COUNT Zit - ti, zit - ti, pia - no, pia - no, non fac-cia-mo con-fu - sio - ne
If we all go ve - ry soft - ly, one by one with care de - scend - ing

[38]

No. 20 Finale

Allegro

FIGARO Di si fe-li-ce in - ne - - sto ser-biam me-mo-ria e - ter - - na,
This lan-tern I have light - - ed to guide a rash e - lope - - ment

35

Act One of the 1985 production of 'The Barber of Seville' at Covent Garden with (above) Alicia Nafe as Rosina and Domenico Trimarchi as Doctor Bartolo and (below) Thomas Allen as Figaro and Keith Lewis as Count Almaviva (photo: Catherine Ashmore)

The Barber of Seville
Il Barbiere di Siviglia

A Comic Opera in Two Acts by
Gioachino Rossini

Text by Cesare Sterbini
English version by Edward J. Dent

Il Barbiere di Siviglia was first performed as *Almaviva o sia L'Inutile Precauzione* at the Teatro Argentina, Rome on February 20, 1816. The first performance in England was at the King's Theatre, Haymarket, London on March 10, 1818. The first performance in the United States was in New York on May 3, 1819.

The Italian text follows the verse layout and scene divisions of the libretto printed in Rome for the 1816 Carnival première. This is also the basis for Alberto Zedda's critical edition of the score (1969) where the actual text Rossini set is printed in the modern Italian manner which we have adopted here.

The English version of E.J. Dent was made for performances by Sadler's Wells Opera. He modified and condensed the recitatives, and often added new lines to the original verse. Where appropriate, therefore, we have supplied additional literal translations in square brackets for passages he chose not to use, and supplemented the Italian text with repeated lines. The distinction between recitative and verse is made in the English by beginning the recitative lines without capital letters.

Dent's original text has been continuously altered by performers over the years, as may be seen by comparing this libretto, which purports to be the most recent ENO version, with that first printed in 1940. Nevertheless the pace and style of this text, many of whose lines have passed into English operatic lore, make it a classic example of Dent's exceptional qualities as a translator, and of the qualities upheld by the Sadler's Wells Opera in its early years.

The stage directions are literal translations of those in the libretto and do not represent either Dent's version or any particular production. The musical sections, and their numbers, follow after an oblique. The numbers in square brackets relate to the Thematic Guide.

CHARACTERS

Fiorello *servant to Count Almaviva*   *baritone*
Count Almaviva   *tenor*
Figaro *a barber*   *baritone*
Rosina *a wealthy heiress*   *mezzo-soprano*
Doctor Bartolo* *Rosina's guardian*   *bass*
Berta† *housekeeper to Doctor Bartolo*   *soprano*
Ambrogio *servant to Doctor Bartolo*   *bass*
Don Basilio *a music-master and hypocrite* *bass*
An Officer
A Notary
An Alcalde or Magistrate
Musicians, Watchmen and Constables, Soldiers

The action covers one day and takes place outside and inside the house of Doctor Bartolo in Seville.

* In the original, Bartolo is a doctor of medicine. Dent altered his profession to that of the law.

† Dent altered the housekeeper's name to Marcellina in order to tie the opera into Beaumarchais' trilogy and the character in *The Marriage of Figaro*. Thus Rosina had to wrap up sweets not for Marcellina but for Barbarina.

Teresa Berganza as Rosina in 'The Barber of Seville' at Covent Garden in 1960 (Royal Opera House Archives)

Overture. [1, 2, 3]

Act One

Scene One. *It is just before sunrise. A square in Seville. On the left is the house of Doctor Bartolo; on the upper floor it has a practicable balcony enclosed by a jalousie, which can be locked or unlocked at will.*

Enter Fiorello, with a lantern, followed by a number of musicians with instruments. Then Count Almaviva, wrapped in a cloak. / No. 1 Introduction.

FIORELLO
(coming forward cautiously)

Softly now, softly there, lest we be heard;   Piano, pianissimo! senza parlar,
Come, follow me, never a word!   Tutti con me venite qua.

MUSICIANS

Softly now, softly there, lest we be heard.   Piano, pianissimo! eccoci qua.

FIORELLO

Hush now, be quiet, still as a mouse!   Piano, pianissimo! senza parlar,
Here lives the lady, this is the house.   Tutti con me venite qua.
Now is the moment, no soul about,   Tutto è silenzio, — nessun qui sta;
To spoil our music or put us out.   Che i nostri canti possa turbar.

COUNT
(sotto voce)

Fiorello, I say!   Fiorello — olà!

COUNT

My lord, I'm here.   Signor, son qua.

COUNT

Your friends now, where are they?   Ebben; gli amici?

FIORELLO

They're waiting near.   Son pronti già.

COUNT

Bravo, that's excellent; we can go on then.   Bravi, bravissimi; fate silenzio.

FIORELLO, THEN MUSICIANS

Softly now, softly there, say not a word!   Piano, pianissimo! Senza parlar.

The musicians tune their instruments and the Count begins to sing accompanied by them. / Cavatina.

COUNT

Far in the Eastern heaven   [4] Ecco ridente in cielo,
  Brightly the dawn is breaking;   Spunta la bella aurora,
  Time is that you were waking,   E tu non sorgi ancora —
  O loveliest light of all!   E puoi dormir così?
Rise, rise and leave your pillow,   Sorgi, mia dolce speme,
  New light to heaven lending,   Vieni, bell'idol mio;
  And from your window bending,   Rendi men crudo, o Dio!
  Oh, hear a lover's call!   Lo stral che mi ferì;
Oh, moment of rapture!   O sorte! già, veggo
  If only she'd hear me,   Quel caro sembiante;
  Allow me to capture   Quest'anima amante
  One sight of her face!   Ottene pietà?
Oh, moment entrancing!   O, istante d'amore!
  Could I but behold her   Felice momento!
  And softly enfold her   O, dolce contento
  In love's fond embrace!   Che eguale non ha.

It grows lighter gradually. / Continuation and Stretta of Introduction.

COUNT

Oh, Fiorello!   Ei, Fiorello!

FIORELLO

Did you speak, sir?   Mio signore?

COUNT

Say, did you see her?   Di', la vedi?

FIORELLO

Not at all.   Signor, no.

COUNT

All in vain is all my pleading.   Ah, ch'è vana ogni speranza!

FIORELLO

Please your lordship, daylight is breaking.   Signor Conte, il giorno avanza.

COUNT

What do I care? Hope is gone.   Ah, che penso — che farò?
All is useless. You musicians!   Tutto è vano. Buona gente!

MUSICIANS
(*sotto voce*)

Here, my lord.   Mio signor?

COUNT

Fiorello, you pay them.   Avanti, avanti;
He gives his purse to Fiorello, who distributes money among the musicians.
That will do now, no more music.   Più di suoni, più di canti,
No more music from you today!   Io bisogno ormai non ho.

FIORELLO

Now, good fellows, you can leave us;   Buona notte a tutti quanti;
There's no more for you to play.   Più di voi che far non so.

The musicians surround the Count, thanking him and kissing his hand and his cloak; he is annoyed and tries to drive them away. Fiorello does the same.

MUSICIANS

Thank you kindly — wish you luck, sir,   Mille grazie, mio signore;
Thank you kindly — Heaven preserve you!   Del favore, dell'onore,
Always glad to wait upon you,   Ah! di tanta cortesia
We can come, sir, night or day.   Obligati in verità!
For a gentleman like you, sir,   O che incontro fortunato
We are always pleased to play.   E un signor di qualità!

COUNT

Gently, gently, what's the matter?   Basta! basta! non parlate,
Do be quiet, stop your chatter!   Ma non serve, non gridate,
Curses on you! The devil take you!   Maledetti, andate via,
Dirty blackguards, go away!   Ah canaglia, via di qua!
What with all the noise you're making,   Tutto quanto il vicinato,
All the neighbours you'll be waking;   Questo chiasso sveglierà.
'Tis enough to drive one crazy!   Zitti! Zitti! che rumore!
What will all the people say?   Ma che onore — che favore!

FIORELLO

Do be quiet, stop your chatter!   Zitti, zitti . . . che rumore!
Dirty blackguards, go away!   Ah canaglia, via di qua!
'Tis enough to drive one crazy!   Ve', che chiasso indiavolato!
What will all the people say?   Ah, che rabbia che mi fa?

Exeunt musicians.

40

recitativo

COUNT

The devil take them!   Gente indiscreta!

FIORELLO *

With all	Ah quasi,
the noise they were making	Con quel chiasso importuno,
they'll have roused the whole street.	Tutto quanto il quartier han risvegliato.
[At last they've gone.]	Alfin son partiti!

COUNT
(*looking at the window*)

I can't see her!	E non si vede!
My hopes are at an end.	È inutile sperar; eppur qui voglio

He walks about, thinking.

No, I'll wait a bit longer. Every morning	Aspettar di vederla. Ogni mattina
at sunrise she comes out	Ella su quel balcone
On the balcony to take the air.	A prender fresco viene in sull'aurora.
I'll wait. Fiorello,	Proviamo — Olà tu ancora
you may retire.	Ritirati, Fiorell'!

FIORELLO

[I'll go over here	Vado, là in fondo
And await your orders.]	Attenderò suoi ordini.

Fiorello withdraws.

COUNT

[If I do speak with her,]	Con lei, se parlar mi riesce,
I want no witnesses. She must have discovered	Non voglio testimoni. Che a quest'ora
that I come every day	Io tutti i giorni qui vengo per lei
at the same hour to look for her.	Dev'essersi avveduta. Oh vedi, amore
I know she is beneath me in rank;	A un uomo del mio rango
I care not. I adore her.	Come l'ha fatta bella! Eppure! eppure!
She must be mine — my wife!	Oh! dev'esser mia sposa —

Figaro is heard singing, offstage, and approaching.

Who is this? What impudent fellow	Chi è mai quest'importuno? —
comes here to disturb me?	Lasciamolo passar; sotto quegli archi
I'll step aside a moment	Non veduto vedrò quanto bisogna;
and wait till he goes by.	Già l'alba è appena, e amor non si vergogna.

He withdraws under the portico.

Scene Two. *Enter Figaro, with a guitar slung round his neck.* / *No. 2 Cavatina.*

FIGARO

La ran la lera, la ran la la!	La ran la lera, la ran la la!
I am the busiest man in the town,	[5] Largo al factotum della città
Off to my shop I must go at the dawn.	Presto a bottega che l'alba è già.
La ran la lera, la ran la la!	La ran la lera, la ran la la!
Yes, there's a livelihood,	Ah che bel vivere,
No trade so fine!	Che bel piacere
For I'm a barber,	Per un barbiere
First in my line!	Di qualità.
My name is Figaro, take heed.	Ah, bravo, Figaro; bravo bravissimo!
No one to equal me, no one indeed.	Fortunatissimo per verità,
La ran la lera, la ran la la!	La ran la lera, la ran la la!
Ready from daylight into evening,	Pronto a far tutto, la notte e il giorno —
That's what a barber always must be.	Sempre d'intorno in giro sta.
But of all trades a barber's the finest;	Miglior cuccagna, per un barbiere,
There's not a man more important than me.	Vita più nobile, nò, non si dà!
La ran la lera, la ran la la!	La ran la lera, la ran la la!

---

* Dent gave Fiorello's speech to the Count.

Brushes and combs for you, scissors and
   razors too,
Patches and powders, best that are made;
Shave you and blister you, bleed you and
   bandage you,
If it's a case for surgical aid.

And I may tell you, I can be useful
To pretty ladies and their admirers.
Everyone sends for me, everyone calls for
   me,
Married or single, youthful or aged;
Periwig powdered — shave in a hurry —
Quick with a lancet — quick with a letter —
And all are so insistent
And so impatient.
One at a time please, for pity's sake!
   Figaro! I'm here!
   Hey Figaro! I'm here!
   Figaro here, Figaro there,
   Figaro quick, Figaro slow,
   Figaro high, Figaro low,
   Figaro come, Figaro go!
   Lord how they hurry me!
   Lord how they flurry me!
   I am the busiest man in the town,
Ah, bravo Figaro! Bravo, bravissimo!
You'll make your fortune before you have
   done!
La ran la lera, la ran la la!

Recitative.

[Ha, ha, what a wonderful life!
Not much work and lots of fun;
always with some money in my pocket,
the well-earned fruit of my reputation.
It's like this: without me
no girl in Seville would marry.
It's me the young widow
consults about marriage, and what with
cutting hair all day and
playing the guitar all night
I can honestly say —
without exaggeration — I please everyone.
Oh, what a life! What a profession!
Ah well, back to work —]

Rasori, e pettini, lancette, e forbici —
Al mio comando tutto qui sta.
Lancette, e forbici, rasori, e pettini, —

Al mio comando tutto qui sta.

V'è la risorsa poi del mestiere
Colla donetta, col cavaliere.
Tutti mi chiedono, tutti mi vogliono,

Donne, ragazzi, vecchi, fanciulle:
Qua la parrucca! presto la barba!
Qua la sanguigna! presto il biglietto!
Ahimè! ahimè che furia!
Ahimè! che folla!
Uno alla volta per carità!
   Figaro! son qua.
   Ehi Figaro! son qua.
   Figaro qua, Figaro là!
   Figaro su, Figaro giù!
   Figaro qua, Figaro là!
   Figaro su, Figaro giù!
   Pronto, prontissimo —
   Son come il fulmine —
   Sono il factotum della città.
Ah, bravo Figaro! bravo, bravissimo!
A te fortuna, non mancherà.

La ran la lera, la ran la la!

Ah! ah! che bella vita!
Faticar poco, a divertirsi assai;
E in tasca sempre aver qualche doblone,
Gran frutto della mia reputazione.
Ecco qua: senza Figaro
Non si accasa in Seviglia una ragazza;
A me la vedovella
Ricorre per marito: io colla scusa
Del pettine di giorno,
Della chitarra col favor la notte,
A tutti onestamente —
Non fo per dir — m'addatto a far piacere.
Oh, che vita, che vita! oh, che mestiere!
Orsù, presto a bottega —

COUNT
(aside)

Why surely that must be my old friend
   Figaro!

(È desso, o pur m'inganno?)

FIGARO
(aside)

Where can I have seen him?

(Chi sarà mai costui?)

COUNT

No, I'm sure there's no mistake.
Figaro!

Oh, è lui senz'altro,
Figaro!

FIGARO

   At your service!
(recognising the Count)
Oh, his lordship, Count Almaviva!

   Mio padrone!

Oh, chi veggo? — Excellenza!

42

COUNT

Hush! I beg you, be careful!	Zitto, zitto! prudenza:
I am unknown here,	Qui non son conosciuto,
and wish to remain so.	Nè vo' farmi conoscere — per questo
I have my reasons.	Ho le mie gran ragioni.

FIGARO

I understand, sir; I understand, sir;	Intendo, intendo —
I will leave you to your private meditations.	La lascio in libertà.

COUNT

No!   No!

FIGARO

[I'm sorry . . .?]   Che serve?

COUNT

No, stay here;	No, dico, resta qua;
I may have need of you.	Forse ai disegni miei
[— But damn it!	Non giungi inopportuno. — Ma cospetto!
Tell me, old friend,	Dimmi un po', buona lana,
what brings you here, for goodness sake!	Come ti trovo qua? — poter del mondo!
You look fat and well!]	Ti veggo grasso e tondo —

FIGARO

[Almost destitute, sir!]   La miseria, Signore!

COUNT

[Ah rascal!]   Ah birbo!

FIGARO

[Thanks!]   Grazie.

COUNT

[Have you reformed at last?]   Hai messo ancor giudizio?

FIGARO

[Oh, and how!] — and you, my lord,	Oh, e come! — Ed ella,
how do you come to be in Seville?	Come in Siviglia?

COUNT

[I'll tell you.] One day in Madrid	Ora te lo spiego. Al Prado
at the Prado, I saw the loveliest creature —	Vidi un fior di bellezza — una fanciulla,
daughter of an old brute of a doctor,	Figlia d'un certo medico barbogio,
who has just come to live here.	Che qua da pochi dì s'è stabilito.
I left my home and my relations,	Io di questa invaghito
posted off to Seville, and here I am,	Lasciai patria e parenti; e qua men venni,
spending my days and nights	E qui, la notte e il giorno,
gazing up at that balcony . . .	Passo girando a que' balconi intorno.

FIGARO

At *that* balcony? A doctor? [Good heavens!]	A que' balconi? — un medico? Oh cospetto!
Then you're in luck, sir;	Siete ben fortunato:
[It couldn't be better.]	Sui maccheroni il cacio v'è cascato.

COUNT

How so?   Come!

FIGARO

Yes, sir! In that house	Certo. — Là dentro
I'm barber, surgeon, apothecary —	Io son barbiere, parucchier, cirurgo,
[. . . I see to the health of the plants and the animals —]	Botanico, spezial, veterinario —
. . . and general factotum.	Il faccendier di casa.

COUNT	
What good fortune!	Oh, che sorte!

FIGARO

There's more to come, sir.	Non basta: la ragazza
The young lady is not the Doctor's daughter	Figlia non è del medico — è soltanto
but his ward.	La sua pupilla.

COUNT

[Oh, what a relief!]	Oh, che consolazione!

FIGARO

And what is more, he means to . . . hush!	Perciò — zitto!

COUNT

[What is it?]	Cos'è?

FIGARO

[Someone's coming onto the balcony!]	S'apre il balcone!

He pushes the Count under the portico.

Scene Three. *Enter Rosina, then Bartolo, on the balcony.*

ROSINA
She looks about.

I cannot see him anywhere. [Perhaps —]	Non è venuto ancora. Forse —

COUNT
(*running out*)

My beloved, my adored one!	Oh, mia vita! mio nume! mio tesoro!
[I see you, at last, at last!]	Vi veggo alfine — alfine —

ROSINA
(*startled*)

[Oh how embarrassing!]	(Oh che vergogna!
I must give him the letter.	Vorrei dargli il biglietto.)

She takes a letter from her bosom.

BARTOLO
(*from within*)

Well, then . . .	Ebben, ragazza,

The Count hurriedly retires. Enter Bartolo above.

What's the weather like? And what's that paper?	Il tempo è buono? Cos'è quella carta?

ROSINA

Oh, nothing, sir, only the words	Nulla signore: sono le parole
of my song in 'The Guardian Outwitted'.	Dell'aria dell' 'Inutil Precauzione'.

COUNT
(*to Figaro*)

Did you hear? — 'The Guardian Outwitted'?	Ma brava: — dell' 'Inutil Precauzione'!

FIGARO
(*to the Count*)

That's good!	Che furba!

BARTOLO

What's that? 'The Guardian Outwitted'?	Cos'è questa
What's that, miss?	'Inutil Precauzione'?

ROSINA

Why, it's the name
of the new opera . . .

Oh bella! è il titolo
Del nuovo Dramma in Musica.

BARTOLO

[An opera? . . . That's good!
It will be the usual dramma semiserio;
A long, melancholy, boring,
poetic farrago of nonsense.
Barbarous taste! What depraved times!]

Un Dramma? . . . bella cosa!
Sarà al solito un dramma semiserio;
Un lungo malinconico, noioso,
Poetico strambotto.
Barbaro gusto! Secolo corrotto!

Rosina drops the paper onto the ground below.

ROSINA

Oh dear! I've dropped it!
Won't you go and pick it up for me?

Oh me meschina! l'aria m'è caduta:
Raccoglietela presto.

BARTOLO

I think I'd better.

Vado, vado.

Exit.

ROSINA
(*to the Count*)

Pst, pst!

Pst! pst! —

COUNT

[I understand you —]

Ho inteso —

ROSINA

Be quick!

Presto!

COUNT

[Don't worry!]

Non temete.

He picks it up and retires. Enter Bartolo below.

BARTOLO
(*to Rosina*)

Well, where is it?

Son qua. Dov'è?

ROSINA

Oh, the wind
has blown it away —
over there!

Ah, il vento
Se l'ha portato via. —
Guardate.

She points in the distance. Bartolo looks for it, then returns.

BARTOLO

I can't find it. Well, miss?
I don't like this.

Io non la veggo; — ehi, signorina?
Non vorrei.
(*to himself*)

[The devil!
If this is some trick —]

(Cospetto!
Costei m'avesse preso!)
(*to Rosina*)

Go indoors,
go in at once, I tell you.

In casa! in casa!
Animo, sù! A chi dico?
In casa presto!

ROSINA

Oh, what a fuss about nothing!

Vado, vado; — che furia!

BARTOLO
(*to himself*)

I'll have that window walled up.

Quel balcone voglio far murare.
(*to Rosina, angrily*)

Go indoors, miss.

Dentro, dico!

ROSINA
(to herself)

Oh! What a life!   Ah, che vita da crepare!

She goes in. Bartolo goes in at the house door.

Scene Four.

COUNT

[Poor little thing!   Povera disgraziata!
Her unhappiness   Il suo stato infelice
makes her even more interesting to me.]   Sempre più m'interessa.

FIGARO

         Quick,   Presto, presto —
Let us see what she says!   Vediamo cosa scrive.

COUNT

     Come on then! Read it.   Appunto, leggi.

FIGARO
(reading)

'Your assiduous attendance has excited   'Le vostre assidue premure hanno
my curiosity. As soon as my guardian   eccitata la mia curiosità. Il mio tutore è
has gone out, find some means of telling   per uscir di casa: appena si sarà
me your name, your condition, and your   allontanato, procurate con qualche
intentions. I am never allowed on the   mezzo ingegnoso di indicarmi il vostro
balcony except in the company of my   nome, il vostro stato, e le vostre
tyrant; but rest assured that I shall do   intenzioni. Io non posso giammai
all I can to break my chains.   comparire al balcone senza l'indivisibile
Your unfortunate Rosina.'   compagnia del mio tiranno. Siate però
  certo che tutto è disposta a fare per
  rompere le sue catene, la sventurata
  Rosina.'

COUNT

Break her chains! She *shall*. [What sort   Sì, sì, le romperà; — su, dimmi un poco
of man is this tyrant of a guardian?]   Che razza d'uomo è questo suo tutore!

FIGARO

Oh, he's the very devil!   Un vecchio indemoniato!
An old miser, suspicious and ill-tempered.   Avaro, sospettoso, brontolone;
He must be nearly a hundred,   Avrà cent'anni indosso
But he still thinks to play the gallant,   E vuol fare il galante: indovinate?
[can you imagine it?]   Per mangiare a Rosina
And to swallow Rosina's inheritance.   Tutta l'eredità s'è fitto in capo
He intends to marry her.   Di volerla sposare.

A door opens below.

       Look out!   Aiuto!

COUNT

[What?]   Che?

FIGARO

    [The door.]   S'apre la porta.

Figaro pushes the Count behind the door. Enter Bartolo, speaking to someone inside the house.

BARTOLO

I shall be back directly.   Ehi; fra momenti io torno.
You are not to open the door to *anybody*.   Non aprite a nessuno. Se Don Basilio
If Don Basilio calls, he must wait.   Venisse a ricercarmi, che m'aspetti.

He shuts the door and locks it.

And now for my wedding with Rosina.   Le mie nozze con lei meglio è affrettare.
I'll have it all settled this very day.   Sì, dentr'oggi finir vo' quest'affare.

Exit.
46

COUNT

The wedding today?
He's in his second childhood!
But tell me, who is this Don Basilio?

Dentr'oggi le sue nozze con Rosina.
Ah vecchio rimbambito!
Ma dimmi or tu, chi è questo Don Basilio?

FIGARO

The Reverend Don Basilio? He's a
matrimonial agent;
a crooked fellow, a regular scoundrel,
and always short of money.
He teaches singing too —
teaches Miss Rosina.

È un solenne imbroglion di matrimoni —
Un collo torto, un vero disperato,
Sempre senza un quattrino.
Già è maestro di musica,
Insegna alla ragazza.

COUNT

[Good, good.]
It's as well to know everything.

Bene, bene!
Tutto giova sapere.

FIGARO

Now, sir, you must think
how to satisfy
the wishes of the young lady.

Ora pensate
Della bella Rosina
A soddisfar le brame.

COUNT

I shall not tell her my
name or my rank. I want to make sure that
she loves me, loves me for myself alone,
not for my fortune, or for the title of
Count Almaviva. Now, couldn't *you* —

Il nome mio
Non le vo' dir, nè il grado. Assicurarmi
Vo' pria ch'ella ami me, me solo al mondo,
Non le richezze e i titoli
Del Conte Almaviva. Ah! tu potresti —

FIGARO

I, sir? Oh no, my lord; you must do that
yourself.

Io? — no, Signor: voi stesso dovete —

COUNT

Myself? But how?

Io stesso? E come?

Rosina appears on the balcony.

FIGARO

Hush, sir! Now is the moment.
Look! She's coming out on the balcony.
[Good Lord, I'm not mistaken, she's
behind the shutters.]
Quick, no-one is looking.
[Sing her a song.]

Zi — zitto. Eccoci a tiro.
Osservate — per Bacco, non mi sbaglio.
Dietro la gelosia sta la ragazza.

Presto, presto all'assalto: niun ci vede.
In una canzonetta,

He offers the Count his guitar.

Yes, sir. You can explain it all
to her in a song.

Così, alla buona, il tutto
Spiegatele, Signor.

COUNT

[A song?]

Una canzone?

FIGARO

[Yes, sir.]
Take my guitar. [Quickly, go on.]

Certo!
Ecco la chitarra, presto, andiamo.

COUNT

How can I?

Ma, io —

FIGARO

(*insistently*)

Go on, sir, sing!

O che pazienza!

May love inspire me.   Ebben, proviamo.

The Count takes the guitar and sings to his own accompaniment. / No. 3 Canzone.

Would you know who comes here to implore you.	[6] Se il mio nome saper voi bramate,
Let me tell you my name and condition.	Dal mio labbro il mio nome ascoltate.
I'm a poor student, my name is Lindoro,	Io son Lindoro
And oh! I adore you,	Che fido v'adoro,
To madness adore you,	Che sposa vi bramo,
And I dream of you	Che a nome vi chiamo,
All the day long;	Di voi sempre parlando così
Only Rosina's the theme of my song.	Dall'aurora al tramonto del dì.

Rosina's voice is heard from within repeating the ritornello of the song.

ROSINA

Oh, beloved Lindoro, sing on!   Segui, o caro, deh segui così!

FIGARO

You heard her? You are in luck, sir.   Sentite? — A che vi pare?

COUNT

Oh, happy moment!   O me felice!

FIGARO

Well done, sir! That's right, sir, go on, sir!   Da bravo, a voi, seguite.

COUNT

Your adoring, your loving Lindoro,	L'amoroso e sincero Lindoro
Cannot offer you wealth or position;	Non può darvi, mia cara, un tesoro.
Nothing beside what I now lay before you,	Ricco non sono,
A heart to adore you,	Ma un coro vi dono,
Yes, madly adore you,	Un'anima amante
And to sigh for you	Che fida e costante,
All the day long;	Per voi sola sospira così
Only Rosina's the theme of my song.	Dall'aurora al tramonto del dì.

ROSINA

Your beloved, your loving Rosina,	L'amorosa e sincera Rosina
Her Lindoro cannot —	Del suo core a Lindo —

The sound of a window being closed is heard.

COUNT

[Oh, heavens!]   Oh cielo!

FIGARO

[She's gone in;	Nella stanza
Someone else is there.]	Convien dir che qualcuno entrato sia.
	Ella si è ritirata.

COUNT
(*emphatically*)

[Damn it!	Ah cospettone!
I'm desperate!] I must see her,	Io già deliro — avvampo! — Oh ad ogni costo
I *must* speak to her [at any price].	Vederla io voglio — vo' parlarle: ah, tu,
Can't you help me?	Tu mi devi aiutar —

FIGARO
(*hesitantly*)

[Lord, what a haste you are in!]	Ih, ih, che furia!
Yes, I might help you —	Si, si, v'aiuterò.

Good.	Da bravo: entr'oggi
You must get me into that house today.	Vo' che tu m'introduca in quella casa.
How can you do it?	Dimmi, come farai? — via! — del tuo spirito
I want a sample of your wit.	Vediam qualche prodezza.

FIGARO

A sample of my wit?	Del mio spirito! —
My lord, *I* too want a sample of —	Bene — vedrò — ma in oggi —

COUNT

I understand,	Eh via t'intendo,
[Don't worry.] You shall be handsomely rewarded.	Va là, non dubitar; di tue fatiche Largo compenso avrai.

FIGARO

On your honour?	Davver!

COUNT

On my honour.	Parola.

FIGARO

A small subsidy now and then?	Dunque oro a discrezione?

COUNT

As much as you like,	Oro a bizzeffe.
Only hurry.	Animo, via.

FIGARO

My lord, I'm your man. [Ah, you've no idea the prodigious effect the thought of a little gold produces in me.]	Son pronto. Ah, non sapete I simpatici effetti prodigiosi Che, ad appagare il mio signor Lindoro, Produce in me la dolce idea dell'oro.

No. 4 Duet.

When I hear your lordship mention Such a generous intention,	[7]	All'idea di quel metallo Portentoso onnipossente,
Then my brain begins to boil like Mount Vesuvius, And is throwing up suggestions thick and fast.	[8]	Un vulcano, un vulcano la mia mente Già comincia, già comincia a diventar.

COUNT

Yes, I thought that the effect might be surprising,	Si, su vediamo, su vediam di quel metallo
That ideas in your head would soon be rising.	Qualche effetto, qualche effetto sorprendente
If your brain begins to boil like Mount Vesuvius,	Del vulcano, del vulcan della tua mente
Something wonderful I hope to hear at last.	Qualche mostro, qualche mostro singolar.

FIGARO

We shall have to dress you up, sir.	Voi dovreste travestirvi —
Yes, I have it. As a soldier.	Per esempio, da soldato.

COUNT

As a soldier?	Da soldato?

FIGARO

The very thing, sir.	Si, signore.

COUNT

Yes, but why? Tell me why? Da soldato! — e che si fà? che si fà?

FIGARO

There's a regiment arriving. Oggi arriva un reggimento.

COUNT

And the colonel is my cousin. Sì, è mio amico il Colonnello.

FIGARO

Very good. Va benon!

COUNT

What then? E poi?

FIGARO

I'll tell you. Cospetto!
If your billet's on the Doctor, Dell'alloggio col biglietto
He will have to let you in. Quella porta s'aprirà.
How will that do? Do you like it? Che ne dite, mio signore?
That's the way to do the trick, sir. Non vi par? non l'ho trovata?

I'm a marvel at invention; [9] Che invenzione prelibata!
Bravo, bravo, that's the way. Bella, bella in verità!

COUNT

You're a marvel at invention; Che invenzione prelibata!
Bravo, bravo, that's the way. Bravo, bravo in verità.

FIGARO

Wait now, wait now, I've something Piano, piano — un'altra idea:
   better —
Funny thing how money stimulates the brain! Veda l'oro cosa fa!
You'll be tipsy, yes, Ubriaco! si, ubriaco,
You'll be tipsy, sir, as well. Mio signor, si fingerà.

COUNT

I'll be tipsy? Ubriaco?

FIGARO

Half seas over. Si, signore.

COUNT

Half seas over? Yes, but why? Tell me why? Ubriaco? — ma perchè? ma perchè?

FIGARO
(*imitating without exaggeration the actions of a drunken man*)

When the Doctor sees that you Perchè d'un ch'è poco è in se —
Have a drop too much on board, Che dal vino casca già,
He will think, believe me, sir, Il tutor, credete a me,
You're a safe man to meet his ward. Il tutor si fiderà.

FIGARO AND THE COUNT

You're a marvel at invention; [9] Che invenzione prelibata!
Bravo, bravo, that's the way. Bravo! bravo! in verità!

COUNT

Well then? Dunque?

FIGARO

To work, sir. All'opra.

COUNT

I'm ready. Andiamo.

FIGARO

That's right, sir.   Da bravo.

COUNT

Come, then. Oh, but I forgot to ask you   Vado. — Oh, il meglio mi scordavo;
Where you live? Where can I find you?   Dimmi un po', la tua bottega?
When I want you, are you near?   Per trovarti dove sta.

FIGARO, THEN COUNT

Where to find me? You look there, sir!   La bottega? — non si sbaglia.
Can't mistake it: my shop there.   Guardi bene, eccola là.

He points offstage.

Fifteen my number is; turn to the right, sir.   Numero quindici, a mano manca,
Four steps in front of it — house painted   Quattro gradini, facciata bianca —
  white, sir,
Wigs of all sizes stand in the window,   Cinque parruche nella vetrina,
Lotions and ointment if your hair's thin.   Sopra un cartello, 'Pommata Fina',
Over the doorway my name in blue, sir,   Mostra in azzurro alla moderna,
Pole with a basin ready for you, sir,   V'è per insegna una lanterna.
And when you want me you'll find me there.   Là senza fallo mi troverà.

COUNT

I understand you.   Ho ben capito.

FIGARO

Time that you did, sir.   Or, vada presto.

COUNT

You must be careful.   Tu guarda bene.

FIGARO

I will indeed, sir.   Io penso al resto.

COUNT

Then I can trust you?   Di te mi fido.

FIGARO

Safe as a house, sir.   Colà l'attendo.

COUNT

And of course, Figaro —   Mio caro Figaro!

FIGARO

Of course, of course, sir.   Intendo, intendo.

COUNT

I shall bring with me —   Porterò meco —

FIGARO

— money in plenty.   La borsa piena.

COUNT

You're sure to want it, if no one else does.   Sì, quel che vuoi. Ma il resto poi —

FIGARO

You may be certain I'll see it through.   Oh! non si dubiti che bene andrà.

COUNT

Love burns within me,   [10]   Ah, che d'amore
New joy inspiring,   La fiamma io sento,
Promising happiness   Nunzia di giubilo
Past all desiring;   E di contento!
I feel a flame in me   D'ardore insolito
All my blood firing,   Quest'alma accende,

51

Love knows no barriers,	E di me stesso
Love leads the way.	Maggior mi fa.

FIGARO

Out of this business	Delle monete
I'll make a profit;	Il suon già sento!
He'll have his pleasure,	L'oro già viene,
He'll have to pay.	Viene l'argento.
He has the money,	Eccolo in tasca scende,
Thinks nothing of it;	Eccolo quà;
I'll make my fortune,	D'ardore insolito
I know the way.	Quest'alma accende.

Figaro enters the Doctor's house. Exit the Count.

Scene Five. *A room with four doors in the house of Doctor Bartolo; ahead is the window with the jalousie seen in the first scene. A writing desk to the right. Rosina is discovered; she has a letter in her hand. / No. 5 Cavatina.*

ROSINA

Once a song at break of day	[11] Una voce poco fa;
In my heart did light a flame;	Qui nel cor mi risuonò!
He that sang was young and gay,	Il mio cor ferito è già,
And Lindoro, that was his name.	E Lindor fu che il piagò.
And Lindoro shall be mine;	Sì, Lindoro mio sarà.
Yes, I swear it, I'll win the game.	Lo giurai, la vincerò.
Doctor Bartolo may think	Il tutor ricuserà,
I'm to marry him one day;	Io l'ingegno aguzzerò.
But I know a thing or two	Alla fin s'acchetterà
And I mean to have my way.	E contenta io resterò.
And Lindoro shall be mine;	Sì, Lindoro mio sarà.
Yes, I swear it, I'll win the game.	Lo giurai — la vincerò.
I know my proper place,	[12] Io sono docile.
Know what's expected,	Son rispettosa,
I know my guardian	Son ubbidiente,
Must be respected.	Dolce, amorosa,
I'm quite affectionate	Mi lascio reggere,
As long as I can have my way;	Mi fo guidar.
But if I may not do	[13] Ma se mi toccano
Just what I want to do	Dov'è il mio debole,
Then I'll have something else to say.	Sarò una vipera, sarò,
And Doctor Bartolo	E cento trappole,
Will very shortly know	Prima di cedere, farò giocar.
That I've a thousand tricks to play.	E cento trappole farò giocar.
And I will make it clear,	E cento trappole,
If he should interfere,	Prima di cedere, farò giocar.
That I've a thousand tricks to play.	E cento trappole farò giocar,
For I'm in readiness now for a fray.	Farò giocar, farò giocar, farò giocar.

Recitative.

[Yes, yes, I'll have my way.	Sì, sì, la vincerò. Potessi almeno
If only I could send this letter! But how?	Mandargli questa lettera! — Ma come?
I can trust no one here:	Di nessun qui mi fido:
My tutor has a hundred eyes . . . What a	Il tutor ha cent'occhi. Basta, basta,
nuisance! At least I can seal it.	Sigilliamola intanto.

She goes to the desk and seals the letter.

From the window I saw him talking with	Con Figaro, il barbiere, dalla finestra
Figaro, the barber, for more than an hour.	Discorrer l'ho veduto più d'un ora; —
Figaro is a good fellow,	Figaro è un galantuomo,
an honest young man.	Un giovin di buon cuore.
Who knows if he wouldn't protect our love?]	Chi sà ch'ei non protegga il nostro amore?

52

Scene Six. *Enter Figaro.*

FIGARO

Good morning, Miss Rosina. | Oh, buon di, Signorina!

ROSINA

Good morning, Master Figaro. | Buon giorno, signor Figaro!

FIGARO

Ah, pray, how are you? | Ebbene, che si fa?

ROSINA

Bored to death! | Si muor di noia.

FIGARO

Bored to death? | Oh, diavolo! possibile!
And such a pretty young lady. | Una ragazza bella e spiritosa.

ROSINA

[I know you're just laughing at me.] | Ah, ah, mi fate ridere,
What's the good of being pretty, | Che mi serve lo spirito, —
[how does it help me,] | Che giova la bellezza,
if I'm always shut up in this house? | Se chiusa io sempre sto fra quattro mura
I might just as well be buried alive. | Che mi par d'esser proprio in sepoltura.

FIGARO

Buried alive! Oh dear. | In sepoltura! Ohibò!
(confidentially)
Now listen, I want to tell you... | Sentite, io voglio —

ROSINA

There's my guardian! | Ecco il tutor!

FIGARO

No, no. | Davvero?

ROSINA

Here he comes. I can hear his step. | Certo, certo; è il suo passo!

FIGARO

Then goodbye. [We must meet | Salva, salva; fra poco
very soon.] — But I've something to tell you. | Ci rivedremo — ho a dirvi qual' cosa.

ROSINA

And so have I, Master Figaro. | E ancor io, signor Figaro.

FIGARO

[Bravissima!] | Bravissima!
I'll be back! | Vado.

He hides behind the first door on the left but shows himself from time to time.

ROSINA

I'm sure he'll help me. | Quanto è garbato.

Scene Seven. *Enter Bartolo.*

BARTOLO

Lord, lord, that fool of a Figaro! | Ah disgraziato Figaro!
[That worthless man! That cursed rogue! | Ah indegno! Ah maledetto! Ah scellerato!
That rascal!]

ROSINA
(aside)

[Here he is, complaining as usual.] | (Ecco qua! sempre grida.)

53

[You can't imagine anything worse.]　　　Ma si può dar di peggio!
The house is like a hospital.　　　　　　Un ospedale ha fatto
He's given the servants　　　　　　　　Di tutta la famiglia
All the wrong medicines —　　　　　　A forza d'oppio, sangue e stranutiglia.
a sleeping-draught to Ambrogio　　　　Signorina, il Barbiere
and a sneezing powder to Berta. That　　Lo vedeste?
barber, have you seen him?

[Why?]　　　　　　　　　　　　　　　Perchè?

[Because I want to know.]　　　　　　Perchè lo vo' sapere.

[So you've taken against him too?]　　Forse anch'egli v'adombra?

[And why not?]　　　　　　　　　　　E perchè no?

*[Alright, I'll tell you. Yes, I have seen him.　Ebben, ve lo dirò. Si, l'ho veduto,
I have spoken to him and I like him;　　Gli ho parlato, mi piace, m'è simpatico.
I find his conversation genial, and his　Il suo discorso, il suo gioviale aspetto.
　　company pleasant.
(Go jump in the lake, you dirty old man.)]　(Crepa di rabbia, vecchio maledetto.)

Exit, to the second room on the right.

The minx!　　　　　　　　　　　　　Vedete che grazietta!
The more I'm in love with her, the more　Più l'amo e più mi sprezza la briccona.
　　she disdains me.
I'll be bound it's that Figaro　　　　　Certo, certo è il Barbiere
sets her against me.　　　　　　　　　Che la mette in malizia.
I wonder what he's told her.　　　　　Chi sa cosa le ha detto!
†[H'm, I'll soon find out,　　　　　　Chi sa! Or lo saprò.

(calling)

Berta! Ambrogio!　　　　　　　　　　Ehi, Berta, Ambrogio!

Enter Berta sneezing and Ambrogio yawning.

Achoo!　　　　　　　　　　　　　　　Ecci!

Aah . . . you called?　　　　　　　　Aah — che commanda?

(to Berta)

Tell me —　　　　　　　　　　　　　Dimmi —

Achoo!　　　　　　　　　　　　　　　Ecci!

Has that barber been talking to Rosina?　Il Barbiere parlato ha con Rosina?

---

* Dent has: 'Yes, I have, I like Figaro; he's very well-mannered, and (*pointedly*) he's most agreeable and always in a good humour.'

† This whole scene is usually cut in ENO performances.

BERTA

Achoo!   Ecci!

BARTOLO
(*to Ambrogio*)

Well, *you* answer me, you fool.   Rispondi almen tu, babbuino!

AMBROGIO

Ahhh...   Aah —

BARTOLO

O Lord, O Lord!   Che pazienza!

AMBROGIO

Ahhh — how sleepy I am!   Aah — che sonno!

BARTOLO

Well?   Ebben? —

BERTA

He came — but I —   Venne — ma io —

BARTOLO

Rosina...   Rosina —

AMBROGIO

Aah...   Aah...

BERTA

Achoo!   Ecci!

AMBROGIO

Aah!...   Aah...

BERTA

Achoo!   Ecci!

AMBROGIO

Aah...   Aah!...

BARTOLO

Well, he's half killed you both, I think.   Che serve! eccoli qua, son mezzi morti.
Come, out with it!   Andate.

AMBROGIO

Ahh...   Aah...

BERTA

Achoo!   Ecci!

BARTOLO

Oh, the devil take you both!]   Eh, il diavol che vi porti!
He chases them both out.
Curses on that barber!   Ah! Barbiere d'inferno!
But I'll make him pay for it.   Tu me la pagherai.

Scene Eight. *Enter Don Basilio.*

BARTOLO

Oh, Don Basilio,   — Qua, Don Basilio!
you're in the nick of time.   Giungete a tempo. Oh! lo voglio,
Basilio bows very obsequiously and goes on bowing.
By hook or by crook, before this day is   Per forza o per amor, dentro domani
ended, I mean to marry Miss Rosina. You   Sposar la mia Rosina — avete inteso?
understand?

55

BASILIO
(*bowing*)

The very best thing you can do, sir.	Eh, voi dite benissimo;
And I just came in to tell you —	E appunto io qui veniva ad avvisarvi.

(*mysteriously*)

Do your know who has arrived in Seville?	Ma segretezza! — è giunto
Count Almaviva!	Il Conte d'Almaviva!

BARTOLO

What! Rosina's unknown admirer?	Che! l'incognito amante
	Della Rosina?

BASILIO

The very man, sir.	Appunto quello.

BARTOLO

Oh, the devil!	Oh, diavolo!
We must see about this.	Ah qui ci vuol riparo.

BASILIO

Of course, sir; but — discreetly...	Certo; ma, alla sordina...

BARTOLO

You mean to see...	Sarebbe a dir...

BASILIO

We must invent some pleasant little story about him, which will get him into bad odour as a man of evil reputation — of evil reputation. You leave all that to me. In three days, I give you my word, we shall have him hounded out of town.	Cosi con buona grazia Bisogna principiare a inventar qualche favola Che al pubblico lo metta in mala vista, Che comparir lo faccia un uomo infame, Un'anima perduta. Io, io il servirò: Fra quattro giorni, Credete a me, Basilio ve lo giurà, Noi lo farem sloggiar da queste mura.

BARTOLO

You think so? But — it's slander!	E vorreste? — Ma una calunnia —

BASILIO

Precisely.	Ah, dunque,
Slander. Do you know what that is?	La calunnia cos'è voi non sapete?

BARTOLO

I do not, sir!	No, davvero.

BASILIO

Listen to me, and I will tell you.	No? — Uditemi e tacete.

No. 6 Aria.

Start a slander — the merest nothing — [14]	La calunnia è un venticello,
Just a story — oh, quite amusing —	Un'auretta assai gentile
Start it circulating gently,	Che insensibile, e sottile,
Oh, so lightly, oh, so lightly,	Leggermente, dolcemente,
In a whisper round it goes.	Incomincia a sussurrar.

'Dare I tell you?' — 'Don't repeat it!' [15]	Piano piano, terra terra,
'Contradict it where you meet it!'	Sotto voce sibilando,
So from one to another flying,	Va scorrendo, va scorrendo,
Some believing, some denying,	Va ronzando, va ronzando;
No one knows who first averred it	Nelle orecchie della gente
Or remembers how he heard it,	S'introduce destramente,
But with every repetition	E le teste ed i cervelli
It receives a fresh addition;	E le teste ed i cervelli
If it's true or if it's fiction	Fa stordire, fa stordire
No one knows and no one cares.	Fa stordire e fa gonfiar.

In the wrong place out it's blurted,	Dalla bocca fuori uscendo
Yes, quite openly asserted;	Lo schiamazzo va crescendo;
'Tis the talk of all the city,	Prende forza a poco a poco,
And the country, more's the pity;	Vola già di loco in loco;
As the tempest at a distance	Sembra il tuono, la tempesta,
Nearer draws with more insistence,	Che nel sen della foresta
Rumbling louder, ever louder,	Va fischiando, brontolando,
Till the storm is at its worst.	E ti fa d'orror gelar.
Then a mighty flash of lightning	Alla fin trabocca, e scoppia,
(Yes, it's positively frightening)	Si propaga, si raddoppia
Tears the vault of heaven asunder	E produce un esplosione
With an awful clap of thunder,	Come un colpo di cannone,
And with rending and with roaring	Un tremuoto, un temporale,
Comes the rain in torrents pouring,	Un tumulto generale,
For the cataclysm's burst.	Che fa l'aria rimbombar.

Then the victim of your slander	E il meschino, calunniato,
Can do nothing but surrender	Avvilito, calpestato,
To the public indignation	Sotto il pubblico flagello
At his impropriety;	Per gran sorte va a crepar.
Though the tale was quite unfounded,	E il meschino calunniato,
He's defenceless, he's confounded,	Avvilito, calpestato,
And inexorably hounded	Sotto il pubblico flagello
Out of all society.	Per gran sorte va a crepar.
Now, sir, what do you think of that?	Ah, che ne dite?

BARTOLO

[That's all very well, but] I can't say;	Eh! sarà ver, ma intanto
it would take too much time; and I'm in a	Si perde tempo e qui stringe il bisogne.
hurry [to get married]. Come into my room;	No, vo' fare a mio modo;
we'll have the contract drawn up this very	In mia camera andiam. Voglio che insieme
instant. Once Rosina is my wife, I can look	Il contratto di nozze ora stendiamo.
after all these amorous young gentlemen	Quando sarà mia moglie,
quite well myself.	Da questi zerbinotti innamorati
	Metterla in salvo sarà pensier mio.

BASILIO

I am always at your service . . .

(aside)

for a consideration.   (Vengan danari: al resto son qua io.)

Exeunt Bartolo and Basilio.

Scene Seven. *Enter Figaro and Rosina.*

FIGARO

[Well done! That's excellent!	Ma bravi! ma benone!
I heard everything. Long live the good	Ho inteso tutto. Evviva il buon tutore!
guardian! Poor baboon!	Povero babbuino!
Your wife! — Go on! Wash your mouth out.	Tua sposa? — Eh via! Pulisciti il bocchino.
Now they're locked up in there together	Or che stanno là chiusi,
it would be a good time to speak with the	Procuriam di parlare alla ragazza;
girl; and there she is.]	Eccola appunto.

ROSINA

Well, Master Figaro?   Ebbene, signor Figaro?

FIGARO

Well, Miss Rosina.   Gran cose, Signorina.

ROSINA

[Really?]   Sì, davvero?

FIGARO

[We'll be hearing wedding bells.]   Mangeremo dei confetti.

ROSINA

[What do you mean?]　　　　　　　　　Come sarebbe a dir?

FIGARO

　　　　　[I mean to say]　　　　　　　　　　Sarebbe a dire
Your amiable guardian has made up　　Che il vostro bel tutore ha stabilito
his mind to marry you this very day.　Esser dentro doman vostro marito.

ROSINA

What nonsense!　　　　　　　　　　　Eh, via!

FIGARO

　　　You may think so:　　　　　　　　Oh, ve lo giuro:
He's just gone in there with　　　　　A stender il contratto
your reverend music-master　　　　　Con maestro di musica
to draw up the contract.　　　　　　La dentro or s'è serrato.

ROSINA

[Oh yes? He's made a mistake there!]　Si? Oh l'ha sbagliata affè!
Poor old ninny! He'll have to settle with　Povero sciocco! L'avrà da far con me.
me first. But tell me, Figaro,　　　　Ma dite, signor Figaro,
weren't you talking just now —　　　Voi poco fa sotto le mie finestre
under the window — to a gentleman?　Parlavate a un signore —

FIGARO

　　　　Oh yes, my cousin.　　　　　　　　Ah, un mio cugino —
He's a good lad —　　　　　　　　Un bravo giovinotto; buona testa,
just come to finish his studies　　　Ottimo cuor; qui venne
at the University, and thinks he's going　I suoi studi a compire, e il poverin
to make his fortune.　　　　　　　Cerca di far fortuna.

ROSINA

Oh! I'm sure he will.　　　　　　　Fortuna? — oh, la farà.

FIGARO

Well, *I* don't think so. [Between us,　Oh, ne dubito assai; in confidenza,
he has one major problem.]　　　　Ha un gran difetto addosso.

ROSINA

　　　[A major problem?]　　　　　　　　Un gran difetto?

FIGARO

　　　　[Yes, major.]　　　　　　　　　　　　Ah, grande,
He's [madly] in love.　　　　　È innamorato morto.

ROSINA

　　　In love? In love!　　　　　　　　　Si, davvero?
[This young man, you see, interests me　Quel giovane, vedete,
　very much.]
How very interesting!　　　　　　M'interessa moltissimo.

FIGARO

　　You think so?　　　　　　　　　　　Per Bacco!

ROSINA

Don't you agree?　　　　　　　　Non ci credete?

FIGARO

　　　Oh yes!　　　　　　　　　　　　Oh si!

ROSINA

　　And the young lady —　　　　　　　　E la sua bella —
Tell me, does she live a long way off?　Dite, abita lontano?

FIGARO

Oh no, she lives here.
I mean — quite close by.

Oh nò! — cioè —
Qui! due passi —

ROSINA

Is she pretty?

Ma è bella?

FIGARO

Of course she is. Shall I describe her?
On the plump side. (Most attractive.)
Black hair — rosy cheeks —
a very speaking eye —
and the sweetest little hand in all the world!

Oh, bella assai — eccovi il suo ritratto,
In due parole:
Grassotta, genialotta,
Capello nero, guancio porporina,
Occhio che parla, mano che innamora.

ROSINA

And her name?

E il nome?

FIGARO

Oh, you want to know *that*, do you?
Let me think — what *is* her name?
Let me think...

Ah, il nome ancora?
Il nome? — Ah, che bel nome! —
Si chiama —

(*hesitating, as if trying to remember*)

ROSINA

What letter does it begin with?

Ebben? si chiama?

FIGARO
(*hesitating, then suddenly*)

Ah!

Si chiama R - o - ro - si - rosi - Rosina.

ROSINA

Oh!

FIGARO

Yes!

ROSINA

I —

FIGARO

Ro -

ROSINA

- sina!

No. 9 Duet.

Then it's me? You really mean it?
   Then it's me that he's in love with?
   (But of course I always thought so;
   No, it's nothing new to me.)

[16] Dunque io son — tu non m'inganni?
   Dunque io son la fortunata!
[17]   (Già me l'ero immaginata,
   Lo sapevo pria di te.)

FIGARO

Yes, Lindoro's lovely lady
   Is no other than Rosina;
   Now you know it, Miss Rosina.
   (What a crafty little schemer!
   But she'll find her match in me.)

Di Lindoro il vago oggetto
   Siete voi, bella Rosina,
   Siete voi, bella Rosina.
   (Oh, che volpe sopraffina,
   Ma l'avrà da far con me.)

ROSINA

Tell me, tell me, can't I somehow
   With Lindoro have a talk?

Senti, senti, ma a Lindoro
   Per parlar come si fa?

FIGARO

You will see him very shortly,	Zitto, zitto, qui Lindoro
Soon into this house he'll walk.	Per parlarvi or sarà.

ROSINA

Come to see me? Oh how lovely!	Per parlarmi? Bravo! bravo!
But you know he must be careful.	Venga pur, ma con prudenza;
I am dying with impatience —	Io già moro d'impazienza!
What's he doing? Why delay?	Ma che tarda? cosa fà?

FIGARO

He is waiting for some token,	Egli attende qualche segno,
Poor young man, of your affection,	Poverin, del vostro affetto;
If you send him just a letter	Sol due righe di biglietto
He would come this very day.	Gli mandate, e qui verrà.
Well, and won't you?	Che ne dite?

ROSINA

I don't know.   Non vorrei.

FIGARO

Why so timid?   Su, coraggio!

ROSINA

It might look —   Non saprei —

FIGARO

Quite a short one —   Sol due righe.

ROSINA

Not quite proper —   Mi vergogno.

FIGARO

What of that? What of that? Come on!	Ma di che? — di che? — si sa?
Here, sit down and write the letter.	Presto, presto, qua il biglietto.

Rosina takes the letter from her pocket and gives it to Figaro.

ROSINA

Write the letter? Here you are.	Un biglietto? eccolo qua.

FIGARO

What, ready written? Did you ever?	Già era scritto! — ve' che bestia!

(astonished)

Who'd have thought it? You're a minx, upon my word!	Ve' che bestia! Il maestro faccio a lei!
I begin to think I'm learning	Ah, che in cattedra costei
How a girl can use her pen.	Di malizia può dettar.
Woman, woman, who can read you?	Donne, donne! eterni Dei,
You're a mystery apart.	Chi v'arriva a indovinar?
He'll be here very shortly . . .	Qui verrà. A momenti
Very shortly he'll be here.	Per parlarvi qui sarà.

ROSINA

Now at last my luck is turning,	Fortunati affetti miei!
I begin to breathe again.	Io comincio a respirar.
Ah, 'tis love, 'tis love, love only	Ah, tu solo, amor, tu sei
That can satisfy my heart.	Che mi devi consolar!
Tell me, tell me, my Lindoro . . .	Senti, senti ma Lindoro . . .
But you know he must be careful.	Venga pur, ma con prudenza.

Exit Figaro.

Scene Eight. *Enter Bartolo. / Recitative.*

ROSINA

Oh, now I feel happier.
Figaro is a very nice young fellow.

Ora mi sento meglio.
Questo Figaro è un bravo giovinotto!

BARTOLO
(*amorously*)

Well, and won't Rosina tell me
what Figaro was doing here
this morning?

Insomma, colle buone,
Potrei sapere dalla mia Rosina
Che venne a far colui questa mattina?

ROSINA

Figaro? *I* don't know.

Figaro? — Non sò nulla.

BARTOLO

Did he talk to you?

Ti parlò?

ROSINA

He did.

Mi parlò.

BARTOLO

What did he say?

Che ti diceva?

ROSINA

All sorts of things —
talked about the latest Paris fashions —
and how little Marcellina was not very well.

Oh, mi parlò di cento bagatelle:
Del figurin di Francia,
Del mal della sua figlia, Marcellina.

BARTOLO

Yes. And I'll wager
he brought you the answer to your letter.

Davvero? Ed io scommetto
Che portò la risposta al tuo biglietto.

ROSINA
(*taken by surprise*)

What letter?

Qual biglietto?

BARTOLO

No use pretending! The words
of your song in 'The Guardian Outwitted',
that you let fall from the balcony this
morning. [You're blushing!] If only I had
guessed in time.
Your finger is inky!

Che serve! L'arietta
Dell' 'Inutil Precauzione',
Che ti cadde staman giù dal balcone.
Vi fate rossa — (Avessi indovinato!)
Che vuol dir questo dito
Cosi sporco d'inchiostro?

ROSINA

Inky? [Oh, it's nothing!]
Oh, I burnt it
and put ink on it to take the pain away.

Sporco? — Oh, nulla.
Io me l'avea scottato,
E con l'inchiostro or or l'ho medicato.

BARTOLO
(*looking at the table*)

H'm! There are only
five sheets of paper here now; there *were* six.

(Diavolo!) E questi fogli?
Or son cinque — eran sei.

ROSINA

[What paper? Oh, that's right:]
I took one to wrap up
some lollipops for Marcellina.

Quei fogli? È vero:
D'uno mi son servita
A mandar de' confetti a Marcellina.

BARTOLO

Very kind of you. And the new pen —
is inky too?

Bravissima! E la penna —
Perchè fu temperata?

61

ROSINA

[(Curses!) The pen?]
I used it to draw a flower for my embroidery.

(Maledetto!) La penna?
Per disegnare un fiore sul tamburo.

BARTOLO

[A flower?]

Un fiore?

ROSINA
(indignantly)

[A flower.]

Un fiore.

BARTOLO
(imitating her)

For my embroidery!

Un fiore!

Oh, you hussy!

Ah, fraschetta!

ROSINA

Sir!

Davver.

BARTOLO

Be quiet!

Zitto!

ROSINA

I beg you —

Credete.

BARTOLO

Not a word more!

Basta cosi.

ROSINA

[Sir —]

Signor —

BARTOLO

I know all about it!

Non più — tacete.

No. 8 Aria.

Really now, my dear young lady,
Your excuses won't deceive me;
I'm a lawyer of experience;
I'm a lawyer of experience.
After my investigation
Nothing's ever left in doubt.
Now be careful, very careful!
And in cross-examination
You are sure to be found out.

[18] A un dottor della mia sorte
Queste scuse, signorina?
A un dottor della mia sorte
Queste scuse, signorina?
Vi consiglio, mia carina,
Un po' meglio a imposturar,
Meglio, meglio, meglio, meglio.
Vi consiglio, mia carina,
Un po' meglio a imposturar.

Lollipops for Marcellina?
Drew a pattern to embroider?
Burnt your finger? Of course, I know.
Most ingenious explanation,
But it will not do for me.
Most ingenious, most inegenious.
Circumstantial information,
Quite fictitious, I can see.

I confetti alla ragazza?
Il ricamo sul tamburo?
Vi scottaste? Eh via! Eh via!
Ci vuol altro, figlia mia,
Per potermi corbellar,
Altro, altro, altro, altro.
Ci vuol altro, figlia mia,
Per potermi corbellar.

Where's that missing sheet of paper?
For what purpose did you use it?
I suggest you wrote a letter;
Otherwise how could you lose it?
Tell the truth, it's always better.

Perchè manca là quel foglio?
Vo' saper cotesto imbroglio.
Perchè manca là quel foglio?
Sono inutili le smorfie;
Ferma là, non mi toccate.

Ah, what a tangled web it is we weave,
When first we practise to deceive.
I'm a lawyer of experience —
I shall always find you out.

No, figlia mia, non lo sperate
Ch'io mi lasci infinocchiar.
No, figlia mia, non lo sperate
Ch'io mi lasci infinocchiar.

Really now, my dear young lady,	A un dottor della mia sorte
Your excuses won't deceive me.	Queste scuse, signorina,
You'll be kept in isolation,	Vi consiglio, mia carina,
Safely under lock and key.	Un po' meglio a imposturar.

Come, Rosina, tell the truth now;	Via, carina, confessate.
I'll forgive you if you'll confess.	Son disposto a perdonar.
Won't you tell me? What does this mean?	Non parlate? Vi ostinate?
So pigheaded! Miss, how dare you?	Non parlate? Vi ostinate?
Now I know what I must do.	So ben io che ho da far.

For the future, let me tell you,	Signorina, un'altra volta
More precautions will be taken.	Quando Bartolo andrà fuori,
'Tis the duty of your guardian	Signorina, un'altra volta
To protect your reputation.	Quando Bartolo andrà fuori,
I shall give the servants orders	La consegna ai servitori
That you're never to be free.	A suo modo dar saprà.

And whenever it may happen	Signorina, un'altra volta
That I have to quit the mansion,	Quando Bartolo andrà fuori,
To perform the many duties	Signorina, un'altra volta
Of my legal occupation,	Quando Bartolo andrà fuori,
You'll be kept in isolation,	La consegna ai servitori
Safely under lock and key.	A suo modo dar saprà.

Not a word or look shall shake me,	Eh, non servono le smorfie;
All in vain is your protesting.	Faccia pur la gatta morta,
Let me tell you, don't mistake me,	Faccia pure, faccia pure,
Lamentations you are wasting.	Faccia pur la gatta morta.

Every door and every window	Cospetton! per quella porta,
Shall be locked and barred and bolted.	Cospetton! per quella porta,
Not a fly shall enter in.	Nemmen l'aria entrar potrà.

Only chaste incarceration	E Rosina innocentina,
Can relieve you of temptation.	Sconsolata, disperata . . .
All in vain is your protesting;	Eh, non servono le smorfie;
Lamentations you are wasting.	Faccia pur la gatta morta.
Not a breath of air shall enter	Cospetton! per quella porta
If I am not there to see.	Nemmen l'aria entrar potrà.
Not a word or look shall shake me;	E Rosina innocentina,
All in vain is your protesting.	E Rosina innocentina,
Let me tell you, don't mistake me,	Sconsolata, disperata,
Lamentations you are wasting.	Sconsolata, disperata,
Only chaste incarceration	In sua camera serrata,
Can relieve you of temptation;	In sua camera serrata
You'll be kept in isolation,	Fin ch'io voglio star dovrà.
Safely under lock and key,	Si, si, si, si, si si, si.
Yes, safely under lock and key.	Fin ch'io voglio star dovrà.

Scene Eleven. *Rosina alone.*

ROSINA

[Rage at me all the day.	Brontola quanto vuoi,
Lock the doors, lock the windows.	Chiudi porte e finestre. Io me ne rido.
Much good that will be! If you want	Già di noi femmine alla più marmotta
to sharpen the wits of a woman,	Per aguzzar l'ingegno
all you need to do	E farla spiritosa, tutto a un tratto
is to turn the key upon her!]	Basta chiuderla a chiave e il colpo è fatto.

Exit into the second room on the right.

Scene Twelve. *Berta alone.*

BERTA

| [I thought I heard the sound of voices | Finora in questa camera |
| just a moment ago from this room. | Mi parve di sentir un mormorio; |

It must have been the tutor. With his pupil,
he never has a moment's peace. Young girls
nowadays don't want to understand.]

Sarà stato il tutor. Colla pupilla
Non ha un'ora di ben. Queste ragazze
Non la voglion capir.

A sound of knocking is heard.

Someone's knocking.   Battono.

COUNT

[Open up!]   Aprite!

BERTA

[I'm coming... Achoo! It never stops.
That tobacco will be the death of me.]

Vengo... Ecci! Ancora dura.
Quel tabacco m'ha posto in sepoltura.

She opens the door and leaves.

Scene Thirteen. *The Count enters dressed as a soldier pretending to be drunk; then Bartolo. / No. 9 Finale Primo.*

COUNT

Oh, good morning! Who's at home here? [20]
Can't you hear me? All asleep there?
No one answers!

Ehi, di casa! — Buona gente — buona gente —
Ehi, di casa! niun mi sente!

BARTOLO

Who's that knocking? A drunken soldier!
Ugly fellow! Why's he here? Why's he here?

Chi è costui? — Che brutta faccia!
È ubriaco! chi sarà? chi sarà?

COUNT

Ho, good people! Devil take you!
Plague upon you!

Ehi, di casa! — Maledetti!
Maledetti!

BARTOLO

What the devil do you want, sir?   Cosa vuol, signor Soldato?

COUNT

(*Seeing Bartolo, he feels for something in his pocket.*)

Ah! That's right. Your humble servant!   Ah! Si, si! — bene obligato.

BARTOLO

What on earth can this man want?   Qui costui! — che mai vorrà?

COUNT

Aren't you Doctor — just wait a moment —
Aren't you doctor — yes — Doctor
  Buffalo?

Siete voi — aspetta un poco!
Siete voi — Dottor Balordo?

BARTOLO

Sir, how dare you call me Buffalo?   Che Balordo? Che Balordo?

COUNT

(*looking at his paper*)

No, no — it's Buttercup —   Ah, ah! Bertoldo —

BARTOLO

Sir, how dare you call me Buttercup?   Che Bertoldo? Che Bertoldo?
Go to the devil, sir!   Eh, andate al diavolo!
Doctor Bartolo, Doctor Bartolo!   Dottor Bartolo! Dottor Bartolo!

COUNT

Oh, I've got it now —   Ah, bravissimo!
Doctor Buttonhole. Delighted, sir —   Dottor Barbaro; benissimo; ...

BARTOLO

How dare you?   Un corno!

64

Now we've got it right.	Va, benissimo.
Well, it's much the same whichever way you write it.	Già v'è poca differenza.

(aside)

Where's she got to? What's she doing?	(Non si vede! Che impazienza!
Oh, where is she? Is she here?	Quanto tarda! — Dove sta?)

BARTOLO
(aside)

Now I mustn't let myself get too excited;	Io già perdo la pazienza.
I must handle him with care.	Qui prudenza ci vorrà.

COUNT

Well, at any rate you're a doctor?	Dunque voi — siete Dottore?

BARTOLO

Yes, I am, sir, I'm a doctor.	Son dottore — sì, signore.

COUNT

Glad to hear it! So am I, sir.	Ah, benissimo! Un'abbraccio —
Pleased to meet you.	Qua collega.

He tries to embrace Bartolo.

BARTOLO

Hands off, sir!	Indietro.

COUNT
(embracing him by force)

There!	Qua!
As you see I'm in the forces,	Sono anch'io dottor per cento,
A physician to the horses.	Ma niscalco al reggimento:
And I'm billeted on you, sir;	Dall'alloggio sul biglietto
Here's the paper, you look at that!	Osservate, eccolo qua.

He shows him the paper.

Ah, if I could only find her,	Ah venisse il caro oggetto,
Love would show me what to do.	Della mia felicità!

BARTOLO
(aside)

This is really most annoying	Dalla rabbia — dal dispetto
But I don't know what to do.	Io già crepo in verità;
By refusing to receive him	Ah, ch'io fo, se mi ci metto,
I may get into a stew.	Qualche gran bestialità!

COUNT
(aside)

Ah, if I could only find her,	Vieni, vieni; il tuo diletto,
Love would show me what to do.	Pien d'amor, t'attende già.

Scene Eleven. *Enter Rosina; seeing a stranger, she stops short.*

ROSINA

There's a soldier with the Doctor;	Un soldato! — il tutore! —
Oh, what can he mean to do?	Cosa mai faranno qua?

She comes forward on tiptoe.

COUNT
(seeing Rosina)

There's Rosina; now what's the next move?	È Rosina! Or son contento.

ROSINA

Why, the soldier's coming nearer!	Ei mi guarda, e s'avvicina!

COUNT
(*softly to Rosina*)

I'm Lindoro.   Son Lindoro.

ROSINA

        I'm all a-tremble!   Oh ciel! che sento?
Do be careful now, I pray.   Ah, giudizio, per pietà!

BARTOLO
(*seeing Rosina*)

Miss Rosina, why are *you* here?   Signorina, che cercate?
Go away at once, I tell you.   Presto, presto, andate via.

ROSINA

Oh, I'm going, sir, directly.   Vado, vado, non gridate.

BARTOLO

Go away, miss, go away!   Presto, presto, via di qua.

COUNT

Wait a moment, I'll come with you.   Ehi, ragazza, vengo anch'io.

BARTOLO

Pray, where d'you think you're going?   Dove, dove, Signor mio?

COUNT

To my billet — and it's a soft one.   In caserma: oh, questa è bella!

BARTOLO

To your billet? Stuff and nonsense!   In caserma? Bagatella!

COUNT

Dearest!   Cara!

ROSINA

    How dare you?   Aiuto!

BARTOLO

   You don't come here!   Olà, cospetto!

COUNT

Then I'm settled.   Dunque vado —

BARTOLO
(*holding him back*)

    No, no, by no means.   Oh no, signore!
In this house you cannot stay.   Qui d'alloggio non può stare.

COUNT

Why not? Why not?   Come, come?

BARTOLO

    Why? Let me tell you, sir;   Eh, non v'è replica;
I've a warrant of exemption.   Ho il brevetto d'esenzione.

COUNT
(*angrily*)

Of exemption?   Il brevetto?

BARTOLO

    Wait a moment.   Mio padrone,
Wait a moment, you shall see.   Un momento e il mostrerò.

He goes to look in his papers.

66

COUNT
(to Rosina)

If he will not let me stay here, Take this letter —	Ah, se qui restar non posso, Deh, prendete —

ROSINA
(to the Count)

No, no! He's looking!	Ahimè! ci guarda.

BARTOLO
(rummaging in his desk)

Where's the thing? I cannot find it.	Ah, trovarlo ancor non posso.

ROSINA
(to the Count)

Be careful!	Prudenza!

BARTOLO

Somewhere here it ought to be.	Ma si, si, lo troverò.

ROSINA AND THE COUNT

Now I know there will be trouble Very soon for you and me.	Cento smanie io sento addosso! Ah, più reggere non so.

BARTOLO

Ah, here it is.	Ah! ecco qua.

He comes forward with a document and reads.

'We hereby certify that Doctor Bartolo, etcetera, from the billeting of all military personnel is exempt —'	'Con la presente, Il dottor Bartolo, etcetera, Esentiamo' —

COUNT
(tossing the document up in the air)

That for your exemption, sir! How do I know if it's true?	Eh, andate al diavolo! Non mi state più a seccar.

BARTOLO

What the devil are you doing?	Cosa fa, signor mio caro?

COUNT

Hold your tongue, you doddering idiot! I am billeted on you, sir, And I mean to stay with you.	Zitto là, dottor Somaro! Il mio alloggio è qui fissato, E in alloggio qui vo' star.

BARTOLO

Stay with me?	Vuol restar!

COUNT

I do indeed, sir.	Restar sicuro.

BARTOLO

This is more than I can stomach; If you do not go this instant You'll be beaten black and blue.	Oh, son stufo, mio padrone; Presto fuori, o un buon bastone Ti farà di qua sloggiar.

COUNT
(in earnest)

Then you're asking to see some fighting? Good! For battle I'm your man. 'Tis a grand thing to fight a battle; I'll explain to you the plan.	Dunque lei — lei vuol battaglia? Ben. battaglia le vo' dar. Bella cosa è una battaglia! Ve la voglio or qui mostrar.

He approaches Bartolo in a friendly way.

Come, look here, sir, here are the trenches; We'll suppose that you're the enemy,	Osservate! questo è il fosso, L'inimico voi sarete.

67

On your guard! Here are our men.	Attenzion! e gli amici —

(aside to Rosina, showing her the letter)

Just drop your handkerchief.	(Giù il fazzoletto.)

(continuing to Bartolo)

All in order here they stand.	E gli amici stan di qua.
On your guard!	Attenzion!

He drops the letter; Rosina lets her handkerchief fall upon it.

BARTOLO

What's that paper?	Ferma, ferma!

COUNT

What is it? Ah!	Che cos'è? — Ah!

Turning around, he pretends to notice the letter, which he picks up.

BARTOLO

Let me see.	Vo' vedere.

COUNT

Oh, it's just a piece of paper.	Sì, se fosse una ricetta!
No, it's a letter. Permit me, madam.	Ma un biglietto — e mio dovere —
It's addressed to you, I see.	Mi dovete perdonar.

He gives the letter and handkerchief to Rosina.

ROSINA

Thank you, thank you.	Grazie, grazie!

BARTOLO

Thanks indeed! Give me that letter,	Grazie, un corno! Qua quel foglio,
Give it to me, you forward hussy!	Qua quel foglio, impertinente!

COUNT

Would you fight, sir? Shoulder arms! 'Shun!	Vuol battaglia? Attenzion . . . ih! . . .

BARTOLO
(to Rosina)

Give it me, you forward hussy! Don't you hear me?	Qua quel foglio, impertinente!
Hand it over here to me.	A chi dico? — presto qua!

ROSINA

If you want to see the paper,	Ma quel foglio che chiedete,
You are welcome, sir, with pleasure;	Per azzardo m'è cascato,
It's the linen for the laundry —	È la lista del bucato.

Enter on one side Basilio holding a paper; on the other side Berta.

BARTOLO
(tearing the paper out of Rosina's hand)

Don't suppose that you'll deceive me,	Ah, fraschetta, ah, fraschetta,
Give it me, miss, give it me.	Ah, fraschetta, presto qua!
Shirts and stockings, cravats and nightgowns —	Ah, che vedo? — ho preso abbaglio!

BERTA

Here's the barber. Who are these folk?	Il barbiere! Uh, quanta gente!

BARTOLO

'Tis the washing for the laundry.	E la lista, son di stucco!
They have caught me in a pitfall;	Ah, son proprio un mammalucco!
I'll be even with them yet.	Oh, che gran bestialità!

ROSINA AND THE COUNT

Ha! The Doctor's nicely fallen	Bravo! bravo! il mammalucco!
Right into the trap we set.	Che nel sacco entrato è già.

What's the cause of all this trouble?	Non capisco, son di stucco;
What's the cause of all the fuss?	Qualche imbroglio qui ci sta.

BASILIO

Do re mi fa sol la si do,	Do re mi fa sol la si do,
There'll be more to follow yet.	Ma che imbroglio è questo qua.

ROSINA
(*in tears, to Bartolo*)

There you are, the usual story!	Ecco qua! Sempre un istoria,
You suspect me every moment and ill-treat me.	Sempre oppressa e maltrattata;
It's unbearable, past endurance,	Ah, che vita disperata —
And I wish that I were dead.	Non la so più sopportar.

BARTOLO
(*approaching her*)

Come, Rosina, come, Rosina —	Ah, Rosina! — Poverina!

COUNT
(*threatening Bartolo and grabbing his arm*)

Let her be, she cannot bear you.	Vien qua tu! Cosa le hai fatto?

BARTOLO

I'm her guardian, sir! How dare you?	Ah, fermate — niente affatto —

COUNT

You old ruffian, let me teach you —	Ah, canaglia, traditore —

ROSINA, BERTA, BASILIO AND BARTOLO
(*Rosina restraining the Count*)

Sir, be careful, I beseech you.	Via, fermatevi, signore.

COUNT

I've a mind to break your head!	Io ti voglio subissar!

ROSINA, BERTA AND BASILIO

Call the neighbours, help, he'll murder him!	Gente, aiuto — ma chetatevi —
Help, before it is too late!	Gente, aiuto, per pietà!

BARTOLO

Call the neighbours, help, he'll murder me,	Gente, aiuto — soccorretemi —
Help, before it is too late!	Gente, aiuto, per pietà!

COUNT

I'll break his head.	Lasciatemi!

Scene Fifteen. *Enter Figaro with a basin under his arm.*

FIGARO

Hold your hand!	Alto là!
Ladies and gentlemen, what is the matter? [21]	Che cosa accade? — Signori miei,
What are you doing? Why, goodness gracious!	Che chiasso è questo? Eterni Dei!
What's all this turmoil? What's all this noise about?	Già sulla strada a questo strepito
Everyone's asking what's going on.	S'è radunata mezza città.
Crowds are collecting out in the square below,	Già sulla strada a questo strepito
There must be nearly half of the town.	S'è radunata mezza città.

(*aside to the Count*)

You've gone too far, sir, indeed you have.	(Signor, giudizio, per carità!)

BARTOLO
(pointing to the Count)

This drunken fellow —   Questo è un birbante!

COUNT
(pointing to Bartolo)

This filthy scoundrel —   Questo è un briccone!

BARTOLO

Murderous ruffian!   Ah disgraziato! —

COUNT
(threatening Bartolo with a drawn sword)

Foul-mouthed old blackguard!   Ah maledetto!

FIGARO
(pretending to threaten the Count)

Now, Mister Soldier, you mind your   Signor Soldato, porti rispetto,
  language!
You're not in barracks, you must be civil;   O questo fusto, corpo del diavolo,
So mind your manners, and be a gentleman,   O questo fusto, corpo del diavolo,
Or I'll soon teach you how to behave.   Or le creanze le insegnerà.
(aside to the Count)
You've gone too far, sir, indeed you have.   Signor, giudizio, per carità.

COUNT
(to Bartolo)

Ugly old monkey!   Brutto scimmiotto —

BARTOLO
(to the Count)

You foul-mouthed blackguard!   Birbo malnato —

ROSINA, BERTA, FIGARO AND BASILIO

Doctor, be quiet!   Zitto, Dottore —

BARTOLO

I don't care what I say!   Voglio gridare —

ROSINA, BERTA, FIGARO AND BASILIO

Do keep your temper!   Fermo, Signore!

COUNT

Let me get at him!   Voglio ammazzare.

ROSINA, BERTA, FIGARO AND BASILIO

Can't you be quiet? Do stop this row!   Fate silenzio! Per carità!

COUNT

Damn you, I'll murder him, murder him   No, voglio ucciderlo, non v'è pietá!
  now.

ROSINA, BERTA, FIGARO AND BASILIO

Can't you be quiet? Do stop this row!   Fate silenzio! Per carità!

A loud knocking is heard at the street door.

ALL

Who is that knocking there? Who can it be?   Zitti, chi battono? Chi mai sarà?

BARTOLO
(spoken)

Who's there?   Chi è?

70

MILITIA
(*offstage chorus*)

We charge you! We charge you!	La forza, la forza.
Come open the door!	Aprite qua!

ALL

The watchmen! Confound it all!	La forza! — Oh, diavolo!

FIGARO AND BASILIO
(*to the Count, Rosina and Bartolo*)

Now we are done for!	L'avete fatta!

COUNT AND BARTOLO

I'm not afraid of them.	Niente paura.
Let them all come!	Vengan pur qua.

ALL EXCEPT THE LADIES

What explanation have we to offer them? what can we say?	Quest' avventura, ah, come diavolo mai finirà!

ROSINA AND BERTA

Now we shall all be taken to prison.	Quest' avventura, ah; come diavolo mai finirà!

Last Scene. *Enter an officer and militia.*

MILITIA

In the King's name, stay where you are now!	Fermi tutti! Niun si muova.
No evasions, don't you try!	Miei signori, che si fa?
What's the cause of all this trouble?	Questo chiasso donde è nato?
We must know the reason why.	La cagione presto qua.

BARTOLO

This intoxicated soldier	Quesa bestia di soldato,
Is a daring desperado	Mio signor, m'ha maltrattato,
And has threatened me with murder.	Mio signor, m'ha maltrattato.
Yes, indeed.	Si, signor.

FIGARO

I looked in as I was passing	Io qua venni, mio signore,
When this shouting caught my ear.	Questo chiasso ad acquetar.
Yes, indeed.	Sì, signor.

BASILIO THEN BERTA

Yes, he threatened him with murder	Fa inferno di rumore,
And in most improper language	Parla sempre d'ammazzare,
For a clergyman to hear.	Parla sempre d'ammazzare,
Yes, indeed.	Si, signor.

ROSINA

You can understand it quicker	Perdonate, poverino,
When you see the man's in liquor.	Tutto effetto fu del vino.
Just a drop too much he's taken,	Perdonate, poverino,
That's why all this noise he's making.	Tutto effetto fu del vino.
Yes, indeed.	Si, signor.

OFFICER

Yes, I see now.	Ho inteso.

(*to the Count*)

Come along,	Galantuom',
I must arrest you:	Siete in arresto:
Off to prison	Fuori presto,
You must go.	Via di qua.

The soldiers advance to surround the Count.

71

Off to prison? You'd arrest me?   In arresto? In arresto?
Read that! Now you know.   Io? fermi, olà.

He shows a paper to the officer who, much surprised, orders the militia to stand back. All are amazed.

ROSINA, BERTA, BASILIO AND BARTOLO

I don't know what to think;   [23] Fredd } ^o_a ed immobile

'Tis indeed a mystery,   Come una statua.
Quite takes my breath away,   Fiato non restami
'Tis all so queer.   Da respirar.

COUNT

They know not what to think;   Freddo ed immobile
'Tis indeed a mystery,   Come una statua,
Quite takes their breath away,   Fiato non restagli
'Tis all so queer.   Da respirar.

FIGARO

Poor old Doctor Bartolo   [24] Guarda Don Bartolo,
Doesn't know what to do.   Sembra una statua!
Look at old Bartolo!   Guarda Don Bartolo!
Can't even puff and blow;   Guarda Don Bartolo!
I never saw a man   Ah, ah, dal ridere
Looking so queer.   Sto per crepar.

BARTOLO
(to the Officer)

Please allow —   Ma, signor —

MILITIA

     Not a word!   Zitto tu!

BARTOLO

Really now!   Ma un dottor —

MILITIA

     That's absurd.   Oh, non più.

BARTOLO

Wait, I say!   Ma se lei —

MILITIA

     Say no more.   Non parlar.

BARTOLO

Who's to pay?   Ma vorrei —

MILITIA

     As before.   Non gridar.

BERTA, BARTOLO AND BASILIO

Yes, but we —   Ma se noi —

MILITIA

     That may be.   Zitto tu.

BERTA, BARTOLO AND BASILIO

But 'twas he —   Ma se poi —

MILITIA

     Hold your tongue!   Pensiam noi.

High time all this nonsense ended;
Stop this noise and all go home.

Vada ognun pe' fatti suoi,
Si finisca d'altercar.

BARTOLO

I demand an explanation
Of this awkward situation.
I insist on satisfaction.
You may drive me to distraction.
I repeat what I have stated:
That the man's intoxicated.
I'd have been assassinated
If you people had not come.

Ma sentite, ma sentite,
Ma sentite, ma sentite,
Ascoltate, ascoltate.
Ma sentite, ma sentite,
Ma sentite, ma sentite,
Ascoltate, ascoltate.
Ma sentite, ma sentite,
Ascoltate, ascoltate.

BERTA, ROSINA, COUNT, FIGARO AND BASILIO

Really now! Please allow!
But 'twas he!

Zitto su! Zitto giù!
Zitto qua! Zitto là!

ALL

All this noise and this commotion
Makes me feel as if I were upon the ocean,
Rolling, lurching, pitching, tossing,
On a rough and stormy crossing,
Staggering, toppling, stumbling, falling,
And in all directions calling,
Everyone has lost his head.
Everyone reiterating
What already they were stating
Cursing, swearing, shouting, bawling,
Till the noise is quite appalling,
And repeating and repeating
Like a thousand hammers beating
To the din of horrid orgies
In the Fiend's infernal forges
With a clattering and clanging
And a shattering and banging,
Roaring and reverberation
With a din to wake the dead —
All this wild unending chatter,
What the devil does it matter?
This eternal pitter-patter,
'Tis enough to drive one mad.

[25] Mi par d'esser con la testa
In un'orrida fucina,
Mi par d'esser con la testa
In un'orrida fucina,
Dove cresce e mai non resta
Dell'incudini sonore
L'importuno strepitar.
Alternando questo e quello
Pesantissimo martello,
Alternando questo e quello
Pesantissimo martello,
Fa con barbara armonia,
Muri e volte, muri e volte,
Muri e volte rimbombar, sì,
Alternando questo e quello
Alternando questo e quello
Pesantissimo martello,
Fa con barbara armonia,
Muri e volte rimbombar.
E il cervello, poverello,
Già stordito, sbalordito,
Non ragiona, si confonde,
Si riduce ad impazzar.

End of Act One.

Frederica von Stade as Rosina in 'The Barber of Seville' at La Scala in 1985 (photo: Lelli and Masotti)

Act Two

Scene One. *A room in Doctor Bartolo's house with a piano, on which there are various sheets of music. Doctor Bartolo is alone.*

BARTOLO

I wish I knew who that soldier was!	Ma vedi il mio destino! Quel soldato,
Not a soul knows him	Per quanto abbia cercato,
in the regiment.	Niun lo conosce in tutto il reggimento.
I wonder . . . No, I'm sure	Io dubito — oh, cospetto!
that gentleman was sent here	Che dubitar? — Scommetto
by Count Almaviva	Che dal Conte Almaviva,
to find out how the land	E stato qui spedito quel Signore,
lay with Rosina.	Ad esplorar della Rosina il core.
A man can't be safe	Nemmeno in casa propria
even in his own house!	Sicuri si può star! ma io —

(*knocking*)

Who's there?	Chi batte?

(*more knocking*)

Who can that be? Berta! Ambrogio!	Ehi! chi è di là? battono, non sentite?
Can't you hear? Open the door!	

(*turning upstage*)

I'm at home. There can be no danger.	In casa io son; non v'è timore, aprite.

Scene Two. *The Count enters disguised as a music master in clerical dress. / No. 12 Duettino.*

COUNT

Heaven send you peace and gladness!	[26] Pace e gioia sia con voi!

BARTOLO

Reverend Father, much obliged to you!	Mille grazie, non s'incomodi.

COUNT

Bless this house and all within it!	Gioia e pace per mill'anni!

BARTOLO

Very welcome. Pray take a chair.	Obbligato in verità.
Pray be seated. What brings you here?	Mille grazie, non s'incomodi.

(*aside*)

I've a sort of recollection,	(Questo volto non m'è ignoto;
Though I don't see the connection,	Con ravviso — non ricordo —
That I've seen the fellow somewhere,	Ma quel volto — ma quell'abito —
But I can't remember when.	Non capisco che sarà.)

COUNT
(*aside*)

Though my first attempt was wasted	(Ah, se un colpo è andato a vuoto
And I nearly got arrested,	A gabbar questo balordo,
I'll not let myself be bested,	Un novel travestimento
So I mean to try again.	Più propizia a me sarà.)

(*to Bartolo*)

Heaven send you peace and gladness!	Gioia e pace; pace e gioia.

BARTOLO

Yes, exactly. (The man's a nuisance!)	Ho capito. — (Oh! ciel! che noia!)

COUNT

Bless this house and all within it!	Gioia e pace, ben di cuore.

BARTOLO

Reverend Father, that's enough of	Basta, basta, basta, basta,
Peace and gladness for today.	Basta, basta! per pietà!

Heaven bless you!   Gioia, pace!

BARTOLO

Devil take you!   Gioia, pace.
Heaven bless you! The man's a nuisance.   Ho capito, ho capito.
Stop it! That will do, I say!   Oh ciel, che noia!

COUNT
(*aside*)

I'm quite safe in this disguising   (Il vecchion non mi conosce:
From the Doctor's recognizing.   Oh, mia sorte fortunata!
How to talk with fair Rosina   Ah, mio ben! Fra pochi istanti
I shall shortly find a way.   Parlerem con libertà.)

sillabato

BARTOLO
(*aside*)

After all the morning's riot   Me che perfido destino!
I could do with peace and quiet.   Ma che barbara giornata!
This is not the sort of diet   Tutti quanti a me davanti!
I can stomach all the day.   Che crudel fatalità!
          (*to the Count*)
And now, sir,   Insomma, mio Signore,
may I ask who you are?   Chi è lei, si può sapere?

COUNT

Don Alonzo,   Don Alonso,
Professor of music and singing,   Professore di musica, ed allievo
and pupil of Don Basilio.   Di Don Basilio.

BARTOLO

What's your business?   Ebbene?

COUNT

Don Basilio   Don Basilio
is somewhat indisposed so he has sent me   Sta male, il poverino, ed in suo vece —
to give ...

BARTOLO

Indisposed? I'll see him at once.   Sta mal? — Corro a vederlo.

COUNT

Indeed, sir,   Piano, piano.
it is nothing very serious.   Non è un mal così grave.

BARTOLO
(*aside*)

I don't trust this man.   (Di costui non mi fido.)
          (*to the Count*)
Come, sir, we must go.   Andiamo, andiamo.

COUNT
(*confidentially*)

But, sir —   Ma, Signore!

BARTOLO
(*brusquely*)

What is it?   Che c'è?

COUNT
(*in a low voice, drawing Bartolo aside*)

Don Basilio desired me —   Voleva dirvi —

BARTOLO

Speak up! I'm deaf.   Parlate forte.

75

COUNT
(more confidentially)

Don Basilio desired me to tell you —   Ma —

BARTOLO
(angrily)

Louder, I tell you!   Forte, vi dico.

COUNT
(also angrily)

Very well, then, as you please.   Ebben, come vuole.
(aside)
But he'll soon have to learn who Don   Ma chi sia Don Alonso apprenderete.
  Alonzo is.
(raising his voice)
Sir, the Count Almaviva —   Vo' dal Conte Almaviva —

BARTOLO

Gently, gently —   Piano, piano —
He takes him on one side.
              Yes — I'm listening.   Dite, dite, v'ascolto.

COUNT
(very loudly and angrily)

The Count! —   Il Conte —

BARTOLO

Hush, for Heaven's sake!   Pian, per carità.

COUNT
(calming down)

              This morning   Stamane,
I happened to see him at the inn where he   Nella stessa locanda
lodges and just by chance there came into   Era meco d'alloggio, ed in mie mani
my hands
(producing a letter)
this little letter, written by your ward   Per caso capitò questo biglietto
to Count Almaviva.   Dalla vostra pupilla a lui diretto.

BARTOLO
(taking the letter and looking at it)

Heavens! It's her handwriting!   Che vedo? È sua scrittura!

COUNT

Don Basilio knows nothing of this letter.   Don Basilio nulla sa di quel foglio,
And as he sent me to give a music lesson   Ed io per lui venendo a dar lezione
to the young lady, well, I thought that —   Alla ragazza,
(with feigned embarrassment, as if to justify himself)
if you thought it worthwhile —   Voleva farmene un merito con voi —
with the letter — in my hands —   Perchè, con quel biglietto, si potrebbe . . .

BARTOLO

              The letter?   Che cosa?

COUNT

              I'll explain.   Vi dirò,
If I could have just a word with the young   S'io potessi parlare alla ragazza,
lady, I think I might induce her to believe   Io creder, verbigrazia, le farei
that it was given to me by another lady;   Che me lo die' del Conte un'altra amante:
that would be proof enough that the Count   Prova significante
was merely trifling with her affections.   Che il Conte di Rosina si fa gioco,
And then, of course —   E perciò —

Wait a moment!   Piano un poco.
A slander! — Oh bravo!   Una calunnia! — oh, bravo!
I see you are a worthy pupil of Don Basilio!   Degno e vero scolar di Don Basilio!

He embraces him and pockets the letter.

I shall recompense, as it deserves,   Io saprò come merita
your valuable suggestion.   Ricompensar sì bel suggerimento.
I will call the girl in.   Vo a chiamar la ragazza;
[Since you've shown such an interest in my   Poichè tanto per me v'interessate,
affairs, I will put my trust in you.]   Mi raccomando a voi.

COUNT

I don't doubt it.   Non dubitate.

Bartolo enters Rosina's room.

I didn't mean to tell him   L'affare del biglietto
all that story of the letter when I came in.   Dalla bocca m'è uscito non volendo.
But what could I do? Without an excuse of   Ma come far? Senza un tal ripiego
some sort I'd have had to go away and look   Mi toccava andar via come un baggiano.
a fool, too. However, I can explain   Il mio disegno a lei
the whole thing to Rosina now. If she agrees,   Ora paleserò; s'ella acconsente,
my happiness is assured.   Io son felice appieno.
Here she comes; and now, now to prepare   Eccola. Ah, il cor sento balzarmi in seno.
her rescue!

Scene Three. *Doctor Bartolo re-enters with Rosina.*

BARTOLO

Come in, come in, Rosina. Don Alonzo,   Venite, Signorina. Don Alonso,
this gentleman here, will give you your   Che qui vedete, or vi darà lezione.
    singing lesson.

ROSINA
(seeing the Count)

Ah!   Ah!

BARTOLO

What's the matter?   Cos'è stato?

ROSINA

I've got cramp in my foot.   È un granchio al piede.

COUNT

[It's nothing.   Oh nulla!
Come and sit next to me, my sweet child.]   Sedete a me vicin, bella fanciulla.
May I have the honour of hearing you sing?   Se non vi spiace, un poco di lezione
                          Di Don Basilio invece io vi darò.

ROSINA

Oh, certainly. I am delighted.   Oh, con mio gran piacer la prenderò.

COUNT

What will you sing for me?   Che vuol cantare?

ROSINA

I'll sing, if you'll allow me,   Io canto, se le aggrada,
The song from 'The Guardian Outwitted'.   Il Rondò del 'L'Inutil Precauzione'.

BARTOLO

She's always talking of   Eh, sempre, sempre in bocca
'The Guardian Outwitted'.   'L'Inutil Precauzione'.

ROSINA

[I've told you before;   Io ve l'ho detto

it's the title of the new opera.]   E il titolo dell'opera novella.

She looks through various sheets of music on the piano.

BARTOLO

[Yes, well; understood; let's begin.]   Or bene; intesi; andiamo.

ROSINA

There it is.   Eccola qui.

COUNT

Oh bravo! Come, let me hear you!   Da brava, incominciamo.

The Count sits at the piano; Rosina stands by him and sings. Bartolo sits and listens. /
No. 13 Aria.

ROSINA

'When a heart by Cupid's arrow	Contro un cor che accende amore
Has with fire of love been lighted,	Di verace invito ardore,
Every tyrant power united,	S'arma invan poter tiranno
Every torment is in vain.	Di rigor, di crudeltà.
Love's a force there's no resisting,	D'ogni assalto vincitore
Love will shatter every chain.'	Sempre amore trionferà.

Bartolo falls asleep.

Dear Lindoro, let me tell you,	(Ah, Lindoro — mio tesoro —,
You already know my secret;	Se sapessi — se vedessi —
How that odious Doctor treats me	Questo cane di tutore,
Is too dreadful to relate.	Ah, che rabbia che mi fa!
'Tis to you I turn for rescue,	Caro, a te mi raccomando,
Save me from the man I hate.	Tu mi salva, per pietà.)

COUNT

There's no need to be so nervous,	Non temer, ti rassicura,
Our good luck, I'm sure, will serve us.	Non temer, ti rassicura,
Trust Lindoro, 'tis not too late.	Sorte amica a noi sarà.

ROSINA

I may hope then?   Dunque spero? —

COUNT

Yes, yes, believe me!   A me t'affida.

ROSINA

And my heart?   E il mio cor —

COUNT

Belongs to me by law of fate.   Giubilerà, giubilerà.

ROSINA

All my sorrow now is over,	[27] Cara immagine ridente,
Fortune smiles on me at last.	Dolce idea d'un lieto amor,
Oh, what rapture to find a lover,	Tu m'accendi in petto il core,
In his arms who'll hold me fast!	Tu mi porti a delirar.

COUNT

Yes, take heart and trust Lindoro;	Non temer, ti rassicura,
Fortune's with us, so have no fear.	Sorte amica a noi sarà.

ROSINA

I may trust you?   Dunque spero? —

COUNT

Trust your Lindoro.   A me t'affida.

ROSINA

You'll be true?   E il mi cor —

Of course, my dear.   Giubilerà!

Bartolo wakes up.

ROSINA

Oh what rapture to find a lover,	[27] Cara immagine ridente,
In his arms who'll hold me fast!	Tu mi porti a delirar.
All my sorrow now is over,	Caro, a te mi raccomando,
Fortune smiles on me at last.	Tu mi salva per pietà.

Recitatative.

COUNT

Your voice is charming! Bravissima!   Bella voce! bravissima!

ROSINA

You are too kind, sir.   Oh, mille grazie!

BARTOLO

Yes, quite a pleasant little voice;	Certo, bella voce!
but I can't stand this modern music.	Ma quest'aria, cospetto! E' assai noiosa.
Now in my young days music was quite	La musica a miei tempi era altra cosa:
another thing. You should have heard	Oh! quando, per esempio, cantava Cafariello
Cafariello in that wonderful song —	Quell'aria portentosa —

famous castrato

(trying to remember the tune)

           La, la, la. How did it go?   'La, la, la!'
You listen, Don Alonzo, I'll sing it now.   Sentite, Don Alonso, eccolo qua.

No. 14 Arietta.

'Tell me if you have seen her,	[28] Quando mi sei vicina,
My fair, my sweet Rosina.'	Amabile Rosina,

(interrupting himself)

'Tis Giannina in the song,	L'aria dicea Giannina,

(with a gesture towards Rosina)

But I always sing Rosina.	Ma io dico Rosina;
'Tell me if you have seen her,	Quando mi sei vicina,
My fair, my sweet Rosina;	Amabile Rosina,
When I spy her advancing	Il cor mi balza in petto,
My heart for joy is dancing.'	Mi balla il minuetto.

Bartolo dances. Figaro enters with a basin under his arm; he stands behind Bartolo and mimics him. Bartolo suddenly turns round and sees Figaro dancing. Rosina laughs. /
Recitative.
Bravo, Master Barber, bravo!   Bravo! Signor Barbiere, bravo!

FIGARO

           Oh, not at all, sir.   Eh, niente affatto.
Dancing's a weakness of mine.   Scusi son debolezze.

BARTOLO

           Well, well!   Ebben, guidone,
What have you come for?   Che viene a far?

FIGARO

           Why,   Oh bella!
to shave you sir; this is your day.   Vengo a farvi la barba — oggi vi tocca.

BARTOLO

I won't be shaved today.   Oggi non voglio.

FIGARO

           [Not today?]   Oggi non vuol?
I can't shave you tomorrow, sir.   Domani non potrò io.

BARTOLO

           Why not?   Perchè?

FIGARO

I've too much business on. Let me see —	Perchè ho da fare.

(looking in his book)

I've got to attend all the officers	A tutti gli Ufficiali
of the regiment;	Del nuovo reggimento barba e testa —
Marchesa Andronica's wig;	Alla Marchesa Andronica
then Count Bombè's hair to be dressed	Il biondo parruchin coi maronè —
in the very latest fashion;	Al Contino Bombè
Lawyer Bernardone...	Il ciuffo a campanile —
a dose of castor oil —	Purgante all'avvocato Bernardone
[for his indigestion.	Che ieri s'ammalo d'indigestione —
And then — and then — well, anyhow,]	E poi — e poi — che serve?
Tomorrow's out of the question.	Doman non posso.

BARTOLO

Oh, stop your chatter;	Orsù, meno parole.
I tell you I won't be shaved today.	Oggi non vo' far barba.

FIGARO

That's a nice way to treat me!	No? — Cospetto!
I come this morning	Guardate che avventori!
And there's the devil's own row going on.	Vengo stamane: in casa v'è l'inferno.
I come this afternoon and you say	Ritorno dopo pranzo:

(imitating him)

'I won't be shaved today!'	'Oggi non voglio.'
What sort of a barber do you take me for?	Per un qualche barbier da contadini?
You can send for somebody else, I'm going home.	Chiamate pur un altro; — io me ne vado.

BARTOLO

Oh, well, have your own way!	Che serve? — a modo suo —
	Vedi che fantasia!
There, go and get the towels.	Va in camera a pigliar la biancheria.

He fumbles for the keys.

No, I'll get them myself.	No, vado io stesso.

Exit.

FIGARO
(aside)

If he'd only give me	(Ah, se mi dava in mano
that bunch of keys!	Il mazzo delle chiavi, ero a cavallo.)

(to Rosina)

Tell me, isn't	Dite, non è fra quelle
the key of the balcony there?	La chiave, che apre quella gelosia?

ROSINA

Yes, it's the new one.	Sì, certo; è la più nuova.

Bartolo re-enters.

BARTOLO
(aside)

I was a fool to leave her alone,	(Ah, son per buono
to leave her alone with that barber.	A lasciar qui quel diavolo di barbiere!)

(to Figaro)

Here! *You* go!	Anime, va tu stesso.

He gives him the keys.

You'll find the linen at the top of the	Passato il corridor, sopra l'armadio
cupboard at the end of the passage. Take	Il tutto troverai.
care. Don't touch anything else.	Bada non toccar nulla.

FIGARO

Trust me, sir.	Eh, non son matto.

(aside)

Hurrah!	(Allegri!)

(to Bartolo)

I'll be back.   Vado e torno.

(aside)

That's done.   (Il colpo è fatto!)

Exit.

BARTOLO
(to the Count)

That's the rascal who took   È quel briccon, che al Conte
Rosina's letter to the Count.   Ha portato il biglietto di Rosina.

COUNT

He looks a most dangerous character.   Mi sembra un imbroglion di prima sfera.

BARTOLO

[Eh, I don't care a fig.]   Eh, a me non me la ficca —
There is a loud noise of smashing crockery, offstage.
Oh, all my best china!   Ah, disgraziato me! —

ROSINA

[What a racket!]   Ah, che rumore!

BARTOLO

[What a rogue! I'll go and see what's   Oh, che briccon! Me lo diceva il core.
happened.]

Exit.

COUNT

[Figaro's a good fellow.]   Quel Figaro è un grand'uomo.

(to Rosina)

At last we are alone;   Or che siamo soli,
tell me, will you be mine?   Ditemi, o cara; il vostro al mio destino
                                     D'unir siete contenta? Franchezza! —

ROSINA
(enthusiastically)

O Lindoro!   Ah, mio Lindor!
Of course I will.   Altro io non bramo —

She composes herself as Figaro re-enters with Bartolo.

COUNT

[Well?]   Ebben? —

BARTOLO

He's broken everything —   Tutto m'ha rotto, tutto:
Six plates, eight glasses, and a soup-tureen!   Sei piatti, otto bicchieri, una terrina!

FIGARO

What a piece of luck! If I hadn't   Vedete che gran cosa! ad una chiave,
held on to this key   Se io non m'attaccava per fortuna,
I should have broken my head   Per quel maledettissimo
in that cursed passage.   Corridor, così oscuro,
It's as black as your hat in there! Spezzato mi sarei la testa al muro.
[He keeps all his china in the dark, so —]   Tiene ogni stanza al buio; e poi — e poi —

BARTOLO

[That's enough!]   Oh, non più.

FIGARO

[Right, let's get on with it.]   Dunque, andiam.

(aside to the Count and Rosina)

[Be careful.]   (Giudizio.)

81

BARTOLO

Come on, shave me. A noi.

Bartolo sits down to be shaved.

Scene Four. *Enter Don Basilio. / No. 15 Quintet.*

ROSINA

Don Basilio! (Don Basilio!)

COUNT

Oh, the devil! (Cosa veggo?)

FIGARO

Now for trouble! (Quale intoppo!)

BARTOLO
(to Basilio)

Why it's you. Come qua?

BASILIO

Peace and joy be on this dwelling! Servitor di tutti quanti.

BARTOLO

I thought he was ill in bed. (Che vuol dir tal novità!)

ROSINA

What ever shall we do? (Ah, di noi che mai sarà!)

COUNT
(to Figaro)

I must leave the case to you. (Qui franchezza ci vorrà.)

FIGARO
(to the Count)

This time please to keep your head. (Qui franchezza ci vorrà.)

BARTOLO

Don Basilio, are you better? Don Basilio, come state?

BASILIO

What d'ye mean? Come sto?

FIGARO

Make up your mind, sir, Or che s'aspetta?
Shall I shave you or not? Questa barba benedetta?
Shall I shave you, sir, or not? La facciamo sì or no?

BARTOLO

Wait a moment. Ora vengo.
(to Basilio)
Now, is it settled? Ehi il curiale —

BASILIO
(puzzled)

Is what settled? Il curiale! —

COUNT
(to Basilio, interrupting)

I've told the Doctor Io gli ho narrato
That the whole affair is settled. Che già tutto è combinato;
(to Bartolo)
That is so? Non è ver?

82

BARTOLO

Yes, yes, that is so.   Sì, tutto io so.

BASILIO

Doctor Bartolo, explain yourself.   Ma, Don Bartolo, spiegatevi —

COUNT
(interrupting, to Bartolo)

Doctor Bartolo, I beg you,   Ehi, dottore, una parola.
Just a word with you in private.   Ehi, dottore, una parola.
(softly, to Basilio)
Don Basilio, wait a moment,   Don Basilio, son da voi.
Just a word with you, I say.   Ascoltate un poco qua.
(softly to Bartolo)
You must not let him discover   (Fate un po' ch'ei vada via.
All the business of the letter.   Ch'ei ci scopra ho gran timore.)

ROSINA

There'll be trouble, I'm afraid.   (Io mi sento il cor tremar.)

FIGARO
(softly to Rosina)

There's no need to lose your head.   (Non vi state a disperar.)

COUNT
(aside to Bartolo)

All the business of the letter   Della lettera, signore,
Is unknown to him as yet.   Ei l'affare ancor non sa.

BARTOLO
(aside)

There's a nasty tangle somewhere,   (Ah, qui certo v'è un pasticcio,
But the clue I cannot get.   Non s'arriva a indovinar.)
That's a very good idea,   Dite bene, mio signore,
We will send him off to bed.   Or lo mando via di qua.

COUNT
(aside to Bartolo)

All the business of the letter   Ch'ei ci scopra ho gran timore:
Is unknown to him as yet.   Ei l'affare ancor non sa.
Figaro listens carefully, ready to back up the Count's story.
You've a fever, Don Basilio,   Colla febbre, Don Basilio,
Don't you think it's rather rash   Chi v'insegna colla febbre
To leave your house?   A passeggiar?

BASILIO

I've a fever?   Colla febbre?

FIGARO

You have indeed, sir!   E che vi pare?
You are yellow! Looks like jaundice!   Siete giallo come un morto.

BASILIO
(astonished)

I am yellow! Looks like jaundice!   Sono giallo come un morto?

FIGARO
(feeling his pulse)

Goodness gracious!   Bagatella!
Oh, my stars! Why, this is dreadful!   Cospetton! — che tremarella! —
It's a bad case, very serious,   Bagatella! bagatella!
Yes indeed, sir, you're infectious,   Tremarella! tremarella!
Here's a case of scarlet fever!   Questa è febbre scarlattina!

BARTOLO

Scarlet fever?	Scarlattina!

COUNT
(slipping a purse into Basilio's hand)

You must take a dose of medicine,	Via, prendete medicina.
Or it may affect the brain.	Non vi state a rovinar.

FIGARO

Off to bed with you this minute!	Presto, presto, andate a letto —

COUNT

You're as yellow as a guinea.	Voi paura in ver mi fate —

ROSINA

Take a drink with something in it.	Dice bene, andate a letto —

BARTOLO THEN ALL

Stay there till you're well again.	Presto andate a riposar.

BASILIO
(puzzled)

For a fever — an odd prescription!	(Una borsa! – Andate a letto! —
Well, at any rate, they all are in agreement.	Ma che tutti sian d'accordo.)

ALL

Off to bed with you!	Presto a letto.

BASILIO

You need not shout so.	Eh, non son sordo,
I suppose I'd better do as you all say.	Non mi faccia più pregar.

FIGARO

You're as yellow —	Che color — eh!

COUNT

— as a guinea.	Che brutta cera.

BASILIO

Am I really?	Brutta cera?

FIGARO, COUNT AND BARTOLO

Your case is serious.	Oh brutta assai.

BASILIO

Well, I'm going.	Dunque vado.

ALL THE OTHERS

Go, sir, go, sir!	Vada, vada.

COUNT

Reverend Father, must you leave us?	[29] Buona sera, mio signore,
You've a fever, do take care, sir,	Buona sera, mio signore.
Now get home and go to bed!	(Presto andate via di qua.)

ALL THE OTHERS

Must you really now be going?	Buona sera, mio signore,
Reverend Father, you must leave us?	Buona, sera, mio signore.
'Tis too soon to go away.	(Presto andate via di qua.)

BASILIO

Yes, I really must be going,	Buona sera — ben di core —
I'll come back another day.	Obbligato — in verità.
Yes, I'm going. I can hear you.	Poi diman si parlerà.

Plague upon the man, he's always
    interfering;
Yes, he's really past enduring.
For your health we all will pray,
If you'll only go away.

(Maledetto seccatore!)

Buona sera, mio signore,
Buona sera, mio signore,
Pace, sonno e sanità.

BASILIO

I can hear you, I can hear you,
Do not shout so loud, I pray.
Peace and gladness on this dwelling!

Non gridate, ho inteso già.
Buona sera, mio signore.
(Ah, che in sacco va il tutore!)

ALL THE OTHERS

Off to bed with you I say.

Presto andate via di qua.

Exit Basilio.

FIGARO

Now then, Signor Don Bartolo.

Orsù, signor Bartolo.

BARTOLO

Alright, come on.

Son qua, son qua.

Bartolo sits down. Figaro ties a towel round his neck and begins to shave him, standing so as to screen the Count and Rosina from his view.

BARTOLO

Tighter. Yes, that will do.

Stringi. Bravissimo.

COUNT

Rosina, Rosina,
Here, I must talk to you.

Rosina, Rosina,
Deh, ascoltatemi.

ROSINA

I'm listening, I'm listening,
Come, talk away.

V'ascolto, v'ascolto,
Eccomi qua.

She pretends to study the music.

COUNT
(softly, to Rosina)

At midnight I shall come for you,
At twelve o'clock precisely;
This key unlocks the balcony,
And we shall run away.

(A mezzanotte in punto,
A prendervi qui siamo:
Or che la chiave abbiamo
Non v'è da dubitar.)

FIGARO

Oh dear, oh dear!

Ahi! Ahi!

BARTOLO

What is the matter?

Che cosa è stato?

FIGARO

I don't quite know;
I've something on my eyelid.
Don't touch it! You look there, sir;
Just blow it off, I pray.

Un non so che,
Un non so che nell'occhio!
Guardate, non toccate —
Soffiate per pietà.

ROSINA AND THE COUNT

Do, re, mi, fa, so, la.

Do, re, mi, fa, sol, la.

ROSINA
(softly to the Count)

At twelve o'clock precisely	A mezzanotte in punto,
I will be waiting for you;	Anima mia, t'aspetto;
Indeed I'm all impatience,	E già l'istante affretto,
I cannot bear to stay.	Che a te mi stringerà.

COUNT

Dearest, I ought to tell you,	Ora avvertir vi voglio,
I had to invent a story,	Cara, che il vostro foglio,
Or else I could not justify	Perchè non fosse inutile
This queer disguise I'm wearing.	Il mio travestimento.

BARTOLO
(having overheard, rising)

This queer disguise he's wearing!	Il suo travestimento!
Ha! Ha! Now I have caught you out,	Ah! ah! Ma bravi, in verità!
Don Alonzo! Bravo! Bravissimo!	Sor Alonso! bravo! bravissimo!
You villains, you scoundrels,	Bricconi! Birbanti!
I know what your game is;	Ah, voi tuttti quanti
You're banded together	Avete giurato
To cheat me somehow.	Di farmi crepar!
But now I've caught you	Su, fuori, furfanti!
You shall not escape me	Vi voglio accoppar!
Until I have taught you	Di rabbia, di sdegno
Your duty to know.	Mi sento crepar.

ROSINA, COUNT AND FIGARO

Pray, Doctor, be quiet,	Tacete, tacete,
Your head's in a riot;	Non serve gridare.
You're in such a hurry,	Ma zitto, Dottore,
Be calm and don't worry,	La testa vi gira,
Or you may be sorry	L'amico delira,
For what you say now.	Vi fate burlar.
He's perfectly furious,	Intesi ci siamo,
He'll soon be delirious.	Non va replicare.
Our plans are all settled;	Tacete, partiamo,
It's no good insisting;	Non serve a gridar,
It's no good resisting	Intese ci siamo,
What we mean to do.	Non va replicar.

BARTOLO

With fury I'm bursting,	Di rabbia, di sdegno
For vengeance I'm thirsting,	Mi sento crepare,
And that is the first thing	Su, fuori, furfanti,
I'd have you to know.	Vi voglio accoppar.

Exeunt all except Bartolo. / Recitative.

What a blessed old fool I am!	Ah! Disgraziato me! — Ma come? — Ed io
I never noticed anything. I'll swear Don	Non mi accorsi di nulla! Ah! Don Basilio
Basilio knows something about this.	Sa certo qualche cosa.

(calling, having thought this over)

Ambrogio! Berta!	Ehi! — Chi è di là?

Enter Ambrogio and Berta.

Ambrogio!	Senti, Ambrogio:
Go across to Don Basilio	Corri da Don Basilio qui rimpetto;
and tell him [I'm waiting here for him and]	Digli ch'io qua l'aspetto,
to come here at once, it's most important.	Che venga immantinente,
[And that I have something important to	Che ho gran cose da dirgli e ch'io non vado
tell him and I can't come myself	
because, because . . . Because I have very	Perchè — perchè — perchè ho di gran
good reasons.	ragioni.
Go quickly.]	Va subito.

(Exit Ambrogio, to Berta:)

And you,	Di guardia

go and stand at the front door to keep
    guard, and — no, no —
[I don't trust her.] I'll keep guard myself.

Tu piantati alla porta, e poi — no, no —
(Non me ne fido.) Io stesso ci starò.

Exit Bartolo.

Scene Six. *Berta alone.*

BERTA

He's always suspicious. Keep guard indeed!
You may stay there till you burst.
I never saw such a noisy house as this —
Shouting, crying, quarrelling —
never a moment's peace
with that old gentleman.
[Oh, what a madhouse, what a madhouse
    it is!]

Che vecchio sospettoso! Vada pure
E ci stia finchè crepa.
Sempre gridi e tumulti in questa casa;
Si litiga, si piange, si minaccia . . .
Non v'è un'ora di pace
Con questo vecchio avaro e brontolone.
Oh, che casa! oh, che casa di confusione!

No. 16 Arietta.

Spite of sixty years to carry
Our old Doctor wants to marry;
Miss Rosina wants a husband though she's
    not yet sixteen,
Well, well, crazier folk I've never seen.
For this madness what's the reason?
Love's the cause of it we're told.
Love both in and out of season,
Driving mad both young and old.
It's a universal evil,
An invitation of the devil;
It's a tickling irritation,
It's a torture, it's a passion.
Though I ought not to reveal it,
E'en at my age I can feel it.
And it drives me to despair,
And it makes me tear my hair.

[30] Il vecchiotto cerca moglie,
Vuol marito la ragazza;
Quello freme, questa è pazza —
Tutti e due son da legar.
Ma che cosa è questo amore
Che fa tutti delirar?
Ma che cosa è questo amore
Che fa tutti delirar?
Egli è un male universale,
Una smania, un pizzicore,
Una smania, un pizzicore,
Un solletico, un tormento . . .
Poverina, anch'io lo sento,
Poverino, anch'io lo sento,
Nè so come finirà,
Nè so come finirà.

Some folk always think a woman
After forty isn't human,
But this passion's all too common
In the later years of life.
Well, well, I shall never be a wife.
I shall never find a husband I'm afraid,
So I shall have to die an old maid.

Oh, vecchiaia maledetta!
Son da tutti disprezzata,
E vecchietta disperata,
Si, si, mi convien così crepar,
Così crepar, così crepar,
Mi convien così crepar!

Exit.

Scene Seven. *Enter Bartolo and Basilio. / Recitative.*

BARTOLO

What's that! You don't know
this Don Alonzo?

Dunque voi Don Alonso
Non conoscete affatto?

BASILIO

I never saw him in my life.

Affatto.

BARTOLO

Then the Count must have sent him here!
There's a plot brewing somewhere!

Ah, certo il Conte lo mandò.
Qualche gran trama qui si prepara.

BASILIO

              I venture
to think that our young friend
was the Count himself in person.

                    Io dico
Che quel garbato amico,
Era il Conte in persona.

BARTOLO

        The Count?

                Il Conte?

87

BASILIO

The Count!   Il Conte!
(aside)

His purse told me that.   La borsa parla chiaro.

BARTOLO

Well, whoever it was, I'm going to see the   Sia chi si vuole — amico, al notaro
notary, *now*; I'll have my marriage contract   Vo' in questo punto andare, in questa sera
signed and sealed without a moment's delay.   Stipular di mie nozze io vo' il contratto.

BASILIO

The notary? Are you mad, sir?   Il notar! siete matto?
It's going to rain in torrents; and besides,   Piove a torrenti; e poi
the notary this evening is with Figaro the   Questa sera il notaro
barber to settle about   È impegnato con Figaro; il barbiere
the marriage of his niece.   Marita una nipote.

BARTOLO

His niece?   Una nipote!
That proves it. Figaro   Che nipote? — Il barbiere
Hasn't got a niece.   Non ha nipoti. Ah, qui v'è qualche imbroglio,
They're up to some mischief,   Questa notte i biocconi
this very night. Quick,   Me la vogliono far. Presto, il notaro
fetch the notary at once.   Qua venga sull'istante.
Here's the key of the front door.   Ecco la chiave del portone — andate,
Go, quickly, I beseech you.   Presto, per carità.

He gives the key to Basilio.

BASILIO

Have no fear; I will be back directly.   Non temete; in due salti io torno qua.

Exit.

BARTOLO

If Rosina won't marry me for love,   Per forza, o per amore,
I must marry her by force. The devil!   Rosina avrà da cedere. Cospetto!
Ah! I've an idea.   Mi viene un altra idea.

He takes a letter from his pocket.

This letter   Questo biglietto,
that she wrote to the Count —   Che scrisse la ragazza ad Almaviva,
now for a master-stroke!   Potria servir — che colpo da maestro!
That rascal Don Alonzo   Don Alonso, il briccone,
has done the job for me without knowing it.   Senza volerlo mi die' l'armi in mano.
(calling)
Rosina! Rosina!   Ehi, Rosina! Rosina!
Rosina enters.

Come here.   Avanti, avanti;
Here's a fine sort of lover!   Del vostro amante io vi vo' dar novella.
[Poor deceived one!] Don't you know   Povera sciagurata! in verità
he's playing the fool with you?   Collocaste assai bene il vostro affetto!
You're not the only woman in the case.   Del vostro amor sappiate.
                                   Ch'ei si far gioco in sen d'un altro amante;
He shows her the letter.

Look at that!   Ecco la prova!

ROSINA

Heavens! My letter!   Oh cielo! il mio biglietto!

BARTOLO

Don Alonzo and the barber   Don Alonso e il barbiere
are both in league with him; don't trust   Congiuran contro voi: non vi fidate.
them an inch. They mean to hand you over   Nelle braccia del Conte d'Almaviva
to Count Almaviva's clutches.   Vi vogliono condurre —

To the arms of another! O Lindoro! Faithless traitor!	(In braccio a un'altro — Che mai sento? — Ah, Lindoro! Ah, traditore!

(furious)

I'll show him what I think of him! Sir, you once expressed a desire to marry me —	Ah si! — vendetta! e vegga Quell'empio chi è Rosina.) Dite Signore, di sposarmi, Voi bramavate?

BARTOLO

I desire it indeed.	E il voglio.

ROSINA

Very well, you shall; but you must marry me this minute, for at midnight Figaro is coming here with that scoundrel. They said I was to run away and marry him —	Ebben, si faccia! Io son contenta — ma all'istante. Udite: A mezzanotte qui sarà l'indegno, Con Figaro il barbier; — con lui fuggire Per sposarlo io voleva.

BARTOLO

Oh, the villains! I'll bar the door at once.	Ah, scellerati! Corro a sbarrar la porta.

ROSINA

No use. They're coming by the window. They've got the key.	Ah, mio signore, Entràn par le finestre: hanno la chiave.

BARTOLO

Then I don't move from this spot. But — supposing they have weapons? My dear Rosina, now that you have come to your senses, I'll tell you what to do. You lock yourself into your room. I shall go and call the watch. I'll tell them there are thieves in the house; and thieves they *are*, too! [Shut yourself in quickly, my child; I shall go now.]	Non mi muovo di qui! Ma — e se fossero armati? — Figlia mia, Poichè ti sei si bene illuminata, Facciam cosi. Ti chiudi a chiave in camera, Io vo' a chiamar la forza. Dirò che son due ladri, e come tali, Corpo di Bacco! l'avremo da vedere! Figlia, chiuditi presto: io vado via.

Exit.

ROSINA

Oh! Was there ever a girl so miserable as I am?	Quanto, quanto è crudel la sorte mia!

Exit.

No. 17 A Storm. / During this movement flashes of lightning are seen through the window and thunder is heard. After the storm has subsided, the shutters are opened from the outside. Figaro enters by the window, followed by the Count. Both are wrapped in cloaks; Figaro carries a lantern.
Scene Eight. / *Recitative.*

FIGARO

Here we are at last!	Al fine, eccoci qua.

COUNT

Give me a hand. Heavens, what a storm!	Figaro, dammi man. Poter del mondo! Che tempo indiavolato!

FIGARO

Fine weather for lovers!	Tempo da innamorati!

Light the candles.   Ehi, fammi lume.

Figaro does so.

Where can Rosina be?   Dove sarà Rosina?

Figaro looks about. Enter Rosina.

FIGARO

[We soon shall see her . . .]   Ora vedremo —
Ah, here she is.   Eccola appunto.

COUNT
(*ecstatically*)

My own beloved!   Ah, mio tesoro —

ROSINA
(*pushing him away*)

Stand back,   Indietro,
you miserable wretch! I only came in   Anima scellerata! Io qui di mia
to cast your vile treachery in your teeth!   Stolta credulità venni soltanto
[I scorn to hide away; in order to show you   A riparar lo scorno; a dimostrarti
what I am, what a lover you are losing,   Qual sono, e quale amante
unworthy and ungrateful soul!]   Perdesti, anima indegna, e sconoscente!

COUNT

I'm astounded!   Io son di sasso!

FIGARO

I can't understand a word.   Io non capisco niente.

COUNT

For Heaven's sake!   Ma per pietà —

ROSINA

Not a word! You pretend to love me,   Taci! Fingesti amore,
only that you might sacrifice me   Per vendermi alle voglie
to your profligate friend, Count Almaviva.   Di quel tuo vil Conte Almaviva —

COUNT

To the Count?   Al Conte?
You arre indeed deceived. [Oh, happy me!]   Ah, sei delusa. Oh, me felice! adunque
Then you love Lindoro —   Tu di verace amore
truly and sincerely?   Ami Lindor! — rispondi —

ROSINA

I loved you only too well.   Ah, sì! t'amai pur troppo!

COUNT

Then there is no need   Ah, non è tempo
for further concealment.   Di più celarsi. Anima mia! Ravvisa

He kneels.

Behold the man who followed you   Colui che si gran tempo:
from Madrid, who sighs for you,   Segui tue tracce; e che per te sospira:
worships you and adores you — not   Che suo ti vuol. Mirami, o mio tesoro!
   Lindoro, but —
Count Almaviva!   Almaviva son io: non son Lindoro.

No. 18 Terzetto.

ROSINA

Almaviva! Your romantic intimation   [31] Ah, quel colpo inaspettato,
Of your title, your rank and station   Egli stesso! oh ciel! che sento!
Fills my bosom with wild elation,   Di sorpresa, di contento,
With amazement, and with delight!   Son vicina a delirar!

FIGARO

They were both of them despairing;
Now a world of joy they're sharing,
And they've me to thank for daring
To arrange all this tonight.

Son rimasti senza fiato!
Ora muoian dal contento;
Guarda, guarda il mio talento.
Che bel colpo seppe far!

COUNT

Here's a triumph unexpected!
Happy moment! No more rejected!
For in her eyes I see reflected
All my passion, all my delight!

Qual trionfo inaspettato!
Me felice! oh, bel momento!
Ah, d'amore, di contento,
Son vicino a delirar!

ROSINA

Oh, my lord! Or do I mistake you?

Mio signor — ma voi — ma io —

COUNT

Say no more, no more, I beg you!
Soon my Countess I shall make you;
Dearest, you shall be my wife. Yes!

Ah, non più, non più, ben mio!
Il bel nome di mia sposa,
Idol mio, t'attende già. Si!

ROSINA

What! The Countess Almaviva!
Shall I then be yours for life?

Il bel nome di tua sposa,
Ah, qual gioia al cor mi dà!

COUNT

Are you happy?

Sei contenta?

ROSINA

      Ah, could I tell you!
Oh, what rapture!

      Ah! mio Signore!
Dolce nodo —

FIGARO

    Quick!

    Presto!

ROSINA

    Our troth is plighted,
Now forever —

          — avventurato —
Che fai paghi —

FIGARO

    Let's go now!

    Andiamo.

ROSINA

    — we are united.

    — i miei desiri!

COUNT

Oh, what rapture!

Dolce nodo.

FIGARO
(imitating)

    Rapture!

    Nodo.

COUNT

    Our troth is plighted!

    Avventurato.

FIGARO

Come, sir, no waiting.

Presto, andiamo.

COUNT

    — now forever —

    — Che fai paghi —

FIGARO
(imitating)

    — ever —

    Paghi —

We are united!   — i miei desir!

FIGARO

Please be quick, sir!   Vi sbrigate!

ROSINA AND COUNT

Though I thought my passion slighted   Alla fin de' miei martiri,
Love took pity on my heart.   Tu sentisti, Amor, pietà.

FIGARO

Come, be quick, sir, time is passing;   Presto, andiamo: vi sbrigate,
Keep your rapture for tomorrow.   Via, lasciate quei sospiri;
Please make ready to depart.   Se si tarda, i miei raggiri —
Come along! Not a moment longer wait.   Presto andiamo, per carità —
Your elopement will be ruined   Fanno fiasco in verità.
If you leave it all so late.   Fanno fiasco, fanno fiasco.
Figaro, who has been looking out of the window, now comes forward and drags the Count to the window.
Oh, the devil! You look there, sir,   Ah, cospetto! che ho veduto?
There's a man there —   Cospetto, che ho veduto?
Yes, there are two men,   Alla porta — una lanterna —
Come and look, sir, I see a lantern   Due persone — due persone —
At the entrance — who are they?   Due persone — che si fa?

COUNT

Are you certain?   Hai veduto? —

FIGARO

Yes, indeed.   Sì, signor.

COUNT

There are men there?   — due persone?

FIGARO

Yes, there are.   Sì, signor.

COUNT

And with a lantern?   Una lanterna?

FIGARO

Down below there in the street.   Sì, signor.

ALL THREE

We are lost, we are lost!   Che si fa? che si fa?
If we all go very softly,   [32] Zitti, zitti, piano, piano,
One by one with care descending,   Non facciam più confusione,
By the ladder from the window   Per la scala del balcone,
We may yet escape unseen.   Presto, andiamo via di quà!

They start to leave by the window.

FIGARO

Here's a pretty mess!   Ah, disgraziati noi! come si fa?

COUNT

[What's happened?]   Che avvenne mai?

FIGARO

[The ladder ?]   La scala —

COUNT

[Well?]   Ebben?

FIGARO	
The ladder's gone.	La scala non v'è più.
COUNT	
What!	Che dici?
FIGARO	
Somebody's taken it away.	Chi mai l'avrà levata?
COUNT	
Good heavens!	Quale inciampo crudel!
ROSINA	
Oh, I am lost!	Me sventurata!
FIGARO	
Hush, I hear people coming. We're trapped.	Zi, zitti! sento gente, ora ci siamo.
What are we to do, my lord?	Signor mio, che si fa?
COUNT	
Rosina, be brave!	Mia Rosina, corraggio.
FIGARO	
Here they all are.	Eccoli qua.

Figaro blows out the candles and all retire to a corner of the stage.

Scene Nine. *Enter Basilio with a lantern, introducing the notary with papers.*

BASILIO	
(*calling*)	
Doctor Bartolo! Doctor Bartolo!	Don Bartolo! Don Bartolo.
FIGARO	
(*softly to the Count*)	
That's Don Basilio.	Don Basilio!
COUNT	
Who's the other?	E quell'altro?
FIGARO	
Oh, that's our Notary.	Ve', ve', il nostro notaro. Allegramente.

He goes up to the notary.

Leave it to me. Master Notary,	Lasciate fare a me. Signor Notaro,
you were to draw up	Dovevate in mia casa
a contract of marriage,	Stipular questa sera
this evening at my house,	Un contratto di nozze
between Count Almaviva and my niece.	Fra il Conte Almaviva e mia nipote.
Here is the happy couple.	Gli sposi, eccoli qua! Avete indosso
Have you the document with you?	La scrittura?

The notary shows it.

Excellent!	Benissimo!
BASILIO	
	Ma piano;
But where is Doctor Bartolo?	Don Bartolo dov'è?
COUNT	
Oh! Don Basilio,	Ehi, Don Basilio,

He takes him to one side.

— will you do me the honour of accepting	Questo anello è per voi.
this ring?	
BASILIO	
How dare you!	Ma io —

93

Well, if you don't,   Per voi
you'll have the honour of a   Vi sono ancor due palle nel cervello
bullet through the head.   Se v'opponete.

BASILIO

Thank you, I'll take the ring.   Oibò! prendo l'annello.
Where are the signatories?   Chi firma?

ROSINA AND THE COUNT

Here we are.   Eccoci qua.

They sign.

COUNT

And the witnesses —   Son testimoni
Figaro and Don Basilio.   Figaro e Don Basilio.
Figaro and Don Basilio sign too.
I take this lady as my wife.   Essa è mia sposa.

FIGARO AND BASILIO

All health and happiness!   Evviva!

COUNT

[Oh, what happiness!]   Oh, mio contento!

ROSINA

[Oh, longed-for happiness!]   Oh, sospirata mia felicità!

ALL

[Evviva!]   Evviva!

As the Count kisses Rosina's hand, and Figaro embraces Basilio, enter Bartolo with an alcalde, watchmen, soldiers, etc..

Scene Ten.

BARTOLO

Hands up! There are the villains!   Fermi tutti. Eccoli qua.

FIGARO

Gently, sir, gently —   Colle buone, signor.

BARTOLO
(*to the alcalde*)

Take them in charge;   Signor, son ladri;
They are thieves.   Arrestate, arrestate!

ALCALDE
(*to the Count*)

Your name, sir?   Mio signore, il suo nome.

COUNT

My name is that of a gentleman.   Il mio nome? Egli è quel d'un uom d'onore;
I am the husband of this —   Lo sposo io son di questa —

BARTOLO

Go to the devil, sir!   Eh, andate al diavolo!
Rosina is going to be *my* wife.   Rosina esser deve mia —
(*to Rosina*)
[Aren't you?]   — non è vero?

ROSINA

Your wife?   Io sva sposa?
Not for the world!   Oh, nemmeno per pensiero.

BARTOLO

What, you baggage? Oh, I'm betrayed!   Come, come, fraschetta! Ah, son tradito.

(to the Alcalde)

Take them in charge;   Arrestate, vi dico:
he's a thief!   È un ladro!

FIGARO

[Now, just a moment.]   Or, or l'accoppo.

BARTOLO

[He's a villain and a scoundrel.]   È un furfante, è un briccone.

ALCALDE
(to the Count)

Your name, sir!   Signore?

COUNT

Hands off!   Indietro!

ALCALDE

Your name —   Il nome —

COUNT

Hands off, I tell you!   Indietro, dico; indietro!

ALCALDE

Don't answer me like that, sir;   Ehi, mio signor, quel tuono basso.
I must have your name.   E chi è lei?

COUNT
(taking off his cloak)

My name — Count Almaviva.   Il Conte d'Almaviva io sono.

No. 17 Accompanied Recitative.

BARTOLO

Good heavens! Count Almaviva!   Il Conte! ah, che mai sento! —
Do you say, sir —   Ma cospetto! —

COUNT

Be silent! No protestations,   T'accheta; invan t'adopri,
they are in vain. Your tyranny is ended;   Resisti invan. De' tuoi rigori insani
all resistance is useless. Before the whole   Giunse l'ultimo istante. In faccia al mondo
world I declare my betrothal to this young   Io dichiaro altamente
lady. We now are plighted, Rosina, none can   Costei mia sposa: il nostro nodo, o cara,
part us. 'Twas love that first brought us   Opra è d'amore: amor
together, and, till my dying breath, love   Che ti fe' mia consorte,
shall unite us. You're free at last. Forget   A te mi stringerà fino alla morte.
this house of bondage. Henceforth you   Respira omai: del fido sposo in braccio,
shall be happy — Countess Almaviva!   Vieni, vieni a godere più lieta sorte.

BARTOLO

No, no, sir!   Ma io —

COUNT

Silence!   Taci —

BARTOLO

I tell you —   Ma voi —

COUNT

No more, you scoundrel!   Olà, t'accheta.

No. 18 Aria.

(to Bartolo)

Silence! Resist my will no more,	Cessa di più resistere,
Nor rouse my righteous anger!	Non cimentar mio sdegno:
My bride need fear no danger	Spezzato è il giogo indegno
While I stand by her side.	Di tanta crudeltà.
Though 'twas your will to take her,	Della beltà dolente,
And your poor slave to make her,	D'un innocente amore,
Your monstrous greed and fou desire	L'avaro tuo furore
Must now be mortified	Più non trionferà.

(to Rosina)

And now that all your woes are past	E tu, infelice vittima
And all your suffering ended,	D'un reo poter tiranno,
A new day dawns for you at last,	Sottratta al giogo barbaro,
By all delight attended.	Cangia in piacer l'affanno
And on your lover's bosom	E in sen d'un fido sposo
You may rest in peace,	Gioisci in libertà,
Enjoy the happy moment	E in sen d'un fido sposo
Of rapture, of love's embrace.	Gioisci in libertà.

(to the others)

You are witness —	Cari amici —

CHORUS

We'll bear witness,	Non temete,

COUNT

— to my marriage.	Questo nodo —

CHORUS

Every happiness	Non si scioglie,
every joy be yours today!	Sempre a lei vi stringerà.

COUNT

Where's the man could be so happy	Ah, il più lieto, il più felice
As am I, and so contented,	È il mio cor de' cori amanti! —
Now Rosina has consented	Non fuggite, o lieti istanti,
To become my loving bride?	Della mia felicità.

CHORUS

Every joy in life we wish you,	Annodar due cori amanti
Now the knot is safely tied.	È piacer che egual non ha.

BARTOLO

So I'm in the wrong all the way round!	Insomma, io ho tutti i torti.

FIGARO

I'm afraid you are, Doctor.	Pur troppo è così!

BARTOLO
(to Basilio)

And you, you scoundrel,	Ma tu briccone —
You betrayed me and signed as a witness!	Tu pur tradirmi, e far da testimonio!

BASILIO

My good Doctor Bartolo,	Ah, dottor Bartolo mio,
his noble lordship	Quel signor Conte certe ragioni
brought forward certain arguments	Ha in tasca; certi argomenti
to which there was no resisting.	A cui non si risponde.

BARTOLO

[And I, fool that I am,]	Ed io, bestia solenne,
to make sure of the wedding,	Per meglio assicurare il matrimonio,
took away the ladder myself!	Io portai via la scala del balcone!

FIGARO

| It's a case of 'The Guardian Outwitted'! | Ecco che fa un 'Inutil Precauzione'! |

BARTOLO

| She'll get no dowry from me. | Ma — e la dote? io non posso — |

COUNT

| There's no need of a dowry. | Eh, via; di dote |
| You can keep it yourself. | Io bisogno non ho: va, te la dono. |

FIGARO

[Ha, ha! Now you're smiling?]	Ah, ah! Ridete adesso?
Bravo, Doctor Bartolo!	Bravissimo Don Bartolo!
I'm very glad	Ho veduto alla fin rasserenarsi
to see you look pleasant at last!	Quel vostro ceffo amaro e furibondo
[Eh, the rascals have all the luck in the world.]	Eh, i bricconi han fortuna in questo mondo.

ROSINA

| Come, Doctor Bartolo — | Dunque, signor Don Bartolo — |

BARTOLO

| Yes, yes, I know. | Si, si, ho capito tutto. |

COUNT

| Come, good Doctor. | Ebben, Dottore? |

BARTOLO

| Well — well — [what's done is done.] | Si, si, che serve? Quel ch'è fatto è fatto. |
| Heaven bless you both, peace be with you! | Andate pur, che il Ciel vi benedica! |

FIGARO

| [Well done! Come now, Doctor, | Bravo, bravo, un'abbraccio! |
| Let's embrace.] | Venite qua, Dottore. |

ROSINA

| [Ah, what happiness!] | Oh, noi felici! |

COUNT

| [Ah, Fortune smiles on us!] | Oh, fortunato amore! |

No. 20 Finale.

FIGARO

This lantern I have lighted	[33] Di si felice innesto,
To guide a rash elopement;	Serbiam memoria eterna,
But now that you're united,	Io smorzo la lanterna,
'Tis time to put it out.	Qui più non ho che far!

He blows out his lantern.

BERTA, BARTOLO, BASILIO AND CHORUS

Your troubles now are ended,	Amore e fede eterna
You're free from every care,	Si vegga in voi regnar.
With every joy attended,	Amore e fede eterna
All hail the happy pair!	Si vegga in voi regnar.

ROSINA

Though dreadful fears assailed me	Costò sospiri e pena
Before our troth was plighted,	Un si felice istante
Lindoro never failed me,	Alfin quest'alma amante
His love was ne'er in doubt.	Comincia a respirar!

COUNT

Rosina never doubted
The humble and poor Lindoro,
And now your guardian's routed,
My fortunes you shall share.

Dell'umile Lindoro,
La fiamma a te fu accetta;
Più bel destin ti aspetta —
Su, vieni a giubilar.

CHORUS

Your troubles are all ended,
All hail the happy pair!

Amore e fede eterna,
Si veggar in voi regnar!

The end of the opera

*'The Barber of Seville' at the Bayerische Staatsoper, Munich in the 1974 production by
Ruth Berghaus, designed by Andreas Reinhardt, with Reri Grist as Rosina, Claes-Haaken
Ajnsjö as Almaviva and Hermann Prey as Figaro (photo: Sabine Toepffer)*

Balzac, Stendhal, and Rossini's 'Moses'

Pierluigi Petrobelli

One February 14, 1837, Honore de Balzac left Paris bound for Milan. The French novelist, whose fame was then at its peak, did not, however, go to Italy for artistic or sentimental reasons; he was entrusted with a specific business mission, since he had been given power of attorney for the Count and Countess Guidoboni-Visconti, both resident in Paris, to settle with their remaining relatives in Italy the transactions relating to the estate of the count's mother. It was, therefore, a business trip; but, just as every experience in life immediately and suddenly becomes tinder for the imagination of a writer, so this second 'voyage en Italie' (the first had been to Turin a year before) was to yield Balzac a harvest of experiences and images that he would immediately transform and infuse into his work. Having arrived at Milan on February 19, Balzac was received with all honours by the Milanese — and the Austrian — nobility, and by the cultivated and intellectual circles of the Lombard capital. Andrea Maffei dedicated a copy of his translations of Schiller to 'that man who — after the English tragedian [Shakespeare] — has cast the most profound gaze into the secrets of the heart.' The sculptor Puttinati executed a statue of him, and Balzac also met Manzoni. The strongest and truest friendship that the writer succeeded in establishing during this first Milanese sojourn was that with the Countess Clara Maffei, the wife of Andrea, whose salon was then the centre of the intellectual life of the Lombard city, the very Clarina Maffei who was to provide one of the deepest and most lasting friendships in the life of Verdi. Balzac's feelings were even to assume a rather warm tone, and it was to her that he would communicate his impressions of his journey; to her he would describe his encounter with Venice, at first in a spirit of disillusion and, later, of marked enthusiasm.

Leaving Milan on March 13, the writer arrived in Venice the following day, where he met Baron Galvagna to discuss the transaction and to sign the final papers relating to it. The business mission was fully successful, since the baron accepted all of the proposals formulated by Balzac relating to the succession. From March 21 until the end of the month the writer was again in Milan; he left there bound for Genoa, and then, by sea, reached Livorno in order to move on to Florence. The stay in Florence was dedicated above all to visiting and studying the monuments, but the following stop at Bologna was motivated primarily by his desire to see again someone to whom Balzac — as he himself tells us — was bound by strong ties of friendship: Gioachino Rossini, who in the December before had settled there.

Passing again through Milan, then over the St Gotthard pass, along Lake Lucerne, to Geneva and Basel, the novelist returned to Paris on May 3. On the 25th of the month he delivered to Plon the publisher the manuscript of *Massimilla Doni*, the short novel in which he sublimated the experience of his Italian journey of the preceding months, hinging the plot around a theme which for a long time he had been waiting, perhaps unconsciously, to realise in a framework ideally adapted to it; *Massimilla Doni*, which even today, contains the most minute and penetrating, the richest, and the most detailed analysis of Rossini's *Moses*. The novel is located entirely in Venice, and the novelist assigns to a performance of the opera at La Fenice a pivotal function at the climactic moment of the plot. During the performance the opera is explained by the protagonist, point by point, with enthusiastic comments, to a worldly-wise and attentive French doctor; and the principal singers of the performance are Tinti and Genovese, the singers who, by diverse ways and for various reasons, lead the two principal characters of the story — Massimilla and Count Emilio Memmi — to consummate their love. To be sure, Balzac had put the reader on his guard as to the value and pertinence of the opinions that he expressed on musical matters, at the same time asserting, elegantly but categorically, his own independent judgement on the subject. In a letter to the publisher Maurice Schlesinger, printed on June 11, 1837, in Schlesinger's *Revue et gazette musicale*, replying to the desire expressed by readers of the journal to see in print the new novel and to learn the opinions of the author on matters of music, Balzac declared:

> I belong to the class abhorred by painters and musicians, wrongly called in a contemptuous manner, *men of letters*. (Would you believe that M. de Montesquieu in his time or that M. de Belleyme today would like to receive a letter in which they were labelled *men of law*?)

And after having teased himself, writers, military men, and musicians for their professional sectarianism, he affirmed with conviction:

> I shall always remain attached to that seditious and incorrigible party that proclaims the liberty of the eyes and ears in the republic of the arts, that claims it is qualified to enjoy works created by the brush, the musical score, and the printing press, that believes sacrilegiously that paintings, operas and books are made for the whole world, and thinks that artists would be very much hindered if they worked only for themselves, very unfortunate if they were judged only by themselves...

In this same letter to the publisher Schlesinger we learn that the writer had formed very precise ideas concerning *Moses* some considerable time earlier:

> One day, being at the home of George Sand, we were discussing music (there were several of us); I expressed timidly my ideas on *Moses*. Ah! This word of encouragement will resound for a long time in my ears: 'You ought to write what you have been saying.' But my modesty made me expostulate to the illustrious author that I did not believe it possible to put into literary form the inventions of such a conversation...

Still, through a reading of this letter, which I believe to be fundamental for an understanding of Balzac's attitude toward music, one can establish exactly how the visit to Italy, the sojourn in Milan and above all in Venice, in addition to the Bologna meeting with the composer of *Moses*, fanned the flames of his imagination and allowed him to give literary form to the impressions and sensations inspired by a hearing of the opera, which had taken place long before. This long-standing admiration assumes a certain importance in explaining a rather curious and problematic fact: that in *Massimilla Doni* Balzac describes the first, not the second, version of Rossini's opera; that in his novel the opera performed at La Fenice is *Mosè in Egitto*, written for the Teatro San Carlo of Naples and performed there for the first time on March 5, 1818, and not *Moïse et Pharaon*, which is the French elaboration in four acts, performed for the first time at the Paris Opéra on March 26, 1827. To see this problem clearly, it is necessary above all to remember that at the time of

Rossini's most intense activity, it was still the practice to substitute, to omit and to change the order of certain numbers at every performance (a practice which the composers themselves, be it noted, endorsed). In the second place, it is a proven fact that, after the performances of *Moïse et Pharaon* at the Opéra in Paris, the new version gained the upper hand and became, so to speak, the definitive form of the opera, but *Mosè in Egitto* did not, for this reason, remain unsung. To give a few examples: we have proof, in the librettos printed for the different performances, that the opera was performed in its first version in Venice at the Teatro San Benedetto in 1831, in Mantua and Vicenza in 1832, at Turin in 1833, and at Crema in 1835; this happened not only in Italy but also in Paris, significantly at the Théâtre Italien (not at the Opéra). In this theatre *Mosè in Egitto* was performed every year from 1832 to 1835, and in 1837, and the libretto for the 1832 performances contains the pieces in *exactly* the same order in which Balzac described them in his imaginary performance of the opera at La Fenice. We cannot, however, be absolutely certain that it was this production which he attended; for example, in 1822 *Mosè in Egitto* was performed at the Théâtre Italien as an oratorio for an evening in honour of Giuditta Pasta; the libretto was printed in two languages, with a French translation opposite the Italian text, and this translation coincides literally at several points with the one used by Balzac for the lines of the libretto that he cites in the novel. Moreover, the second 'prima donna' of this performance was Mlle Cinti, who was later to be the leading female singer in *Moïse et Pharaon* — 'la Cinti', famous for her whims and caprices, just as the prima-donna who sings in *Moses* in *Massimilla Doni* is famous, and for the same reasons. In the novel her name is Clarina Tinti (note the similarity of the first name with that of Clarina Maffei and the assonance of the surname with that of the singer!). In any case it is evident from what Balzac declares in his letter to Schlesinger that he became acquainted with the opera for the first time, and received the strongest impressions, not in Italy but in Paris, and it was during the Italian journey of 1837 that the French writer 'discovered' the ideal setting, namely La Fenice, in which to place in his imagination the performance of the opera, and which enabled him to 'put into literary form' his impressions and reactions.

*   *   *

Having taken part, as he was obliged to do, in the capacity of 'maestro al cembalo', at the first three performances of *Adelaide di Borgogna*, which was premièred in Rome at the Teatro Argentina on December 27, 1817, Rossini returned directly to Naples, where he had a contract with the impresario Barbaja. This required him to set to music by the beginning of March 1818 a serious opera on a sacred subject ('azione tragico-sacra', as the libretto calls it), put into verse by Andrea Leone Tottola with the title *Mosè in Egitto*. The composition and the writing out of the score occupied him for about forty-five days; on February 25, 1818, the *Giornale delle Due Sicilie* announced that it had been completed. This is an exceptionally long period, given Rossini's 'working speed' at that time. The necessity of adapting his musical style to the character and plot of the libretto may explain this relative slowness, and at the same time why he indulged in so few 'self borrowings', that is, few pieces written for earlier operas are inserted into the new score. It was not the first time that Rossini had confronted the 'serious' genre; but what was certainly new was the content, the character and the 'tone' of the plot.

This libretto is not concerned with the development and confrontation of individual passions, or the exchange of expressions of affection and straightforward human sentiments; it is, instead, a text in which the supernatural element plays a determining role, decisive at every focal point of the action. It is, moreover, constructed around a violent clash of forces and wills which transcends the sphere of the individual characters: on one side the Israelite people in slavery, whose leader is Moses, interpreter and earthly executor of the divine will and power, and, on the other side, the will of the Pharaoh, determined not to let the Israelites depart, seconded in this by the high priest of Isis and, above all, by the exalted passion of his son for a Hebrew girl. In the libretto of *Moses* we observe two clearly distinct planes which are connected only externally; they are juxtaposed but not coherently fused and amalgamated. The first plane, the 'choral' and collective one, is demonstrated in the scenes in which the Israelites — *all* the people of Israel — weep, pray, lament, raise hymns of joy and gratitude to the Eternal, both through the chorus and through single characters, all of whom feel, in the same manner, similar anguish, similar joy. This plane reaches its greatest point of tension when the Chosen People, in their unity of feeling, guided and inspired by Moses (who, as I have said, symbolises the people), confront the Egyptians, the Pharaoh, his family, the high priest, and the court. The Egyptian group is distinguished from the Israelite group in that it is formed of characters who, taken singly, have well defined individual sentiments. At the moments when the two groups meet, however, every personal element disappears, precisely because they are absorbed by the unified characterisation of the opposed groups. Let me anticipate by saying that this distinction of planes is even clearer in the score. In the libretto the dynamics of the action occur essentially when the two groups confront each other and the plot develops only because the will of the one party prevails momentarily over the other; only the total destruction of the might of Egypt can end it.

In the 'Argument' printed at the beginning of the libretto, Tottola declared:

> ...I believed I could render [the plot] more interesting with the episode of the love of a Hebrew girl for the Pharaoh's first-born son, because he could then with greater fervour urge his father to keep the people of Israel enslaved in Egypt.

This is, then, the second plane, the parallel story which, in the plot of *Moses*, is supposed to be interwoven with the principal one, the liberation of the people of Israel from servitude in Egypt, and to stimulate its development. Tottola's assertion clearly implies that this second element of the story is his own invention; but it is a rash statement, to say the least, since the librettist, in the lines immediately preceding in the same 'Argument', has just declared that he planned his text 'following the development of the well-known tragedy of *Sig. Ringhieri.*' The identification and a reading of this tragedy allow us to state categorically that the amorous sub-plot has in the play an equal, and perhaps still greater, importance than it has in Tottola's libretto. *L'Osiride* of the 18th-century Olivetan monk and 'Reader of Theology' Francesco Ringhieri takes its name precisely from the son of the Pharaoh, and the love of this youth for the young Hebrew girl Elcia, who in the tragedy is simply his 'lover', but in the libretto becomes his 'consort', is the origin of dramatic conflicts between contrasting affections and passions, of the Pharaoh's stubbornness, and, therefore, of the eruption of divine wrath. Let us compare Ringhieri's text with Tottola's libretto, limiting ourselves only to the simple succession of scenes and their content; what has happened? The action that was destined to be expressed purely by means of words has been transformed into a text whose sole function is to be the basis for the scenic and musical realisation of the plot. This metamorphosis has led to the elimination of situations, of characters, and of motivations that furnish a logical and plausible justification for the actions of the principal characters. In other words: many elements tied to the development of the spoken drama have fallen by the wayside, and in this way the characters in the drama have been, so to speak, emptied of rational content for their behaviour; what is left is only their psychological scheme, the abstract characterisation; the logical motivations of their actions have disappeared. The extreme case is the wife of Pharaoh (Amaltea in the tragedy and first version of the opera; Sinaïde in the second version): in the libretto of *Mosè in Egitto*, and even more in *Moïse et Pharaon*, the Egyptian queen openly sides with the Hebrews and asks her husband to let them go. Addressing her in the libretto of the first version, Moses says:

Gentil Regina, oh quanto	Noble queen, how well your fair heart
Mi è noto il tuo bel cor! Tu mia difesa,	is known to me! You are my defence,
Tu scudo al popol mio presso il consorte	you have always been the shield of my
Fosti mai sempre, e se a consigli tuoi	people before your husband; and if the
Ceduto avesse il Re, straziato, afflitto	King had yielded to your advice, Egypt
Da tanti affanni or non sarebbe Egitto.	would not now be scourged, afflicted by
	these troubles.

This attitude of Amaltèa, from the point of view of common logic, is entirely incomprehensible, incoherent and unjustified. In the tragedy of Ringhieri, however, it finds full justification in the fact that the queen desires that her son abandon Elcia, his young Israelite lover, and marry instead an Armenian princess, repeatedly proposed in attractive terms (attractive on the political level as well) by the ambassador Ittaco.

There is no need to insist further on this point; we are facing the nth case of 'violence' done to a literary text in adapting it to the exigencies of the musical theatre. In this way, the balance which we can clearly perceive in Ringhieri's tragedy is entirely compromised. In the spoken tragedy, the two planes that I have tried to identify, the collective and the personal, influence each other, interpenetrate, and form an organic whole, or at least one rather adroitly organised. In the libretto, on the contrary, the fusion of the two planes is practically impossible, since the characters have been deprived of any internal dynamism, and therefore the two spheres of action — that of the whole people and that of the individuals — remain throughout split, differentiated, out of phase with one another.

Such is the dramatic structure which Rossini set to music in forty-five days. How did he react to Tottola's libretto? From a study of the score, especially an analysis of its formal structure, we can say that the major interest of the twenty-six-year-old composer was precisely the most difficult problem, the problem for which he had no direct precedent on which to base and model his own work, namely the musical characterisation of the two peoples, and, above all, the translation of group feelings into Italian operatic terms. Rossini did not try to blunt or to attenuate the inconsistency between what I have called the two planes of the libretto: the subjective individual parts — the inner torment of Elcia-Anaï-Anna, the impatient, juvenile frenzies of Osiride-Amenofi-Amenophis, the various sentiments that from time to time excite the single characters — are resolved in terms that are dramatically neutral and are static musical realisations of 'affects' still understood in the 18th-century sense. The arias, and even more the duets, are very beautiful 'numbers' in the score, rich in splendid melodic ideas that are perfectly developed from a musical point of view, and are authentic models of *bel canto* style transformed into elements of a very individual musical language, but none of these parts has any function in the development of the action. Such being the case, the tension underlying the plot is based on the alternation of one people's domination over the other; and upon the fact that the plagues which the God of Israel, invoked by Moses, sends down on the Egyptians are quickly forgotten by the Pharaoh in order to refuse the Chosen People their promised liberty; we can therefore understand why the revision made by Rossini for the Paris Opéra left the dramatic substance of the score intact. The three acts of the original score became four; the first act was largely new; to the third act was added the ballet music expected for a performance at that theatre; but the plot did not undergo any substantial modification, nor is there any fundamental imbalance in it. The reason is evident: the opera's ground-plan allows the various episodes to be interchangeable.

Laure Cinti-Damoreau who created the role of Anaï (Opera Rara)

The characters in *Moses* are not, as I have said, sufficiently characterised, from a musical point of view, to enable us to distinguish them from other characters in similar dramatic circumstances. This is both true and untrue at the same time; there is one character whose musical and psychological delineation does not undergo any evolution in the course of the action, but who is clearly distinguished from all the others, so as not to be merely an abstract 'affective' figure; this is possibly also because there did not exist in opera any earlier model on which he could be based. This character is Moses, the protagonist, the prophet and liberator of Israel, the one who guides the Chosen People to liberty, the one who reveals to mortals, with the powerful tones of his declamation, the will and threats of the Divinity, to whom he, alone, has the power to address himself directly. When Moses speaks to the Egyptians, threatening in the name of God the heavenly plagues that will immediately come down upon them, then his voice assumes truly superhuman force, and he speaks exactly like the statue of the Commendatore in *Don Giovanni*, that inexhaustible model of perfect dramatic realisation. This kind of declamation, however, goes back to a much older tradition, traceable as far back as the Renaissance; another historical example could be found, for instance, in Gluck's *Alceste*, when the Oracle's voice announces the necessity of a victim offering herself in place of Admeto:

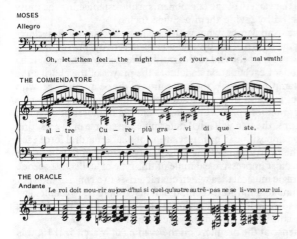

In the same way, however, other superhuman voices speak in the opera. For instance, in the first act of the new version, the voice offstage which calls Moses to receive the tablets of the law:

or the other offstage voice which, in the second act (still referring to the second version), invites the Egyptians to worship the goddess Isis:

But when Moses addresses the Israelites, afflicted and in distress, with words of consolation, his voice, although preserving solemn and hieratic tones, succeeds in becoming persuasive and convincing with a truly apt and entirely new psychological movement. In this sense, from the point of view of the characterisation of the protagonist, *Moïse et Pharaon* is, without any doubt, a refinement in comparison with *Mosè in Egitto*. Significantly, in the French (or, if we prefer, definitive) version of the opera, the character of Moses is not given a single aria: he participates in ensembles, but for the rest the lines entrusted to him are incisive declamations, enunciations of the will of God, threats of plagues, prayers; he is above all the consoler, the guide, the soul of the oppressed people. Massimilla Doni will say to the French doctor, even before the performance begins: 'Moses is the liberator of a people in slavery. Remember that idea, and you will see with what religious hope the entire audience will hear the prayer of the liberated Hebrews, and with what thunderous applause they will respond to it.'

In order to display precisely this character of the protagonist, Rossini created the vast fresco-like scene that opens the new version of the opera; in it, Moses encourages the Israelites 'oppressed by misfortune', repeating their musical statements and transforming them into a song of hope and joy. Already on this solemn opening page the Israelite people is clearly delineated as a composite: the alternation between the male and female parts of the chorus underlines the variety of the components while establishing the unity of their state of mind by giving them a single theme.

After a recitative from Moses, who, with a majestic declamation, declares that he is awaiting the return of the brother and sister sent by him to Pharaoh, the people begin to pray. At the end of this prayer Eleazor, Miriam and Anna enter and their jubilant exclamation concludes the prayer of the chorus: the three characters stamp, so to speak, the invocation of the people of Israel with their expressions of joy, and they are grafted onto the collective plane. This principle assumes grandiose proportions in the closing numbers of each act, where the two groups, the two wills that determine the course of events, find themselves in direct opposition. The intervention of a supernatural force each time determines the overturning of the situation (generally in favour of the Israelites). Yet the most impressive example of this type of 'collective scene', constructed on a single musical idea which characterises in a concise and very clear manner the fundamental state of mind that determines its psychological atmosphere, is the so-called 'scene of darkness', the scene with which *Mosè in Egitto* had begun and which now opens the second act.

Among the audience at the première on the evening of March 5, 1818, was Stendhal, who, in his *Life of Rossini*, having spoken at length of his personal discontent with the choice of a Biblical subject (and having caustically justified the reasons), wrote:

> I arrived then at the Teatro San Carlo, unable to be more ill-disposed, and like a person who pretends to brighten up at a spectacle of the stakes of the Inquisition ... The opera begins with the so-called *scourge of darkness*, a scourge rather too easily executed on the stage, and therefore rather ridiculous; it is enough to turn down the footlights and to dim the chandelier. I laughed at the rise of the curtain; the poor Egyptians formed a group on an immense stage, and, afflicted by the plague of the extinguisher, are in prayer. I had hardly heard twenty measures of this admirable introduction before I saw a great people plunged in grief; for example, Marseilles praying at the announcement of the plague in 1720.

Stendhal's judgement, on the whole based solely on instinctive reactions, and rather impressionistic, is opposed to that of Balzac in *Massimilla Doni*. In that novel the comments concerning what happens on the stage are generally entrusted to the protagonist; for the 'scene of darkness', however, the writer is unable to resist following Massimilla's enthusiastic (and, after all, exaggeratedly nationalistic) comments with some personal observations which are even more penetrating than they are evocative. For the strictly musical part, Balzac declared openly that he had availed himself of the aid of the musician Jacob Strunz, a German residing in Paris, to whom he was to dedicate *Massimilla Doni* when it was finally published in 1839. Whatever may be the contribution of the specialist in these observations, the selection of the parts to be analysed and the value judgements expressed concerning them can only come from the author of the *Comédie humaine*:

The duchess [i.e. Massimilla Doni] had been able to say those words while the curtain was going up. The doctor then heard the sublime introduction, by means of which the composer has opened this vast Biblical scene. It concerns the grief of an entire people. Grief is one in its expression, above all when it relates to physical suffering. Thus, after having understood instinctively, like all men of genius, that there should not be any difference in the ideas there, the musician, once he had found his principal theme, led it from tonality to tonality, grouping the masses and the characters around this motif through modulations and cadences of an admirable flexibility. One recognises the power from this simplicity. The effect of this phrase, which paints the sensations of cold and of the night on a people incessantly bathed by the luminous rays of the sun, and which the people and their kings repeat, is startling. There is something unrelenting in this slow musical movement. This cold and dolorous phrase is like a blade held by that celestial executioner who will drop it on the limbs of all these sufferers in steady rhythm. Hearing it move from C-minor to G-minor, resuming in C to return to the dominant G, and taking root again, *fortissimo*, in the tonic, E♭, to arrive in F-major and return to C-minor, ever more and more charged with terror, with cold and with darkness, the soul of the spectator is, at the end, united with the mood expressed by the musician. In this manner the Frenchman [i.e. the doctor] experienced the strongest emotion when all these combined griefs exploded in the cry:

O nume d'Israël!	O God of Israel!
Se brami in libertà	If you wish to have free
Il popol tuo fedel	your faithful people,
Di lui, di noi pietà.	have mercy on them, and on us.

In ensemble scenes, such as this one, when each of the two peoples appears united by the same mood, the single personalities, the individual psychological characteristics, are annulled, assimilated and absorbed in the manifestation of the collective state of mind that predominates at that moment; the Pharaoh, the queen Amaltéa-Sinaïde-Sinaida, the young Osiride-Aménofi-Amenophis are annihilated, prostrated like all the Egyptians in horror and misery. Pharaoh summons Moses; and we hear Stendhal again:

The Pharaoh, won over by the moans of his people, cried out: Venga Mosè! (Let Moses come forth!) Benedetti, entrusted with the role of Moses, appeared in a simple and sublime costume that he had imitated from Michelangelo's statue in San Pietro in Vincoli, in Rome; he had not addressed twenty words to the Eternal before the lights of my spirit eclipsed themselves; I no longer saw a charlatan changing his cane into a serpent, and playing the fool, but a great man, minister of the Almighty, making a vile tyrant tremble on his throne. I still recall the effect of these words: 'Eterno, immenso, incomprensibil Dio.'

This appeal to the Deity that he placate his wrath is spoken in a tone that only Moses is allowed to use; it is the solemn, hieratic, majestic tone that Rossini founded in the tradition of Italian opera. Apropos this invocation, especially in connection with the following scene, the return of the light, the words of Balzac (this time entrusted to the Duchess) are of extraordinary interest:

With a skilful calculation . . . this invocation is accompanied only by the brass. Those instruments give this piece its great religious colour. Not only is this artifice admirable at this point, but see how the genius is still fertile in resources; Rossini has drawn new beauties from the obstacles that he has created for himself. He has been able to reserve the strings to express the day when it succeeds the darkness, and to arrive thus at one of the most powerful effects known in music.

Massimilla Doni again guides us in understanding the true reasons for the blazing beauty of this page:

What do you think this piece of the sunrise consists of — so varied, so brilliant, so complete? It consists of a simple C chord, repeated time and again, with which Rossini has mingled only a six-four chord. It is here that the magic of his skill shines. He has proceeded to paint the arrival of the light by the same means that he had employed to paint the darkness and grief . . . There is the seal of the great composer: Unity! Being one and varied. One single phrase and a thousand sentiments of grief, the miseries of a nation; a single chord and all the features of nature at its awakening, all the expressions of the joy of a people. These two immense pages are closed by an appeal to God everlasting, author of all things, of this grief as well as of this joy . . . With what art has not the composer constructed this piece? . . . He has begun it by a horn solo of divine sweetness, sustained by harp arpeggios, for the first voices that are raised in this great ensemble are those of Moses and Aaron who thank the true God; their sweet and solemn song recalls the sublime ideas of the invocation and yet is united to the joy of the people.

An extreme simplicity of means, the firmness and equilibrium of the form ('It is above all the marvellous facility with which he varies the form that one admires in Rossini,' Balzac says later), clarity in the articulation of the musical language, which unfolds though the iteration rather than through the development of ideas; the richness and expressive pertinence of the orchestra: these are Rossini's artistic conquests.

It would be out of place to continue to examine Rossini's score under Balzac's guidance. It is enough to point out that the novelist's observations (whether expressed directly or through the mouths of his characters) continually strike home for their penetrating precision. It has seemed to me sufficient to bring together several examples to prove that the 'seditious party' to which Balzac boasted that he belonged, was once more right.

From Sublime to Romantic

Richard Bernas

At once the overture establishes a serious mood. Rather than audience-silencing formulas, we hear the simple motto of an idea, a rhythm-plus-chord progression played by *sotto voce* strings, then carefully decorated. The ear is drawn in, not assaulted. This is Rossini in his Neoclassical rather than Romantic frame of mind. All the D major restraint is soon annihilated by violently dramatic variations in the minor. The contrast between them and, on a larger scale, between a Haydnesque style and the grander but blunter rigours of early 19th-century opera seria, is at the centre of this fascinating, hybrid work.

After the D minor storm settles on a discreet cadential half close, a martial pendant to this prelude at a more decisive tempo and with brighter, more integrated orchestration begins in the related key of F major. This march is used later for moving Hebrew choruses about; here it gives a sense of forward movement. The momentum is arrested by the chorus intervention in F minor. Precisely the same harmonic tactic Rossini used in the overture (D major to D minor) signals the rise of the curtain. The musical perspective has widened to introduce the kernel of the opera, the Hebrews' captivity in Egypt. This recalls the opening of Gluck's *Alceste*, a similarly heartfelt cry by a fearful people. It is no coincidence that this scene was newly composed for the Paris version of *Moses* in 1827, where Gluck's opera had been revived in 1825.

Integration of overture with stage action is reinforced by the reinstatement of a chromatic 'wailing' figure which dramatically coloured the D minor section of the overture during the extension of the chorus outburst. The music slips into a more relaxed tonality (the relative major, A flat) as Rossini pairs off soprano and alto, tenor and bass to begin the gradual (and Handelian) process of individuating the chorus. The mass of sound first presented is now made more personal, preparing the way for the Hebrews' prophet, the extension of the people's voice, Moses. As this protagonist grows out of the chorus, so his accompanying orchestral colour of solemn brass (no trumpets) reinforced by woodwind (no flutes) sounds as a reflection of the block choral writing at the very start of the scene. And the use of such dark primary colour after the larger but less differentiated full orchestra is both dramatically apt and refreshing. Moses' first statement immediately sets out his musical physiognomy: a high bass with a strong sense of declamation and rhythm. Until the last Act, it has little melodic individuality but its effect is unfailingly noble.

Unity of musical and dramatic technique is maintained in the introduction of Anna, Miriam and Eleazor. A slow, majestic C minor chorus grows in tension, resolving in the major at the entry of the three soloists.

Rossini has chosen a massive, architectural approach, and this is leavened, musically and theatrically, by the appearance of a rainbow as a sign of God's approval. To ears accustomed to the nature portraits of Wagner and Richard Strauss, seven bars of solo harp may seem no great inspiration, but quick harmonic changes coupled with continuous instrumental velocity and a fresh timbre do create a sense of elation and of a miraculous occurrence. This is thrown against a choral outburst that rises suddenly in key from E flat to E major, a natural expression of wonder, while once more the perspective is

Adolphe Nourrit for whom Rossini created the role of Amenophis in 'Moïse et Pharaon' (Opera Rara)

widened by an offstage 'mysterious voice', accompanied by the solemn wind and brass familiar from Gluck's and Mozart's oracles.

The unaccompanied ensemble that follows is prefaced by a precis of the opening bars of the overture, raised a tone to E major, a unifying device that once again encourages us to think retrospectively over the grand structures of the scene. In the ensemble proper, Moses' vocal line ascends simply and purposefully, anchoring the changes of chord around him. His held notes are therefore the focus both of the harmony and of the stage picture, a musical/scenic device that admirably represents his steadfastness and faith. Another individual character emerges when, as Moses' bass joins the general movement of the ensemble, Anna becomes very much the solo soprano.

The final chorus of this ambitious opening scene contrasts choral singing in A minor against a solo quartet's response in the major key; a reversal of the major-minor transitions of the overture in a key that is the harmonic dominant of D major. Such relationships are unusually cogent for the period and the genre, and it is worth noting that this is Rossini's second attempt at an opening scene for *Moses* and that he had an extraordinarily fine precedent to better. In Naples 1818, *Mosè in Egitto* opened with the Plague of Darkness, which in Paris 1827 began Act Two, a scene which bound together an even stronger dramatic situation by means of one melodic figure, and which also made spectacular use of the minor/major transition we heard deployed here. For Paris, he chose to concentrate attention on the Hebrews, emphasizing the chorus as a protagonist equal in status to the soloists, and to exploit a greater variety of orchestral sonorities. Furthermore, he saved a great scene for a later act, when we can suppose the Opéra would have been better attended.

But the worth of the Paris opening scene is great. Some measure of its impressiveness may be judged by its influence on younger composers. In the shape and progress of the overture, the emphasis on the chorus as protagonist and its gradual individualisation into a solo voice, the deployment of a love

110

interest to counter the grandeur with intimacy, the Paris *Moses*, especially the first Act, is the compositional and dramaturgical template of Verdi's *Nabucco*.

The love interest is revealed in the duet between Anna and Amenophis. The duet follows a classic pattern, beginning with two complementary and musically equal statements for tenor and soprano, the solo for Amenophis repeated with a different text by Anna; then follows a less urgent *Andantino* in which the voices sing together; finally an energetic, suspense-creating close, motivated by the impending arrival of the chorus, thematically predicts the march which will follow it. The central section is particularly affecting, with a gently rocking cello commentary that links together the soloists' phrases and then discreetly retreats when they sing in close thirds.

The demands of the role of Amenophis are considerable. In the *Andantino* he must blend his high-lying line with low register soprano notes, making sophisticated use of a light head voice. At the start and finish of the scene, his vocal line is heavier, requiring passionate declamation as well as the ability to integrate high As and Bs into a melodic line, not just to launch them bravely onto the admiring public as a species of operatic exclamation mark. Rossini was lucky to have exceptional artists for both the Naples and Paris versions. In 1818 Amenophis was sung by Andrea Nozzari, who was also Rossini's first Otello, and the Paris Amenophis was the great Adolphe Nourrit, later the first Arnold in *William Tell*.

In dramatic terms, the start of the duet presents critical listeners with a quintessentially Rossinian problem of perspective. Amenophis and Anna have different things to say to one another, yet they do so in two musical paragraphs that are identical. We will encounter some pretty extreme measures regarding the allocation of text later, so it might be best to discuss this matter in the context of one of its milder manifestations. (Another striking example is the duet in Rossini's *Otello* between the Moor and Desdemona which is accompanied by the same phrase that furnishes much of the comic impetus for Basilio's 'Slander' aria, and yet was greeted with great excitement by Rossini's contemporaries.) We are used to thinking of this as an apparent insensitivity to the text, indeed, as one of the classic ambiguities of 19th-century opera. For the public of the time, it was obviously nothing of the sort. The libretto, when imaginatively delivered by the singers, was as important as the music and influenced the comic or tragic impact of the music enormously. That eternal defender of the audience, Stendhal, criticised German composers for 'using their instruments to furnish us as crudely as possible with certain necessary information which the singer on the stage should properly speaking convey *with words*.' He also pointed out (concerning 'Di tanti palpiti' from *Tancredi*) that the proper delivery of a line of recitative 'taxes the resources of the human soul. And even in the aria, the passage setting the words *alma* and *gloria* will never really be sung properly by anyone born north of the Alps!' Obviously, such criteria indicate not just the immediate comprehension of the listeners, but also an imaginative contribution by the singer of an importance, equal, during the performance, to that of the composer. This symbiotic relationship can only exist when both singer and composer are living, when composers tailor their music for an artist's capabilities and both, along with their public, inhabit a common set of cultural and social references. It is worth the effort to listen more imaginatively to some of these 'ambiguities' of the past — and of our own time, since that special intensity of communication which Stendhal celebrates can only occur among the artists and public of the same generation.

111

In the last section of Anna and Amenophis' duet, simple declamation is intercut with snatches of the march heard in the next scene. The effect is one of the soloists being overtaken by events. As the chorus marches in, the orchestration is fuller and more open in texture. The music is a stately procession through C major and a few related keys. Anna's character is further developed in her Bellinian duet with Miriam. The gentle 6/8 metre and general cast of the accompaniment link this number to the middle section of Anna's duet with Amenophis.

The Finale of Act One could be described, as Budden does the central finales of Rossini's comic operas, as a large scale 'ensemble of perplexity'. Passages of incisive declamation and swift action are contrasted with ensembles that reflect on these dramatic revelations. It is also, as Philip Gossett has noted, the classic opposition of kinetic and static elements. In this Finale, the dramatic diptych occurs twice: for each kinetic episode the orchestral music is (key apart) very similar, but the two static episodes are different in velocity, texture and shape.

Starting out in the key of the overture (D major), Amenophis and Moses argue in fast, rhythmically pointed *parlando* over an orchestral contribution of great energy, which bears a family resemblance, in its quicksilver rising sixth, to the music that accompanies the mock-drunk Almaviva's invasion of Bartolo's house. We have only to think of 'Donna, chi sei' from *Nabucco* to appreciate the aptness and influence of this musical tactic. A big concerted number follows in A flat major which, as a tonal centre, in terms of traditional harmony, is as far away from D major as you can get. This slow, static element is divided into three distinct parts: an unaccompanied quartet of reflection, a solo of scarcely suppressed hostility for Amenophis, in the minor key and accompanied by pizzicato or tremolo strings; and a summation of the first ensemble, lightly accompanied, elaborated with coloratura expressions of anger by the Pharaoh and his son, and surprisingly capped by a grand choral and orchestral tutti on the penultimate phrase. This 'ensemble of perplexity' ends unaccompanied, immediately launching into another kinetic section, a repeat of much of the first, but transposed into A flat. As Moses' threats are fulfilled by a plague of darkness, a violent C minor, full of unisons whipping through the strings, rushes out of the orchestra. Such is the terror expressed in this static episode that the textures of the writing are much simpler than heretofore: heavy tutti chords, blunt octave doublings and a lot of raw noise.

A noble simplicity and the key of C minor persist in the opening ensemble of the Second Act, Egypt plagued by darkness. As mentioned, this was the very first scene of the Naples 1818 score, a single moment which possibly represents the highpoint of Rossinian opera seria, and a standard which we assume the composer strove to equal in his Paris revisions. After the solemn unisons of the start, Rossini places a series of woodwind and string chords of no clear rhythmic shape and some harmonic adventurousness, falling gently before a winding violin figure begins the first of its many obsessive repetitions. The effect recalls a similar darkness at the beginning of Haydn's *Creation*, which is also in C and uses the same lack of rhythmic plainness. The comparison is not farfetched; Rossini conducted *The Creation* in Bologna at the age of nineteen.

What makes the music operatic, indeed realisable only in the theatre, is the sense of what I can describe as multiple temporal perspectives. Three planes of action are set out: the steady orchestral figuration twisting repeatedly around itself; the solos of the Pharaoh and his family, first evoking and then lamenting their plight; the Egyptian people, reacting as a distant choral backdrop. Solo vocal lines move restlessly within the orchestral frame, and we perceive that the Pharaoh's high bass lines are of a more fluent nature than Moses' grander pronouncements. His entry and invocation, 'Supreme judge and ruler', is set in A flat, a rich and dense sonority enhanced by the now-familiar presence of the heavy brass. As light returns, Rossini bows most convincingly in the direction of *The Creation*, bringing off the most spectacular C minor-into-major transition of an opera in which the use of such harmonic ploys is by no means uncommon. The quintet, 'O You who by Your mercy', is set in a relaxed F major, less bright than the preceding C major blaze, not as rich as the colour of Moses' invocation. After such an ambitious use of full orchestral forces, Rossini refines the accompaniment down to low strings, wind and harp, featuring an opening horn introduction of fresh pastoral beauty. Each vocal entry, building from solo to all five voices, enhances the sonority. We hear the Neoclassical proportions of a gradual procession outwards, sensing a steady, purposeful expansion after the violent contrasts of the Act One finale.

The repetition of rhythmically charged short phrases creating a surge of forward momentum is a Rossinian trademark, and here it is used to round off the ensemble with fast, then faster movement. We also find the first use in this opera of the famous Crescendo (*sotto voce e crescendo poco a poco*), a direct totally visceral device which other composers, including Schubert in the finale of his C major Symphony, appropriated, though rarely with such brilliant results.

The Pharaoh and Amenophis duet appears to recapitulate the Act One Hebrew march, but this reference in fact works in the reverse. Since the Hebrew march was part of the music composed for the Paris version and the duet under consideration written for Naples, Rossini extrapolated this martial tune and developed it retrospectively, thereby reinforcing the links between older and newer music. The second half of the duet closely resembles, in melodic shape and key, that of Amenophis and Anna, and these deliberate recollections reinforce the listeners' perceptions of Amenophis' attachment to her. In the Naples text, the next aria was sung by Anna with interjections by Amenophis and the chorus; its modification is a not entirely convincing example of Rossini's usually superior carpentry.

To a rich string accompaniment, Sinaida, the Pharaoh's wife, persuades Amenophis to consider his responsibilities; this he refuses to do, threatening to kill Moses, until offstage priests, accompanied by low brass and woodwind, summon the faithful to Isis' temple. This seems to influence Amenophis' mood and his mother concludes the Act with a difficult, brilliant and fast cabaletta. All well and good, though these offstage priests, in declamatory profile and orchestral context, do sound very like Moses. We might presume a Voltairian view of religion on Rossini's part, in as much as the voice of ecclesiastical authority, as perceived by the true believer, is the same no matter what the faith. But in Naples these lines were indeed sung by Moses, after the very same aria, sung to a different text by Anna. Amenophis was struck by lightning; his death was depicted in a remarkable passage which featured Rossini's version of the Bartók *pizzicato* (in which the strings of the doublebass are plucked so violently that the string rebounds against the fingerboard, producing a heavy slapping sound) before Anna launched into the cabaletta with which, in Paris, Sinaida expresses her optimism. If it is well performed, this music has energy and excitement whichever character delivers it; the evidence we have seen concerning the importance of the text to Rossini's dramaturgy can certainly be marshalled to defend these revisions. Overall, the Parisian second Act is more consistent and powerful than its Neapolitan equivalent, which loses momentum during a sequence of not very individual arias for the Pharaoh, Sinaida and Moses. Nevertheless, there are occasions when Moses' music is delivered by anonymous choral mouths when the craggy outlines of some very difficult coloratura sit well on neither the words they now accompany nor the emotions they are now intended to convey.

The ballet occupies most of the third Act. It is prefaced by a grand ceremonial scene, during which the Egyptians avoid the smaller, more individual groupings which added variety to the Hebrews' choruses. The High Priest Osiridis is a third bass, narrower in vocal range than Moses or the Pharaoh, he sings a long-breathed phrase that would do credit to Ramfis of *Aida*.

In spite of the care with which Egyptian and Hebrew choruses have been differentiated, the ballet music has little specific regional character. It is the ethnic music of the Parisian boulevards. The second number, with its fulsome orchestral recitative and graceful woodwind solos accompanied by harp, is the most distinguished composition. Interest during the third number is maintained by the brilliance of the high horn parts and its sheer vitality.

The Act Three Finale is one of the most imaginatively scored and flexibly-paced passages composed for 1827. It involves a description of the plagues, further arguments between the Pharaoh and Moses and a contest of wills between Moses and the High Priest, which ends in the destruction of the altar of Isis. In balance of declamation, *parlando* and more measured use of the chorus as an amplifying echo of the soloists' surprise, the contrasts of orchestral sonority — a threatening, dark duet as Moses and the High Priest claim the superiority of their respective religions.

This kinetic element of the Finale is balanced by a static ensemble, once more of classic proportions and steady pace. 'I'm shaken with horror' originated in Naples as a quartet of reaction after Amenophis' public declaration of love for Anna. In this new context, Rossini adds a small contribution for Moses and a concluding amplification by the chorus. After the orchestral tumult, the simple harp accompaniment can sound anti-climactic, too intimate in focus for such matters of State and God. In the ensuing kinetic episode, the Pharaoh finally agrees to allow the Hebrews to depart, and Rossini takes up the rich textures he temporarily abandoned. It is worth considering again the effect these moments had on a 19th-century audience, as Henry Chorley, one of London's most famous critics, recalled:

There is no contrast in music — no, not even in Handel's stupendous *Israel* — stronger than that between the slow, restless moaning Darkness-chorus (a long *andante maestoso*, unlike any other movement existing in Signor Rossini's operas), and the *stretto* following the delicious '*Mi manca la voce*' round, in which a form of *crescendo*, dear to the master, and more than once abused by him, is worked out, with vivacity and climax, in their happiest forms to expression. It is idle to object that the receipt is one well known — that the means are not such as would be employed by a countryman of Bach or Beethoven. The effect produced is resistless, owing to the exceeding felicity of the phrases (in particular the coda), and the amazing animation of the orchestra. The singers sung it in London as if fire, not blood, was coursing through their veins. A storm of delight burst from every corner of the full theatre. I remember no moment of greater musical excitement.

Act Four opens with a sinfonia and final duet for Anna and Amenophis, largely taken from Act Two in Naples, but with modifications of the recitative to suit its new context. A sense of space is conjured up by the opening quiet string unison, which is immediately echoed, faster and higher, by solo horn and clarinet: a *primo ottocento* 'Doppler' effect. In both the introduction and the duet proper Rossini takes care to end phrases with a melodic fall, giving a sense of tiredness and depression to the scene. This is reinforced by a preponderance of G minor within a major key frame — the emotional centre of the duet is in this minor key, its accompaniment enriched by the sort of divided viola lines Bellini appropriated so successfully for *Norma*. Also of a proto-Bellinian nature is the shift back to G major when the soprano and tenor sing in close harmony.

Anna's aria of confusion, then resolution, was newly made for Paris and it is of an inspiration and dramatic seriousness equal to the new opening of the first Act. It begins with declamatory statements, leading headlong into longer vocal lines, reinforced by a continuously busy, seething string accompaniment as Anna's predicament grows in intensity. The aria is cast in the relative minor of the preceding duet, and the vocal line features a number of highly-charged ascending phrases coloured by the plangent interval of a rising sixth. In keeping with the turbulent nature of the music, Rossini avoids symmetrical designs or formal structures. The first verse, for example, avoids harmonic 'balance' by ending in G major, rather than the expected E major, so demonstrating that Anna's predicament is not yet resolved. Instead of a formal repeat of the first verse to conclude the aria, its momentum is dramatically enhanced by interjections by the other characters, including the chorus, which push the music back into E. Her final resolve to rejoin the Hebrews is cast in the dominant of that key; the music rushes into a concerted ensemble in E major and Anna's hard-won freedom is crowned with wide-ranging, expressive coloratura. Though she loses a duet to Sinaida in the Paris version, this aria more than compensates for it, and it rounds off Anna's characterisation in a much more compelling way.

The opening of the renowned Prayer is a good illustration of the small but telling differences in Rossini's orchestral technique between the two versions. In the Naples score (which can be examined in a photocopy of Rossini's manuscript printed by The Garland Press) the first two bars are played by solo harp. For Paris, he reinforces these gently strummed chords with a quiet held chord played by bassoons, horns and trombone, over two gentle tympani rolls. In effect, Rossini underlines the solemnity of the occasion by enhancing the resonant colours of the harp, as a painter would shade a figure in oils with greater care than in watercolours. But the watercolour leaves more to the viewers' participatory imagination.

Moses leads the prayer, and in so doing is granted his first genuinely original melodic inspiration. After so much declamation of unfailing nobility, this lyrical flowering completes his vocal characterisation, and the composer's portrait of the Hebrews. Much has been written about the Prayer's grand conclusion in G major after three verses in the minor, notably by Stendhal. It is worth remarking on the cymbal clash that announces the harmonic shift, as light-giving and spiritually apt as any in Bruckner.

The parting of the Red Sea and the destruction of the Egyptian army are presented in a single nature-poem of Beethovenian proportions and sonic originality, though it is set out with a greater rhythmic regularity than, for example, the storm in the Pastoral Symphony. Noteworthy features include the use of choral recitative (as in Act Three) and the throwing of string unisons against violent tutti explosions as the army is drowned. Once more, a C minor-major transition resolves the musical argument. The Song of Miriam, which is appended to the Paris score but rarely given after the 1827 performances, is an impressive solo and choral tableau that ends the opera, in harmonic terms, in a not-very-congruent F major.

In the following appendix, the order of numbers of the Naples score is summarised and presented in relation to the Paris revisions. Comparing the two, we can see that the significant Paris additions are improvements, notably the very first scene and Anna's fine aria, while the solo arias that are deleted are frankly expendable both in terms of dramatic pace and melodic originality. The grey areas are the modified numbers which have required changes of text and structural carpentry; here Rossinians will always argue the merits of either version. But the major Parisian changes all work towards greater musico/dramatic consistency, despite the fact that the opera loses its original continuity of key structure. Rossini smashed *Moses'* tonal frame and out of the pieces created a fascinating and grand piece of sculpture.

'Mosè in Egitto' and 'Moïse et Pharaon'
A table of the 1818/9 Naples score with the Paris revision.

Note: differences in the connecting recitative, and in the tailoring of the vocal line have not been listed, and should indeed be presumed. In order to simplify comparisons, all the roles are given their names from the Moody translation.

Mosè in Egitto	Moïse et Pharaon
Act One	
No. 1 Introduction: 'The Plague of Darkness'	Act Two, Nos. 7 & 8
No. 2 Moses' Invocation	
Quintet, stretto & recitative	
No. 3 Duet: Anna and Amenophis	Act One, No. 3
No. 4 Aria: Pharaoh/Orginally composed by Carafa, Rossini's aria was first used in Paris in 1822	deleted
No. 5 March	Act One, Nos. 4, 5 & 6
Duet: Anna and Miriam	
Finale	
Act Two	
No. 6 Duet: Pharaoh and Amenophis	Act Two, No. 9
No. 7 Aria: Sinaida/A beautiful early piece borrowed from *Ciro in Babilonia* (1812) cut in the 1819 revival	deleted
No. 8 Scene: Anna and Amenophis	Act Four, No. 13 revised
Quartet: 'Mi manca la voce'	Act Three, No. 12 as part of the Finale revised as quintet plus chorus
Stretto of quintet	deleted
No. 9 Aria: Moses	deleted
No. 10 Finale: Chorus: recitative and Aria of Anna (The Death of Amenophis)	modified to become Duet: Sinaïda and Amenophis
Act Three	
Recitative after the March	Act Four recitative
No. 11 Prayer (composed in 1819) and Finale	Act Four No. 16 without the Rossini crescendo at the end; instead, a quieter close.

116

Thematic Guide

Many of the themes from this opera have been identified in the articles by numbers in square brackets, which refer to the themes set out on these pages. The themes are also identified by the numbers in square brackets at the corresponding points in the libretto, so that the words can be related to the musical themes.

No. 5 Duet ANNA

Andante

God on this joy-ful mor — ning has en-ded all our fears!
Dieu, dans ce jour pro - spè — re ter - mi - ne nos mal-heurs!

[9a]

Finale 1: ANNA (a cappella)

Largo

Oh, what mad-ness! What an out — rage! Do they dare dis-pute his pow — er?
Quel dé - li - re, quel-le o — ffense, on in - sulte à sa pui-ssan — ce?

[9b]

AMENOPHIS

First by love and then by_____ ha — tred turn by
De l'a - mour et de la _____ hai — ne tour à

turn_they both in — flame — — me,
tour__la voix m'en - trai — — ne

[10a]

No. 7 Introduction

Andante maestoso più tosto largo/*sotto voce*

[10b]

No. 8 Invocation MOSES

Moderato

Su-preme judge and ru - ler, the lord of all cre - a — tion!
Ar - bi - tre su - prê - me, du ciel et de la ter — re!

[11a]

MOSES
Andante

O You who by Your mer-cy, gave light to end their dark-ness,
O toi, dont la clé - men-ce a - pai - se leur souf-fran-ce,

[11b]

SINAIDA

Vivace

Our gods no long - er look down in an - ger
Les Dieux font trê - ve à leur co - lè - re,

See all a - round_us the day__shines a - gain,
Un jour pro - spè - re luit à nos yeux.

[12]

No. 9 Duet AMENOPHIS

Moderato

The blow at last has fal - - len yet
Mo - ment fa - tal ... Que fai - - re? Hé -

still I dare not tell_____ him
-las, il faut me tai - - re

[13]

No. 10 Aria SINAIDA

Andante maestoso

Hear what your mo-ther asks_____ you my dear-est son I
Ah, d'u-ne ten-dre mè - re é - cou - te la

beg___you, be mas-ter____ of_your - self_____ prince,
pri - ère tri-omphe_____ de toi mê - - me

[14]

SINAIDA

Allegro

Oh, hear and re-joice, he o-beys me! To hon-our he will be true,
Qu'en - tends - je? Dou-ce i - vre - sse! Il est fi - dèle à l'hon-neur.

[15]

OSIRIDIS

Allegro moderato

Come a-dorn ev' - ry al-tar, and ar-ray them with gar-lands,
Ap - por-tez vos of - fran-des, sus-pen-dez vos guir-lan - des,

[16]

OPHIDIS Allegro moderato

Great king, ____ O save us all from yet an-oth-er plague!
Grand Roi, ____ dé - li - vre-nous de plus cru-els flé - aux!

119

[17]

ANNA

Andante

I'm sha-ken with hor-ror My hope gone for-ev-er
Je trem-ble et sou-pire, Mon cœur se dé-chi-re:

[18]

Andante lento

sotto voce

[19]

ANNA

Andante maestoso

O be-lov-ed, life___to-geth-er from this
Jour fu-nes-te loi___cru-el-le! Mon cou-

cru-el day is ov-er.
-ra-ge, hé-las, chan-celle...

[20a]

No. 14 Aria ANNA

Allegro

I am torn in two al-rea-dy.
Suis-je as-sez in-for-tu-née!

[20b]

ANNA

At my feet___a yawning cha-sm, and my hope turned to des-pair
Sous mes pas___je vois l'a-bî-me tout es-poir fuit sans re-tour.

[21]

ANNA sotto voce

I shall now____o-bey____God's de-cree!
J'o-bé-is____aux lois____du Seig-neur!

[22]

No. 15 Prayer MOSES

Andante

Look down on us from hea-ven Lord God, and guide your chil-dren,
Des cieux où tu ré-si-des Grand Dieu, toi qui nous gui-des,

Moses
Moïse et Pharaon
ou
Le passage de la Mer Rouge

Opera in Four Acts
Music by Gioachino Rossini
Libretto by Victor de Jouy and Louis Balochy
after Andrea Leone Tottola
English translation by John and Nell Moody

Moïse et Pharaon was first performed at the Théâtre de l'Académie Royale de Musique in Paris on March 26, 1827. The first performance in Britain was at Covent Garden on April 20, 1850 as *Zora*. The first performance in the United States was at the Academy of Music, New York, on May 7, 1860.

CHARACTERS

Moses (Moïse) *legislator of the Israelites*	bass
Eleazor (Eliézer) *the son of his brother Aaron*	tenor
Pharaoh (Pharaon) *King of Egypt*	baritone
Amenophis (Aménophis) *his son*	tenor
Osiridis (Osiride) *High Priest of Isis*	bass
Ophidis (Eufide) *Egyptian officer*	tenor
Sinaïda (Sinaïde) *Pharaoh's wife*	soprano
Miriam (Marie) *Moses' sister*	mezzo-soprano
Anna (Anaï) *her daughter*	soprano
A mysterious voice	bass

Israelites, Egyptians, Priests, Guards, Soldiers, Dancers

The action takes place in the camp of the Midianites near Memphis, at Memphis and by the Red Sea.

Translators' Note

John and Nell Moody

When we first translated *Moïse et Pharaon* for Welsh National Opera we used mostly biblical language with which Wales was already usefully familiar, and which gave it a certain 'classical' form. Today, to bring the subject to life the words used need to have a new directness and impact, (no *thee*s and *thou*s, for example).

Rossini in his music had already given the warmth of heart, together with the size and scale, that generates an immediate response from all oppressed peoples. This is not merely a matter for the cause of Italian unity: there have been striking examples in our own century. For instance a huge production of *William Tell* was given at the Berlin State Opera in honour of Hitler. But it boomeranged. In the Act Three finale, as well as the downtrodden Swiss on stage shouting 'Down with Gessler' (the Habsburg Governor in the opera) shouts of 'Down with Hitler' echoed all round the theatre. The production disappeared from the repertory! And in the 1935 Florence Maggio Musicale *Moses* was put on to honour Mussolini's triumphs. Mussolini's guest, Hitler, had to sit and applaud an opera celebrating the triumph of the Jews over their persecutors. The Prayer from *Moses* was further one of the items chosen to re-open La Scala after the Second World War, with Toscanini conducting a concert performance in which the young Renata Tebaldi made her debut in that theatre.

Goethe said that if *he* had written the libretto for the first act of *Moses and Pharaoh*, he would have given it far greater depth of oppression and real conflict, so that Moses' feat of leadership would have been more effective. Act One certainly needs all the directness and tension one can find in words that generate dynamic action and get away from the danger of religious tableaux. Rossini knew that it is the human faces of kings, religious leaders and politicians, rather than their public faces, that really interest and affect us. So in his new Act One, we surmise, he set out to do this. Firstly he removed Aaron. Because in *Exodus*, the Lord had said that Aaron was to do the public speaking with Moses, as Moses thought himself inadequate, Rossini probably felt that Aaron had become rather a bore; besides presenting a musical problem of brotherly duets, or duets in canon! To solve this, and to keep Moses as a dominating character, was not really possible, so Aaron was replaced by his son Eleazor, to act as Moses' assistant and provide the necessary solo tenor in the Israelite ensembles. At the same time, Rossini built up the various family relationships. He changed Prince Amenophis' secret wife Elcia (originally just a 'Hebrew girl') into Miriam's daughter and Moses' niece, Anaï, not yet married to Amenophis. He filled out the relationships between Queen Sinaîda and her son Amenophis, and Amenophis and his father Pharaoh; also Sinaïda's religious relationship with the Israelites in the earlier part of the act. So his development of the family as well as national relationships, we suggest, make the opera a less formal and far more human, interesting and accessible work.

There was one other textual problem; this was the unorchestrated 'Cantique' at the end of the vocal score, which never appeared in the full score. Critical opinions on the origins of this piece are divided, and verified facts are few. It was said that after the disaster on the first night of the staging of the crossing of the Red Sea, Rossini wrote in a number quickly, to counteract any shortcomings in the Red Sea passage production. Some believe this was the famous Prayer (No. 15) placed *before* the Red Sea crossing; this produced such hysterical euphoria in large sections of the audience that they were oblivious to all stage defects. Others believe he wrote the 'Cantique' for use *after* the crossing in case that had been a flop. Anyhow, being a real man of the theatre Rossini saw that the lift of a final chorus of thanksgiving with the picture of the Israelites in prayer on the far shore in the returning light after the storm, was a far more theatrically effective ending, however good the music. He may not have had time to orchestrate it, or he may have thought of it 'a capella', or he just may have heard it with an organ at rehearsal, and said in his nonchalant way that it would do as it was! By then he was too far into his next opera to worry.

Notice

Victor de Jouy and Louis Balochy

What is a parody? It is the sort of work which sets out to criticise a play by imitating its style , pace and structure; parody is to theatre what caricature is to art. So it is quite improper to describe as such a verse translation of a foreign libretto to which the music composed for the original has to be adapted.

It is almost impossible to make an excellent singing translation; not even the most ingenious talent can reconcile the independence of genius with the slavery exacted by every word, syllable and even the value of each letter. The weight of the chains involved in such work is insufficiently appreciated - not to mention the discomfort imposed upon the author as the servile imitation of metre, rhyme, caesura and euphony make him aware at each stage of new constraints. In practice this work demands from the author a profound knowledge of the two languages of the poetry with which he is working, but also of the language of the music, of which he is also an interpreter.

We did not take upon ourselves such a sterile task in the case of *Moïse*, where we only retained some traces of the Italian libretto in order to introduce the most notable passages of the sublime score of *Mosè*. Ourselves inspired by the austere and religious character which M. Rossini has imprinted, without losing any of his brilliant fire, on this work, we have, so to speak, composed our poem on his music, and we have taken the chance to add new beauties to one of the most original works which the art of music can boast.

*Isabella Colbran painted by Waldmüller seated at the pianoforte with the score of 'Moses'
open at the Prayer (Neue Pinakothek, Munich)*

Act One

[1, 2, 3]

Scene One. *The camp of the Midianites beneath the walls of Memphis. In front of the tent of Moses there is a grass altar; to the left, on the edge of a palm grove, there are several bushes, of which one is notable for its shape and density. Israelites and Midianites of both sexes. / No. 1 Introduction.*

ISRAELITES

Mighty God, deliver your children	[4] Dieu puissant, du joug de l'impie
Oh free them today from bondage and woe.	Délivre aujourd'hui tes enfants,
To their land, to the promised country,	Et permets que dans leur patrie
Proud and free, let your people go!	Les Hébreux rentrent triomphants!

OLD MEN

There is no sign, no hope of freedom,	De notre espoir quel est le gage?
With a king who breaks every vow;	Un tyran, un prince sans foi
Who makes his gods in his own image	Qui fit ses Dieux à son image
And tramples on your holy law.	Et foule à ses pieds notre loi.

WOMEN

We all are so close to despairing,	En prioe aux plus vives alarmes,
Life for us here is past enduring.	Est-il temps d'essuyer nos larmes?
Allow us, Lord, to see again	Dieu tout-puissant reverrons-nous
Our children, fathers, and our men.	Nos fils, nos pères, nos époux?

Scene Two. *The same, Moses.*

MOSES

No more of your faithless complaining!	Cessez ces plaintes parjures!
God and Moses both are here.	Dieu, Moïse sont avec vous;
Men of Midian, your complaining	Madianites, vos murmures
Has roused our jealous God to wrath.	Ont offensé le Dieu jaloux.

ISRAELITES

Oh pardon us we pray you	Pardonne à l'infortune
All our tears and entreaties;	Une plainte importune,
For you know how we're oppressed.	Songe aux maux qu'on a soufferts.

MOSES

Filled with love, and with faith undaunted,	Pleins d'amour et de confiance,
Oh lift your hearts in hope to heaven.	Livrez vos cœurs à l'espérance,
God will strike down these stubborn men,	Dieu saura punir les pervers,
The infinite power of Jehovah	De Dieu la puissance infinie
Will guard his children night and day,	Veille toujours sur ses enfants
And to their land, the promised country,	Et les Hébreux dans leur patrie
He will lead them on, proud and free.	Vont bientôt rentrer triomphants.

ISRAELITES

Mighty God, deliver your children	Dieu puissant, du joug de l'impie
From bondage today and from woe.	Délivre aujourd'hui tes enfants
To their land, the promised country,	Et permets que dans leur patrie
Proud and free, let your people go!	Les Hébreux rentrent triomphants!

Recitative.

MOSES

I wait the return of Eleazor;	J'attends le retour de mon frère;
Sent to Pharaoh on our behalf,	Envoyé près de Pharaon,
He is speaking in my name,	Eliézer parle en mon nom.
And he asks that this king, whom all Egypt reveres,	Il demande à ce roi que l'Egypte révère
Shall appease the anger of heaven;	D'apaiser le ciel irrité

That the Hebrews exiled from their land
Shall this day be set free, and restored to
  their country.

Chorus.

ISRAELITES

Father in heaven, Oh let us see again
Our children, our fathers, our homes and
  our men.

Scene Three. *The same, Eleazor, Anna, Miriam.*

ELEAZOR, ANNA, MIRIAM

Glory to God! Honour to Moses!

Recitative.

MOSES

Oh what joy! Is it true?
Anna here! Can it be? And my sister!

MIRIAM

The Lord has ended all our sorrow.

ANNA

We have found once again our support and
  our strength!

MOSES

For all that he has done, give your thanks
  to the Lord.
Eleazor, what have you now to tell us?
Say what we may expect for our people
  from Pharaoh.

ELEAZOR

I saw the great city of Memphis,
Where for fifteen long years
The enslaved tribes of Israel
Have been praying to God for his long
  promised help.
I knelt before the throne,
And I recalled the many honours
Heaped on Jacob, our prophet, and his son
  Joseph too.

'Mighty King', then I said, 'When the great
  judge of all men,
Through the voice of Moses, bids the
  Hebrews be free,
May you and your people be accursed
If you now go back on your word.'
Osiridis, High Priest of Isis,
Preached hatred against us in vain.
For the Lord then came to our aid
And stirred the heart of Queen Sinaîda
Who straightway supported our cause.
She warned the king of the power of Israel's
  God whom they had deceived.
She threatened, importuned, and alarmed
  him,
Striking terror and panic in her husband's
  heart,
So that Pharaoh relented and promised us
  our freedom.

Et de rendre à la liberté
Les Hébreux exilés sur la terre étrangère.

Dieu paternel reverrons-nous
Nos fils, nos frères, nos pères, nos époux?

Gloire au Seigneur! Gloire à Moïse!

Oh bonheur! Oh surprise!
Est-ce vous, Anaï? . . . ma sœur!

Le ciel finit notre misère.

Nous avons retrouvé notre appui, notre
  père!

De ce nouveau bienfait rendons grâce au
  Seigneur.
Eliézer, c'est à toi de m'apprendre
Ce que de Pharaon nous avons droit
  d'attendre.

J'ai vu la superbe Memphis,
Où depuis quinze années
Nos tribus enchaînées
Invoquaient les veneurs qui lui furent
  promis;
Au pied du trône admis,
J'ai rappelé la mémoire
Du prophète Jacob et de Joseph son fils,

Qui tous les deux couverts de gloire
Furent honorés dans Memphis.
Pharaon, ai-je dit, quand le juge suprême

Par la voix de Moïse affranchit les Hébreux,

Sur toi, sur ton peuple, anathème
Si ton cœur repousse nos vœux!
L'indigne grand-prêtre d'Isis,
Fait parler ses dieux ennemis,
L'Eternel en notre faveur
A suscité la Reine Sinaïde
Elle se déclare pour nous;
Du dieu qu'elle a trahi secondant le
  courroux,
Menace, conjure, intimide,

Et jetant l'épouvante au cœur de son époux,

De Pharaon le cœur s'entrouvre à la
  clémence.

126

And as a pledge of the promise he made,	Pour gage du serment qui le lie en ce jour,
He let Miriam come back to us.	Il rend Marie à notre amour.

MOSES

How much she has endured for the God whom she worships.	Marie a su souffrir pour le Dieu qu'elle adore.

MIRIAM

Yet never so much as Anna,	Ma fille a plus fait encore;
For Amenophis,	Du trône de Memphis
The Pharaoh's heir,	La superbe espérance,
Had chosen your niece	Le jeune Aménophis,
For himself.	De ses charmes épris,
Though she returned his love,	N'avait pu sans l'aimer jouir de sa présence.
Yet she never allowed	Anaï, tendre avec candeur,
That love to turn her from Jehovah or her people. *	Ne distingua pas dans son cœur
	L'amour de la reconnaissance.
	Elle aima, mais ce sentiment,
	Que ma tendresse éclaire,
	Ne balança pas un moment,
	Dans cette âme pure et sincère,
	Son ardeur pour son Dieu, son amour pour sa mère.

MOSES

Israel, let us rejoice!	Peuple, réjouis-toi!
Moses' plan is fulfilled by Miriam and Anna.	Anaï de Moïse a rempli l'espérance,
They both have proved their faith in the living God.	Du Dieu vivant Marie a confessé la foi;
Israel, let us rejoice!	Peuple, réjouis-toi!

A rainbow appears.

MOSES

See above in the cloud, Jehovah sends a token,	Voyez-vous dans les airs briller cet arc immense?
A shining rainbow; for today	Avec son peuple l'Eternel
He remembers the	En ce jour solennel
Everlasting covenant between us.	A confirmé son alliance.

A glowing meteor falls upon one of the bushes and shines around it without burning it up.

ISRAELITES

See the sign from the Lord!	Quel prodige nouveau!

MYSTERIOUS VOICE

Moses, approach and hear;	Moïse, s'approche-toi.
The Lord fulfils His promise.	La Seigneur remplit sa promesse,
Hear Him in exaltation,	Dans une sainte ivresse
You shall receive His law.	Viens recevoir sa loi.
My sons! Prepare yourselves for even greater danger,	Hébreux, préparez-vous à des fureurs nouvelles,
Go boldly to the King,	Allez vers Pharaon,
Trust God and He will help you,	Soyez à Dieu fidèles,
For Him it is you fight, you will win in His name!	Vous combattrez pour lui, vous vaincrez en son nom.

---

* The full text literally reads: 'My daughter has done still more. The proud hope of the throne of Memphis, young Amenophis, struck by her beauty, could not see her without loving her. Anna, both susceptible and honest, could not distinguish love from obligation in her heart. She loved him, but this feeling, with I guessed from my own love for her, never for one moment outweighed devotion to her God or love for her mother in her pure and truthful heart.'

Moses takes the Tablets of the Law from the bush, which no longer shines but which is covered with flowers; he carries them and presents them to the Israelites, who prostrate themselves before them. / Quartet and Chorus.

MOSES AND ISRAELITES

Lord God of peace, Lord God of battle,   [5]
Ruler of nations and of kings!
We bow down our faces before You
And we swear to obey Your law.

Recitative.

MOSES

Made strong in the promise from Heaven,
Our hearts are steadfast, come what may!
We must prove to the Lord that we are
truly grateful:
Let our first-born be brought to the altar
of God,
As an offering to Him — the price of our
deliverance!

No. 2 Chorus.

ISRAELITES
(*during the dedication of the first-born*)

This gentle morning
Even now dawning,
Brings us returning
Hope of new day.
God calls the faithful,
His chosen people,
Since their impatience
Melted away!
So let our first-born
Now be the token;
Faith is unbroken,
And we obey.
With such compliance,
This sweet alliance,
Innocent children
With God on high,
Joins our Creator
With us on earth here,
Carrying praises
Back to the sky.

Recitative.

MOSES

Today our slavery is over.
Prepare now to depart from the shores of
the Nile.
Beneath another sky we shall see again
The land where our forefathers sleep.

He leaves, accompanied by Eleazor, Miriam and the Israelites.

Scene Four.

ANNA

O God, forgive my troubled heart,
You who have watched and guided my life!
I'll disown love that betrays my people . . .
He's here — if he finds me, I'm lost!

Dieu de la paix, Dieu de la guerre,
Maître des peuples et des rois,
Le front prosterné vers la terre
Nous jurons d'observer tes lois!

Forts de la divine assistance,
A tout nos cœurs sont préparés;
Témoignons au Seigneur notre
reconnaissance;
Que nos fils premier-nés, aux autels
consacrés,
Soient le gage et la prix de notre délivrance!

La douce aurore
Qui vient d'éclore,
Promet encore
Un plus beau jour.
Peuple fidèle,
Ton Dieu t'appelle,
L'ange rebelle
Fuit sans retour.
Du mariage
Ce premier gage
Est un hommage
De notre amour.
Douce espérance!
Cette alliance
De l'innocence
Avec le ciel,
Rend à la terre
Le roi, son père;
Gloire et prière
A l'Eternel!

Ce jour finit notre esclavage;
Du Nil qu'on se prépare à quitter le rivage.

Bientôt sous d'autres cieux
Nous reverrons les champs où dorment nos
aïeux.

Pardonne au trouble de mon âme,
Dieu clément qui veille sur moi!
J'éteindrai ma coupable flamme . . .
O ciel! Est-ce lui que je vois?

Scene Five. *Amenophis enters with some guards, who take up positions at a distance. Anna begins to leave. Anna, Amenophis.*

AMENOPHIS

Anna? Why run away? | Anaî, toi me fuir?

ANNA

I must leave with my people! | J'obéis à ma mère.

AMENOPHIS

After all I have done, what a way to reward me! | De tous mes bienfaits voilà donc le salaire?
And is this then the love you promised I should have? | Le voilà cet amour que tu m'avais promis.

ANNA

Yes I love you! But oh, Amenophis, | Oui, je vous aime Aménophis,
With you my life would have been far too happy! | Auprès de vous, hélas, j'eusse été trop heureuse;
Yet the stern demand of our duty, | Mais du sort la loi rigoureuse,
Though it may now part us for ever, | En nous séparant à jamais,
Cannot make me forget what you have done for me. | Ne saurait m'imposer l'oubli de vos bienfaits.

AMENOPHIS

Do you believe that I | Crois-tu que je consente
Will allow you to go? | A briser tes liens?
Slave! You belong to me! | Esclave, tu m'appartiens.

ANNA

[I am swayed by the stronger and dearer hand that keeps me captive here.] | Je fléchis sous la main plus puissante Et plus chère qui m'enchaîne en ce lieu.

AMENOPHIS

What do I care for Moses, or for Israel, or your people! | Que m'importe Moïse, et sa race, et ta mère!
Am I not the son of him who rules the world? | Ne suis-je pas le fils du maître de la terre?

ANNA

But he too is ruled by the Lord! | Ce maître a le sien . . . c'est mon Dieu.

AMENOPHIS

I give you one more chance: answer! Will you come with me? | Pour la dernière fois, parle: veux-tu me suivre?

ANNA

I make no attempt to hide | Du combat que l'amour me livre
What is has cost to make such a choice! | Je ne cache pas la rigueur;
Forget now that Anna existed! | Pour vous Anaî ne peut vivre . . .
I cannot stay! Farewell, my love! | Il faut vous fuir. Adieu, seigneur.

No. 3 Duet.

AMENOPHIS

If I lose the girl I've chosen, | [6] Si je perds celle que j'aime,
Lose the girl I've set my heart on, | Mon amour, mon bien suprême!
If you go and leave me broken, | Si tu pars, ó peine extrême,
All shall feel my change of heart! | Tout doit craindre ma fureur.

ANNA

You can see how I am tortured, | Vous voyez quelle est ma peine,
But my love for God now drives me, | Un devoir sacré m'enchaîne,
Far from you where He will guide me | Loin de vous le ciel m'entraîne,
For the Lord condemns our love. | Il condamne notre ardeur.

129

AMENOPHIS

Safe with me, no one can part us,
Dry your tears my lovely Anna,
Come with me, for if we part,
I shall die of despair.

Près de moi, sois sans alarmes,
Anaî, sèche tes larmes;
Suis moi! loin de toi,
Je mourrais de douleur.

ANNA

So shall I if we are parted —
Tears must flow, no one can dry them,
My heart as well, breaks with despair.

O douleur! O jour d'alarmes!
Rien ne peut tarir mes larmes,
Et rien m'égale mon malheur.

AMENOPHIS

Far from me her God will drive her,
Fate condemns us both for our love!

Loin de moi son Dieu l'entraîne,
Sort cruel! Funeste jour!

ANNA

But my love for God now drives me,
For the Lord condemns our love.

Un devoir sacré m'enchaîne,
Dieu s'oppose à notre amour.

The song of the Israelites is heard in the distance.

I can hear our trumpets calling!
And I must go to join my people!

Ah, le signal se fait entendre,
Près de mes sœurs il faut me rendre.

She begins to leave, but Amenophis holds her back.

AMENOPHIS

Where's the man who dares oppose me?
Who would dare take from me what I most
    desire?

Qui pourrait ici prétendre
Me ravir l'objet de ma foi?

ANNA

Ah! Have mercy!

Ah, de grâce!

AMENOPHIS

I'll not release you!

Vaine espérance . . .

ANNA

God decrees it!

Dieu l'ordonne . . .

AMENOPHIS

A cruel decree!
Oh, stay with me and I'll defend you.
I defy your God, He shall not claim you!

Injuste loi!
Ah, viens . . . je veille à ta défense,
De ton Dieu, je brave la puissance.

ANNA

Ah, beware how you offend Him.

Ah, malheur à qui l'offense!

AMENOPHIS

I will brave Jehovah's wrath!
In my arms you'll find protection
From your God however ruthless.
Fear no more the wrath of Heaven,
I take care of your life from today.

Je méprise sa fureur:
Viens, mon bras va te soustraire
Au pouvoir d'un Dieu sévère,
Ne crains plus le ciel contraire,
C'est à moi d'assurer ton bonheur.

ANNA

Ah, do not defy the anger
Of our jealous God Jehovah,
Lord of earth, and Lord of Heaven,
None may brave His mighty power.

Ah, du Dieu que tout révère
Ne bravez pas le colère;
Roi du ciel et de la terre,
Son pouvoir est immortel.

AMENOPHIS

You must brave the anger of your cruel,
    jealous God.
Oh, why these tears now? With me none
    can harm you.

Brave la colère, le pouvoir d'un Dieu cruel.
Pourquoi ces larmes? Bannis tes alarmes!

ANNA

So I must go . . .   Il faut partir . . .

AMENOPHIS

You shall not.   Arrête.

ANNA

Farewell.   Adieu.

AMENOPHIS

I will now defy Jehovah,   Je saurai bien te soustraire
I defy His cruel power.   Au pouvoir d'un Dieu cruel.

ANNA

None may brave His mighty power!   Son pouvoir est immortel.

Recitative.

AMENOPHIS

By Pharaoh's decree   Par les ordres du Roi,
Israel is placed under my sole command.   Tous les Hébreux sont soumis à ma loi.
                    (letting go of her)
I would have set them free, but you've   J'allais les délivrer, tu me rends à la haine;
    made me hate you!
Now there is no containing the tide of my   Non, je ne contrains plus la fureur qui
    anger!   m'entraîne.
I will go straight to Moses and pronounce   Et je vais à Moïse annoncer mes décrets.
    my decree
That they shall live in chains evermore as   Il doivent dans les fers gémir tous pour
    my slaves!   jamais.

ANNA

Ah, what a dreadful thing you're saying,   Ah, quelle horrible destinée!
Condemning us to part, and my people to   Aux coups les plus cruels je suis donc
    suffer!   condamnée!

Amenophis enters Moses's tent.

Scene Six. *Anna, Miriam, Eleazor and the Israelites / No. 4 March and Chorus.*

ISRAELITES

Day of return, O blessed day!   O jour heureux, jour solennel,
We offer praise to God on high!   Offrons nos vœux à l'Eternel!

ELEAZOR

The Lord in His goodness   [7]   Sa bonté paternelle
Sheds bounty on us all.   Nous comble de bienfaits;
Over Your faithful people   Sur ton peuple fidèle, ˙
Oh, keep watch ever more.   Grand Dieu, veille à jamais.

WOMEN

Praise we the Lord, Israel's God,   Dieu d'Israël, gloire à jamais,
And all His works for they are good.   A ta puissance, à tes bienfaits.

MIRIAM

Let us all praise His mercy; as King of   Célébrons la clémence du Roi de l'univers.
    Kings He 1
˙ For He has heard our prayer, and freed us Il a comblé nos vœux, il fait tomber nos
    from our chains!   fers.

ELEAZOR

Great is His power!   A sa puissance
Praise we the Lord!   Gloire à jamais!

131

MIRIAM	
And all His works,	A sa justice,
For they are good!	A ses bienfaits.
ELEAZOR	
All nature shows us the Lord's power and glory!	Tout nous révèle sa gloire immortelle.
MIRIAM	
Come sing his praises, the everlasting God.	Que tout benisse et chante l'Eternel.
ISRAELITES	
Praise to the Lord! Glory to God!	Gloire au Seigneur, Dieu d'Israël!
Oh, let us praise and thank the Lord!	Offrons nos vœux au Roi du ciel.
Honour and glory,	Hommage et gloire,
Praise to the Lord!	Au tout-puissant,
He our protector'	Qui nous protège,
And our guard!	Et nous défend.
Oh, let us praise and thank the Lord,	Offrons nos vœux à l'Eternel,
The King of Kings, our people's God!	Au Roi des Rois, Dieu d'Israël!

The Israelites withdraw to the back of the stage. / No. 5 Duet.

ANNA		
God, on this joyful morning,	[8]	Dieu, dans ce jour prospère,
Has ended all our fears.		Termine nos malheurs!
Only I, oh how cruel the contrast, —		Moi seule, ó peine amère, —
	(sobbing)	
— Cannot hold back my tears.		— Je dois verser des pleurs.
Gracious Lord, oh if my passion		Dieu clément, si ma flamme
In Your eyes is out of place,		Est digne de ta rigueur,
Lord... I beg you take it from me,		Daigne éteindre dans mon âme
This love that brings disgrace.		Un coupable amour.

MIRIAM	
(approaching her daughter)	
My daughter! What's the matter?	Ma fille! O ciel, que vois-je?
ANNA	
All is over, I want to die!	Je succombe à ma douleur.
MIRIAM	
Die! Today, on this happy day?	Quoi! Ce jour de bonheur...
ANNA	
I feel my courage going...	Epuise mon courage.
MIRIAM	
My daughter...	Ma fille...
ANNA	
Desert him? No, I cannot!	O trouble, ó douleur!
Ensemble.	
MIRIAM	
You must forget your love;	Etiens l'ardeur profane
You know that God condemns it!	Que notre Dieu condamne.
ANNA	
God, if you condemn me,	Du ciel qui me condamne,
Help me forget my love!	J'implore la faveur.

132

MIRIAM

| Oh help her, oh help her | Du ciel qui te condamne, |
| To forget her love! | Implore la faveur. |

Scene Seven. *The same, Moses, Amenophis (coming out of the tent) / No. 6 Finale.*

MOSES
(to Amenophis)

| We *can't* go? | Qu'entends-je? |

AMENOPHIS

| That's what I say! | Tel est ton sort. |

MOSES

| Can the word of Pharaoh be broken? | Pharaon trahit sa promesse! |

ELEAZOR
(to Amenophis)

| Fear the might of God the avenger. | Crains de Dieu la main vengeresse. |

AMENOPHIS
(to Eleazor)

You intriguer, fear your death!	Toi, perfide, crains la mort!
Do you dare brave the Egyptians?	Vous braviez notre puissance;
For this arrogance you shall be punished.	On punit votre arrogance,
Do not hope for your deliverance,	Plus d'espoir de délivrance,
You will stay where you are!	Subissez votre sort.

ELEAZOR

| How dare he say that! | Ah, quelle audace! |

ISRAELITES

| O God! | O ciel! |

Ophidis and Amenophis's guards emerge from the trees.

MOSES
(appealing to Heaven)

| I trust to God in His mercy, | J'espère en sa clémence, |
| To shield His people now. | Il nous protégera. |

AMENOPHIS

| Beware of my anger! | Craignez ma vengeance. |

MIRIAM, ELEAZOR

| Fear God! | Tremble! |

ISRAELITES

| He will be avenged! | Dieu vous punira! |

ANNA
(to Amenophis)

Highness, —	Prince, —
(aside)	
Help me Lord!	Ah, le ciel!

AMENOPHIS

| But I defy His vengeance! | Je brave sa colère. |

ANNA

| Oh, have mercy upon us! | Ecoutez ma prière. |

MOSES

| Take care! Take care! | Tremblez, tremblez! |

Or soon the armoured might of Heaven	Bientôt la foudre meurtrière
Shall on Egypt thunder down.	Sur l'Egypte éclatera.

ELEAZOR
(*to the Egyptians*)

Take care!	Tremblez!

AMENOPHIS

How dare he!	Quelle audace!

(*to his guards*)

Then beat him! He has defied us!	Frappez qui nous menace.

ANNA
(*to Amenophis*)

Oh spare him! Have mercy!	Qu'entends-je? De grâce!
O God!	O Dieu!

ISRAELITES

We shall defend him to the death!	Pour sa défense affrontons tous le trépas.

AMENOPHIS
(*to his guards*)

Go on and beat him!	Frappez ce perfide.

MIRIAM
(*to the Israelites*)

Oh, form a shield and save him!	Ah, servez-lui d'égide.

ELEAZOR

We'll form a shield and save him!	Ah, servons-lui d'égide.

ISRAELITES
(*surrounding Moses*)

You shall not pass!	N'espérez pas!

ANNA

They'll kill him!	On ose!

Scene Eight. *The same, Pharaoh, Sinaïda, Ophidis and Pharaoh's retinue.*

PHARAOH

My son! With soldiers! You Gods!	O ciel, que vois-je, soldats?

Ensemble.

ANNA, SINAÏDA, MIRIAM

Lord, how dare they!	Dieu, l'on ose!
Oh let your power, father,	Que ta puissance veille,
Protect the helpless!	Sur l'innocence!
Oh, what madness! What an outrage!	Quel délire, quelle offense!
Do they dare dispute his power?	On insulte à sa puissance!
O protector of the helpless	Défenseur de l'innocence!
Put an end to their revenge!	Mets un terme à leur fureur.
Day of woe! All hope is gone!	Quelle horreur! Jour de douleur!

AMENOPHIS

I'm in trouble!		Ciel, quel trouble!
Oh, what an outrage!		Ah, quelle offense,
They dare to dispute my power!		On doute de ma puissance.
First my love and then my hatred,	[9]	De l'amour et de la haine
Turn by turn they both inflame me		Tour à tour la voix m'entraîne,
And increase my desolation		Tout redouble, hélas, ma peine,
While my anger grows and grows.		Tout augmente ma fureur.
Oh, what madness! What an outrage!		Quel délire! Quelle offense!
All hope is gone, save my revenge.		Qu'ils éprouvent ma fureur,
May they soon endure my anger!		O jour de deuil et de terreur.

134

May they meet with my revenge!	Ah, bientôt de ma vengeance,
All hope is gone, save my revenge!	Qu'ils éprouvent la rigueur.

OPHIDIS, PHARAOH

Dare they do it!	Ciel, on ose!
Oh, what an outrage,	Ah, quelle offense,
They dare to dispute my power!	On doute de ma puissance.
Oh, what madness! What an outrage!	Quel délire! Quelle offense!
Do they dare dispute my power	On insulte à ma puissance.
May they soon endure my anger,	Ah, bientôt de ta vengeance,
May they meet with my revenge!	Qu'ils éprouvent la rigueur.

PHARAOH

May they soon endure my anger,	Le désire de la vengeance
How I burn to take revenge!	Trouble, enflamme tout mon cœur.

MOSES, ELEAZOR

Lord, how dare they!	Dieu, l'on ose!
Oh, what an outrage!	Ah, quelle offense,
Do they dare dispute His power!	Insulter à sa puissance.
Oh, what madness! What an outrage!	Quel délire! Quelle offense!
Do they dare dispute His power!	Dieu, l'on brave ta puissance,
May the Lord take revenge.	Dieu, punis leur fureur.

MOSES, ELEAZOR, ISRAELITES

May they soon endure His anger,	Ah, bientôt de ta vengeance,
May they meet with His revenge!	Qu'ils éprouvent la rigueur.

AMENOPHIS
(*to Pharaoh*)

My father!	Mon père!

MOSES
(*to Pharaoh*)

Great King!	Seigneur.

AMENOPHIS
(*to Pharaoh*)

Avenge us!	Vengeance!
Let them feel our royal power!	Qu'ils éprouvent ta rigueur!

MOSES

Dare you suggest then,	Qu'oses-tu dire? Quoi,
Pharaoh is false, and might betray his word?	Pharaon pourrait trahir sa foi?

PHARAOH
(*to Moses*)

Silence!	Tremble!
For now my heart is hardened!	Tout cède à mon empire.

MOSES

What? Is it true?	Ah, que dis-tu?

PHARAOH

You'll obey me in silence,	Obéis en silence,
Or know my vengeance . . .	Ou ma vengeance . . .

SINAIDA
(*to Pharaoh*)

My lord, try to be calm.	Calmez votre fureur!

AMENOPHIS
(*to his guards*)

Go and deal with him at once!	Qu'on entraîne l'imposteur!

135

ANNA
(to Amenophis)

Oh mercy!	Qu'entends-je?

PHARAOH
(to Moses)

Then kneel and beg for mercy	Implore ma clémence,
Or you will learn my power!	Redoute ma fureur.

MOSES
(to Pharaoh)

Disarm the righteous anger	Du Dieu que tout révère,
Of Israel's Jehovah;	Désarme la colère;
While yet the time allows,	Il en est temps encore,
Renounce the wrong you do!	Abjure ton erreur.

PHARAOH
(to Moses)

Bite the dust that has bred you,	Rentre dans la poussière,
You slave that dares defy me.	Esclave téméraire;
You've yet to learn my power,	Adore ma puissance,
So kneel before me here.	Et tombe à mes genoux.

MOSES

Lord, let them behold Your power!	Dieu, signale de ta puissance,
Let the heathen know Your anger!	Sur celui qui t'offense.
Let them feel the might of Your eternal wrath!	Grand Dieu, fais éclater ton immortel courroux.

Moses stretches out his hand towards the pyramid against which his tent is constructed.

PHARAOH

There! Look! What is it?	O ciel! Que vois-je?

SINAIDA

The sky ... Ah, we are lost!	O jour trop malheureux!

AMENOPHIS

See, the earth is gaping!	Le terre s'ouvre!

ANNA, SINAIDA, MIRIAM, AMENOPHIS, OPHIDIS, PHARAOH

How thick the darkness	Le ciel se couvre
That veils the sky!	D'un voile affreux!

The sky darkens, the earth quakes, the trees break and the pyramid collapses and becomes a volcano, from which a stream of flaming lava pours out, seeming to inundate the plain.

MOSES, ELEAZOR, ISRAELITES

Vile race of Egypt	Race exécrable!
Our God overwhelms you	C'est Dieu qui t'accable;
With fury unyielding.	Terrible, indomptable,
His hand unrelenting	Sa main redoutable
Will strike down the guilty	Punit du coupable
For their black crime!	Les noirs forfaits.

Ensemble.

ANNA, SINAIDA, MIRIAM, AMENOPHIS, OPHIDIS, PHARAOH

Ah, what disaster sent by Jehovah!	Ah, quel désastre épouvantable!
Terror and fear beyond endurance!	O trouble, ô peine insupportable!
Heaven is against you; us } regrets are vain.	Sort déplorable, mortels regrets.

Moses, Eleazor and The Israelites repeat their previous verses.

Act Two

A hall in Pharaoh's palace.

Scene One. *Pharaoh, Sinaïda, Amenophis, Ophidis, Dignitaries of the Court, Priests, Soldiers — standing in groups. The stage is plunged in extreme darkness. / No. 7 Introduction.*

[10]

EGYPTIANS

Ah, the darkness!	Ah, quel désastre!
O Gods, who will deliver us	O ciel qui nous délivrera
From this eternal night?	De cette sombre horreur.

AMENOPHIS

My senses all are numb.	Mes sens sont tous glacés.
I cannot move for fear	Dieux, quel effroi mortel!
It overwhelms me, and bows me down.	Ah, je succombe à ma douleur.

PHARAOH

This everlasting night	Cette effroyable nuit
Is like a shroud to me,	Fait palpiter mon cœur.
It overwhelms and bows me down.	Ah, je succombe à ma douleur.

SINAIDA

Oh, let us pray their God that He will	Du ciel par la prière apaisons la rigueur.
forgive our sin.	

EGYPTIANS

O God of Israel, spare us we pray,	Puissant Dieu d'Israël, épargne nous
Strike down the wicked man	Et frappe l'imposteur
Who tempted him and made	Qui, séduisant le Roi,
The King betray his word.	Lui fit trahir sa foi.

PHARAOH

I weep, I curse the day	Je pleure et je maudis,
When I deceived their God.	Ma trop funeste erreur.
To all our present sorrow	Du trouble qui m'accable
Add not another load.	N'augmentez pas l'horreur.

AMENOPHIS
(aside)

Oh, punishment past bearing,	O peine insupportable,
I know my sin was great.	Le remords me poursuit.

SINAIDA

How can we face a future	O sort épouvantable,
Of everlasting night?	Ah, quelle affreuse nuit!

EGYPTIANS
(kneeling before Pharaoh)

Your people look to you, O King, for hope	De tes enfants, seigneur, ranime l'espérance,
and guidance.	
Obey their God, Jehovah,	Respecte la puissance
Whose vengeance is so great.	Du Dieu qui nous poursuit.

PHARAOH
(to his retinue)

Go in haste, summon Moses!	Qu'on appelle Moïse.

AMENOPHIS
(aside)

He weakens!	Qu'entends-je?

137

SINAIDA

Thank Heaven!	O ciel!

EGYPTIANS

Hope is returning!	Douce surprise!
Bring Moses! Bring Moses!	Moîse, Moîse!

SINAIDA

Ah, you fulfil our prayers!	Ah, vous comblez nos vœux.

PHARAOH

Let Moses come before us!	Allez, qu'on l'introduise.

AMENOPHIS

Those fatal words!	Ordre fatal!

SINAIDA

There's hope now!	J'espère ...

EGYPTIANS

Once more there shines before our eyes a ray of hope!	Un doux rayon d'espoir luit encore à nos yeux.

AMENOPHIS
(aside)

The danger grows, despair returns,	Fatal danger, ô peine amère!
Fate again betrays our hope.	Ah, le sort trahit nox vœux.

ALL

O God of Israel,	Puissant Dieu d'Israël,
Oh, take from us at last	De cette affreuse nuit,
This awful shroud of night.	Dissipe enfin l'horreur.
Once more forget Your wrath,	Fais tréve à ta rigueur,
Now pardon our offence,	Pardonne notre erreur.
Almighty God	O Dieu puissant
Once more we beg You forgive our sin,	Grand Dieu pardonne á notre erreur,
Forget Your wrath.	Suspends ta rigueur.

Scene Two. *The same, Moses, Eleazor, Ophidis.*

MOSES

[Your voice summons me; well, what do you want of me?]	Ta voix m'appelle, eh bien, que me veux tu?

SINAIDA
(aside)

[What harsh language.]	Quel langage sevère.

PHARAOH

Overwhelmed by affliction all my people implore	Sous le poids du malheur tout ce peuple abattu
Your help in their distress.	Implore ton secours.

AMENOPHIS
(aside)

I am burning with anger.	Je frémis de colère.

MOSES
(to Pharaoh)

By all the vows you made and the same day you broke,	Par des serments trompeurs qu'un jour dicte et détruit,
You slave of the high priest Osiridis,	Esclave du prêtre Osiride,
You thought in your presumption,	Prétendrais-tu, perfide,
To brave again the Lord's avenging arm?	Braver encore le Dieu qui te poursuit?

138

AMENOPHIS
(aside)

What an outrage! | Quel outrage!

PHARAOH

By sorcerers and by the wise men, | Séduit par la fatale adresse
I confess I was led, | D'un perfide imposteur,
And then, my heart being hardened, | Souvent je le confesse
Once more I broke my word; | Je t'ai manqué de foi.
In despair and remorse | Mais confus ... agité,
I now admit my fault, | Je reconnais mes torts.
But if you stretch forth your hand | Si ta main nous délivre
And deliver this land from everlasting | Et dissipe l'horreur de cette obscurité
   night |
Then your people may go, | Je te laisse partir,
Their children and their cattle! | Les tiens pourront te suivre.

SINAIDA

[Hope revives!] | Doux espoir!

AMENOPHIS
(aside)

[How I tremble.] | Je frémis.

MOSES
(to Pharaoh)

[I will again implore the Divine Creator | Du divin créateur,
for mercy upon you.] | Pour toi je veux encore implorer la
   | clémence.

ELEAZOR
(to Pharaoh)

[But remember that God reads your heart.] | Mais songe bien que Dieu lit dans ton cœur.

MOSES

[Fear his vengeance.] | Redoute sa vengeance.

ELEAZOR

[Fear his righteous anger.] | Crains sa juste fureur.

AMENOPHIS

[What pride!] | Quel orgueil!

MOSES
(to Pharaoh)

Will you swear to keep faith? | Pharaon, promets-tu?

PHARAOH

Yes, I swear it. | Je le jure.

MOSES
(to Pharaoh)

But God will send a plague | Malheur, malheur à toi
If you dare break your promise ever again! | Si ta bouche parjure osait encore!

PHARAOH

No, do not doubt my word! | Non, compte sur ma foi.

No. 8 Invocation and Quintet.

MOSES

Supreme judge and ruler, the Lord of all | Arbitre suprême du Ciel et da la terre,
   creation! |
O You Almighty God | O toi, Dieu tout-puissant,
Whom we honour and worship, | Qu'on révère et qu'on aime,

Who chastises the guilty, yet saves the pure in heart,
You who reigned King of Kings, before the birth of time,
Fount of eternal truth,
The just God, the divine God,
The one God who has punished the sins of this obdurate race,
Oh, hear my supplication,
And pardon their transgression,
Once again pierce the gloom
Of the cavernous dark,
Once again let them see
In a torrent of light!

Qui punis le coupable et sauves l'innocent;
Roi des rois, qui des ans précédas la naissance;
Source de vérité,
Dieu juste, adorable, immense,
Qui d'un peuple endurci punis l'impiété,
Pardonne leur offense,
Ecoute ma prière,
Et du sein de la nuit
Dont l'horreur les poursuit
A l'instant fais jaillir,
Des torrents de lumière!

The light returns.

ALL

Ah! See, the sky! Wonder of wonders!
For the day is returning!

Ah, quel prodige incomparable!
Il nous rend la lumière!

MOSES, ELEAZOR, SINAIDA

O You, who by Your mercy
Gave light to end their darkness,
Though great Your power and glory,
Yet greater far Your grace.

O toi, dont la clémence
Apaise leur souffrance,
Ta gloire et ta puissance
Egalent ta bonté.

AMENOPHIS

Yet woe to those who wrong Him,
For all must yield before Him,
But silently I curse Him,
His glory and His grace.

Malheur à qui l'offense:
Tout cède à sa puissance.
Mon cœur maudit en silence
Sa gloire et sa bonté.

PHARAOH

O You, who by Your mercy
Gave light to end my darkness,
Though great Your power and glory,
Yet greater far Your grace.
We all bow before Your face.

O toi, dont la clémence
Termine ma souffrance,
Ta gloire et ta puissance
Egalent ta bonté,
Tout cède à ta volonté.

ELEAZOR

King of Egypt!

Roi d'Egypte!

MOSES

You, his people.

Et vous, peuple.

ELEAZOR

Now to the light around you,
Open your eyes at last!

Au jour qui vous éclaire,
Ouvrez enfin les yeux.

MOSES

Offer praise to the Lord, let your gods be foresworn!

Adorez l'Eternel, abjurez les faux dieux.

PHARAOH

Then go! Go this night, Israel,
To your great God Jehovah.
And in the burning desert
There offer Him your praise.

Hébreux, cette nuit même,
Au maître qui vous guide,
Dans le désert aride,
Allez porter vos vœux.

AMENOPHIS
(*to Pharaoh*)

Do not release them!

Songez, mon père.

SINAIDA
(*to Amenophis*)

My son, fear the wrath of Heaven! | Ah, crains le courroux celeste.

MOSES

Blasphemer! | Impie!

ELEAZOR
(*to Amenophis*)

God will chasten the proud! | Dieu punit les pervers.

SINAIDA
(*to Pharaoh*)

Fear the anger of Heaven! | Ah, craignez sa colère!

PHARAOH
(*to Sinaïda*)

Yes, today they shall go! | Oui, je brise leurs fers.

AMENOPHIS

What! You're afraid! | Quoi! vous craignez!

SINAIDA

Our Gods no longer look down in anger, | Les dieux font tréve à leur colère,
See all around us the day shines again. | Un jour prospère paraît à nos yeux.

ELEAZOR, PHARAOH, MOSES

The day shines again! | Paraît à nos yeux.

AMENOPHIS

Mighty Jehovah, | Dieu redoutable,
Your law will break me, | Ta loi m'accable,
All are against me, | Sort deplorable,
Oh, curse the day! | O jour affreux!
I stand alone | Mon cœur succombe
In my desolation, | A sa misère,
How can I bear it? | O peine amère,
Oh, curse the day! | O jour affreux!

SINAIDA, PHARAOH, MOSES, ELEAZOR

The Gods } no longer
Our God } | [11] Les Dieux font } tréve
Dieu, tu fais }

Look(s) down in anger. | A leur } colère,
  ta }

See all around us, | Un jour prospère
Day shines again, | Luit à nos yeux.
A sign to tell us | Tout nous annonce
That all is well! | Un calme heureux,
The heavens are shining | Le ciel promet
Now all is well! | Des jours heureux.

All leave, except Pharaoh and Amenophis.

Scene Three. *Pharaoh, Amenophis. / Recitative.*

PHARAOH

Now my son, you have heard what I have decreed, | Vous avez entendu quelle est ma volonté,
And today you shall learn our fond hopes for your future. | Apprenez maintenant quelle est mon espérance.
It is time you were married, and a fair young princess, | Une jeune princesse à qui le sang nous lie,
The child of the King of Assyria, | La fille du Roi d'Assyrie,

Has been chosen to be your bride.
You have her father's consent, and I

Must let my people know of this today.

What have you to say? You don't seem happy,
I wonder why?

Etait digne de votre choix.
Vous obtenez sa main et de cette alliance
D'Elégyne et d'Aménophis,
Je dois au peuple de Memphis donner
aujourd'hui connaissance.
Vous vous taisez. D'où naît le trouble

Où je vous vois?

No. 9 Duet.

AMENOPHIS

The blow at last has fallen;
Yet still I dare not tell him.
I cannot stand it, the thought appalls me,
I'd rather die than marry her.
It's nothing but a nightmare!

[12] Moment fatal ... Que faire?
Hélas, il faut me taire.
Le sort m'accable, ô peine amère,
Mon cœur succombe à sa douleur.
Ah, plaignez ma misère.

PHARAOH

The Gods who seem unyielding,
Will soon forget their anger,
And soon I hope that they will grant you
A peaceful, calm and happy life again.
And then we hope your spirits may revive.

Le ciel toujours contraire
Met fin à sa colère,
Il te rendra bientôt j'espère,
Il te rendra le calme et le bonheur,
Et ce bienfait doit ranimer ton cœur.

AMENOPHIS

Ah, forgive my silence!

Ah, plaignez ma misère.

PHARAOH

Won't you try to explain it?

Quel est donc ce mystère?

AMENOPHIS

I can't! I can't explain it!

O ciel, je dois me taire.

PHARAOH

Tell me!

Parle.

AMENOPHIS

Oh God, no! This secret
I must keep till I die.

O ciel, non, ce mystère
Doit mourir avec moi.

PHARAOH

What on earth are you hiding?
You might at least explain.
Tell me, my son, tell me.

Quel est donc ce mystère?
De grace, explique-toi.
Parle, mon fils, parle.

AMENOPHIS

If only all I suffer
Could make you understand.
You Gods ... how can you let me die
From love they all condemn?

O ciel, que mon martyre
Apaise ta rigueur.
Grands dieux, vous voulez que j'expire
D'amour et de douleur?

PHARAOH

Whatever strange resentment and confusion
Can so affect his mind?
Confide in me, your father —
You should not fear to tell me all.

Quel trouble, quel délire,
S'empare de tout son cœur?
Viens dans les bras d'un père,
Tu dois, mon fils, m'ouvrir ton cœur.

AMENOPHIS

But I defy the Gods who are against me!
I must defy them all.
O father, I beg you, do not ask.
That unhappy secret must be kept till I die.

Mais du destin contraire
Il faut braver la fureur!
Que dire mon père pourriez-vous
Ce fatal mystère doit mourir avec moi.

PHARAOH

Who caused this trouble?

D'où vient la peine?

What on earth are you hiding?	Parle, quel est donc ce mystère?
You might at least explain.	Mons fils, explique toi.
Tell me, that's an order!	Parle, je l'ordonne.

AMENOPHIS

| But I defy the Gods who are against me, | Mais du destin contraire |
| I'll fight against my fate. | Il faut braver la fureur. |

PHARAOH

| This secret you are hiding, | De cet affreux mystère |
| The cause of all your hate. | Il faut sonder l'horreur. |

Exit Pharaoh.

Scene Four. *Amenophis.*

AMENOPHIS

What a sea of despair!	Quel abîme de maux,
How can I ride the storm?	Quel déplorable sort!
No matter where I turn	Tout me poursuit, hélas,
There is no-one to help me.	Tout accroît ma misère.
Which way can we escape?	Que vais-je devenir?
What can I do to save her?	Que résoudre, que faire?
I betray my beloved!	Moi trahir Anaï?
No, no! I'd rather die!	Non, non, plutôt la mort!

Scene Five. *Amenophis, Sinaïda, Ladies and Nobles of the Court.*

SINAIDA

My son, why is it when all are gathered	Hé quoi! Mon fils, quand tout s'apprête
In the temple of Isis to celebrate our deliverance,	De la Reine des Dieux à célébrer la fête,
Only you stand aside?	Vous restez étranger aux sons d'un si grand jour!

AMENOPHIS

| [You know my heart . . .] | Vous connaissez mon cœur . . . |

SINAIDA

| [I know of your love. | Je connais votre amour. |
| I know what hope you cherish in your soul.] | Je sais quel est l'espoir où votre âme se livre. |

AMENOPHIS

| I cannot live without my Anna! | Sans Anaï je ne puis vivre. |

SINAIDA

[Your duty presents you with a nobler union;	Le devoir vous présente un plus noble lien;
I respect Moses, and his God was once mine.	Je respecte Moïse, et son Dieu fut le mien.
I feel for you as a mother;	Pour vous j'ai le cœur d'une mère;
But think of the state, think of your father;	Mais songez à l'état, songez à votre père;
Your love betrays them both.]	Vote amour les trahit tous deux.
You are heir to the throne of Egypt.	Héritier du pouvoir suprême,
When you forget your duty	En vous perdant vous même,
You destroy Anna too! and Moses, and her people.	Vous perdez Anaï, Moïse et les Hébreux.

No. 10 Aria and Chorus.

Hear what your mother asks you,	[13] Ah, d'une tendre mère
My dearest son, I beg you	Ecoute la prière;
Be master of yourself, Prince,	Triomphe de toi-même et comble enfin,
And then you will fulfil my fondest prayer.	Et comble enfin mon espoir.
How can you make me suffer?	Calme ma peine amère,
Don't forget you are the Pharaoh's heir.	Sois fidèle à l'honneur, au devoir!

Prince, hear the royal mother!   Ah, d'une auguste mère,
Try to fulfil her prayer.   Comblez enfin l'espoir.

SINAIDA

Come now, be true to our country,   Ah, sois fidèle à la gloire,
To the glory of state and of throne.   A la gloire, à l'état, à l'honneur.
Ah! Hear what your mother asks you,   Ah, d'une tendre mère
My dearest son, I beg you.   Ecoute la prière!
Be master of yourself, Prince,   Triomphe de toi-même
And bring me peace at last.   Et calme enfin ma douleur.

Pause.

But my son, you do not answer,   Mais tu gardes le silence
And my tears are still undried.   Et laisses couler mes pleures.

AMENOPHIS

My only thought is vengeance,   J'aspire à la vengeance:
For Moses dared to thwart me.   Moïse qui m'offense
So Moses now must pay for his pride.   Doit payer nos malheurs.

SINAIDA

Be careful! What are you saying?   Qu'entends-je? Ah, quel délire!
My son . . .   Mon fils . . .

AMENOPHIS

We must defy the power   Bravons l'empire
Of this hard hearted fiend.   De ce fourbe inhumain.

SINAIDA

Oh, put out of your mind   Ah, bannis de ton âme
Such a dangerous plan!   Ce funeste dessein.

AMENOPHIS
(*aside*)

That unrepentant liar!   Cet imposteur infâme
I shall kill him myself!   Doit périr de ma main.

SINAIDA

No!   Ciel!

EGYPTIANS
(*off stage*)

Oh, come to Isis' temple!   Allons, allons au temple,
To Isis, mother of Gods!   Fêter la mère des Dieux!
From Heaven, her eye   Du haut des cieux,
Is always upon us,   Isis nous contemple,
Oh, come and bring her thanks!   Allons offrir nos vœux.

SINAIDA
(*to Amenophis*)

Do you hear them? The priests are calling   Ecoute . . . on nous appelle
To a solemn celebration.   A la fête solennelle.

To please me, do what I ask you: Propice à ma prière,
Control that selfish grief,   Ah, calme ta fureur,
Be master of your passions!   Triomphe de ta flamme,
You must forget your love!   Apaise ma douleur,
Forget her, and calm my distress!   Apaise ma douleur!

AMENOPHIS

I will forget her;   Calmez vos alarmes,
I bow to your decree!   Je vais suivre vos pas.

SINAIDA

Oh, hear and rejoice! He obeys me!   [14] Qu'entends-je? Douce ivresse!
To honour he will be true.   Il est fidèle à l'honneur.

His love and his devotion
Have made me happy too.
Gods evermore reward him
With honour that is his due.

Je dois à ta tendresse
Le calme de mon cœur.
Dieux, protégez sans cesse
Sa gloire et son bonheur!

EGYPTIANS
(*off stage*)

Day of glory, of great rejoicing,
As hope drives out our despair.

Jour de gloire et d'allégresse,
L'espoir renaît dans mon cœur.

AMENOPHIS

Day of woe, of black depression;
My life is dark despair!

Jour de deuil et de tristesse,
Oh, sort trop malheureux!

SINAIDA, EGYPTIANS

Oh, come to Isis' temple!
Oh, come to praise the Gods
Who grant our prayer.

Allons au temple,
Allons offrir nos vœux,
Allons fêter nos Dieux.

SINAIDA

He has obeyed my prayer.

Il a comblé mes vœux.

Boris Christoff as Moses (Royal Opera House Archives)

145

Act Three

The portal of the temple of Isis.

Scene One. *Pharaoh, Osiridis, Priests, Dignitaries of the Egyptian Court, Attendants, in procession.* / *No. 11 March and Chorus.*

GENERAL HYMN
(*during the procession*)

Queen of the earth!	Reine des cieux
Queen of the Heavens!	Et de la terre,
You who gave life	De tous les Dieux
To Gods and humans!	Auguste mère,
Answer our prayer.	Comble les vœux
Your people here,	D'un peuple hereux.
Whose lives depend	Soumis au monde,
On your holy Nile,	Du Nil alors,
Pray that her waters	L'urne féconde
Cover the sand	Va sur nos bords
And shed their riches	Verser son onde
Throughout our land.	Et ses trésors.

OSIRIDIS

All men of Egypt,	Que tout respire
Hear me devoutly!	Un saint délire!
People and kings!	Peuples et rois!
Inspired by Isis,	Isis m'inspire,
My words will ring	Et par ma voix
Throughout this empire	A cet empire,
Her law to bring.	Dicte ses lois.

The hymn is sung again. / *Recitative:*

PHARAOH
(*on his throne*)

You who sustain the throne of Egypt,	Divins appuis de ma couronne,
You priests who serve the altars here,	Vous, tous ministres des autels,
Now direct that the Gods shall behold us with favour,	Ordonnez, et des Dieux appelez sur mon trône
In a lasting regard!	Les regards immortels.

OSIRIDIS

May this day be in Memphis a day of rejoicing!	Que ce jour pour Memphis soit un jour d'allégresse!
Now with music and dance and with voices upraised,	Dans les mêmes tribus, dans les mêmes honneurs
Let us join in praise to the Gods!	Unissons nos Dieux protecteurs,
Come, adorn every altar,	[15] Apportez vos offrandes,
And array them with garlands,	Suspendez vos guirlandes,
And with rarest of flowers	Et le front couronné de fleurs
Wreathe in holy exaltation	Dans une sainte ivresse,
The divine Queen of Heaven,	De la grande déesse,
And offer her your thanks for the grace she bestows!	Que tout signale ici les célestes faveurs.

The rites of Isis. Three dances.

Scene Two. *Moses, Eleazor, Miriam, Anna, the Israelites.* / *No. 12 Finale.*

MOSES
(*to Pharaoh*)

I am come here to claim the bargain	Je réclame la foi promise;
Which the Pharaoh does not forget,	Pharaon n'a pas oublié

The promise that he gave
When the land was delivered from
   darkness by Moses!

Par quel serment lié
Il jura d'acquitter le bienfait de Moïse.

PHARAOH

I shall hold to my word.
[Go into the desert;
And, with that delightful prospect,
Offer up your sacrifices
To this God who left you here for twenty
   years in chains!]

Je tiendrai ma parole.
Allez dans le désert,
Sous de tristes auspices,
Offrir vos sacrifices
A ce Dieu qui vingt ans vous laissa dans
   mes fers.

OSIRIDIS
(*to Moses*)

Before your departure from Egypt,
You Hebrews delivered from slavery
Now must appease
The wrath of our Gods.

Avant de quitter ce rivage,
Ton peuple, en sortant d'esclavage,
Doit de nos Dieux
Apaiser le courroux.

(*to the Israelites*)

You will show them respect at last!
You slaves; before great Isis go down on
   your knees!

Rendez-leur un tardif hommage,
Hébreux; devant Isis fléchissez les genoux!

MOSES
(*to Osiridis, stopping the Israelites, who are about to prostrate themselves*)

Who? We? Shall we squander our homage
On the false Gods of Egypt?
Little you know of Moses, or his people, or
   their faith!
For us there is but one God, one master,
   and one law!

Qui? Nous? Prodiguer nos hommages
A de vaines images!
Tu connais mal Moïse, et son peuple, et sa
   foi;
Pour nous il n'est qu'un Dieu, qu'un
   maitre, qu'une loi.

OSIRIDIS

O my lord, will you let this affront go
   unpunished?

Pharaon, c'est l'instant de punir tant
   d'outrages.

MOSES
(*to Osiridis*)

I deride all your threats, and I speak to your
   king!

Je crains peu ta menace, et je parle à ton roi.

OSIRIDIS
(*to Pharaoh*)

Do you hear?

Tu l'entends...

AMENOPHIS
(*to Anna*)

Anna, stay!

Anaï...

SINAIDA
(*aside, to Moses*)

Be careful of Osiridis!

Redoutez Osiride.

Scene Three. *The same, Ophidis.*

OPHIDIS
(*entering*)

Great King, oh, save us from yet another [16]
   plague!
The Nile is turning into blood,
All the water is crimson,
Disgorging as it flows
The bodies of the dying;
And in the air are sounds like the thunder
   of war

Grand Roi, délivre-nous de plus cruels
   fléaux!
Le Nil a vu rougir ses eaux,
Et son urne sanglante
Vomit avec ses flots
La mort et l'épouvante!
L'écho répète au loin les accents de la
   guerre;

147

And rumblings underground now rock the very earth;
And locusts in a cloud that covers all the land
Are swarming on the fields: nothing green will remain;
And the wind from the south, through the night and the morning,
Is poisoned with the stench of the dead and the decaying!

Des foudres souterrains ont ébranlé la terre;
D'insectes destructeurs on voit les tourbillons
S'abattre sur nos champs, dévorer nos moissons,
Et le vent du désert dans sa course rapide
Exhale le poison de son souffle homicide.

PHARAOH
(*descending from his throne*)

Osiridis! Who can save us? The danger threatens all!

Que faire, que résoudre en ce commun effroi?

OSIRIDIS

Be revenged!

Punissez . . .

ANNA, MIRIAM

Let us go!

Pardonnez . . .

SINAIDA

You are a father and King!

Vous êtes père et Roi.

OSIRIDIS
(*to Pharaoh*)

Crush the pride in their hearts!

Etouffez leur fureur.

AMENOPHIS
(*to Anna, aside*)

But you know you are mine!

Tu connais mon ardeur.

MOSES
(*to Pharaoh*)

Do not harden your heart!

Abjure ton erreur.

SINAIDA

Oh, forgive them their pride!

Pardonnez leur erreur.

MOSES
(*to Pharaoh*)

O King, open your eyes while there is time to save you!
Let Egypt now give hommage to Jehovah, the true God!

Monarque, ouvre les yeux, il en est temps encore.
Peuple, rendez hommage au seul Dieu que j'adore.

OSIRIDIS

Foul blasphemer!

Quel blasphème!

SINAIDA

O my Lord . . . We are lost!

Il se peut . . . O douleur!

ANNA, MIRIAM, ELEAZOR

O my country! We are lost!

O patrie! O douleur!

OSIRIDIS, PHARAOH, EGYPTIANS

O Isis! Avenge us!
Osiris, avenge us we pray!

Vengeance, vengeance!
Isis, Osiris, vengez-nous!

SINAIDA, ANNA, MIRIAM, ELEAZOR, ISRAELITES

Mercy! Mercy! Oh mercy!
O Lord, O Lord, we pray to You!

Grace, grace, clémence!
Seigneur, Seigneur, secourez-nous!

O Sérapis!   Sérapis!

MOSES

O Jehovah!   Jéhovah!

OSIRIDIS, MOSES

You light of the whole world,   Dieu de la lumière,
All creation is in Your hand: Tu disposes des éléments:
Reveal now the power of Your anger, Signale ta juste colère,
Strike down then this } priest, he grows insaner,   Confonds } cet Hébreu téméraire
                      } Hebrew profaner,   } ce prêtre sanguinnaire,
Let him know Your judgement will fall.   Fais connaître ton jugement.

MOSES

In great Jehovah's name!   Au nom du Dieu vivant!

As Moses speaks these words, he stretches out his arms towards the altars of the false gods; at the same moment, the fires burning on the altars go out; the statue of Isis collapses, and the sacred rainbow appears, glorious in light, amid a cloud of gold and silver.

PHARAOH, AMENOPHIS, EGYPTIANS

See! The flame! Isis leaves us!   Qu'ai-je vu? Quel prestige?

OSIRIDIS

Egypt's Gods, roused to wrath,   Tous nos Dieux, irrités,
Show you plainly their holy will.   Manifestent leur volonté.

MOSES

Our Jehovah in wrath,   L'Eternel, irrité,
Shows you plainly *His* holy will!   Manifeste sa volonté.

Quartet.

ANNA, SINAIDA

I'm shaken with horror,   [17] Je tremble et soupire,
My hope gone forever,   Mon cœur se déchire;
The shouting and anger,   Funeste délire!
An insult to God!   Mortelle douleur!

AMENOPHIS

The shouting and anger,   Funeste délire!
My hope gone forever,   Mon cœur se déchire;
The whole world surrenders   Tout cède à l'empire
To Moses and God!   D'un lâche imposteur.

ELEAZOR

They're shaken with horror,   On tremble, on soupire,
Their hope's gone forever,   Leur cœur se déchire;
The whole world surrenders   Tout cède à l'empire
To Almighty God.   Du maître des cieux.

SINAIDA

Today despair   Oh jour de deuil
Darkens my heart!   Et de douleur.

ANNA

The shouting and anger,   Funeste délire,
An insult to God!   Mortelle douleur.

OPHIDIS, PHARAOH, EGYPTIANS

The shouting and anger,   Funeste délire!
Defying the Gods!   On brave nos Dieux.

The whole world surrenders
To Almighty God!

Tout cède à l'empire
Du maître des cieux.

AMENOPHIS

The whole world surrenders
To Moses and God!

Tout cède à l'empire
Du maître des cieux.

MOSES
(*to Pharaoh*)

You have sworn, now keep to your word!

Pharaon, remplis la promesse.

OSIRIDIS
(*to Pharaoh*)

Strike down the Hebrew slaves!

Frappe le peuple Hébreu.

EGYPTIANS

Pharaoh speak, time is pressing!

Hâte-toi! Le temps presse.

MOSES

In Great Jehovah's name...

Au nom du Dieu vivant...

OSIRIDIS

In Isis' name...

Au nom d'Isis...

Recitative.

PHARAOH

Have done!

Eh bien!
(*to Moses*)

I obey the decrees of both my Gods and
yours:

J'accomplis les décrets de mes Dieux, et du
tien:
(*to his guards*)

— Let the people of Israel go forth on their
journey,
But as prisoners in chains cast them out
from the city.
Not a slave shall remain within Memphis
today!

— Qu'on les charge de fers, et, dans cette
journée,
Des esclaves hébreux que la foule
enchaînée,
Soit conduite à l'instant hors des murs de
Memphis.

ELEAZOR

O Heaven!

O ciel!

AMENOPHIS

Stay, Anna stay!

Viens, Anaï...

ANNA
(*moving away*)

Ah, no, I cannot stay!

Jamais, Aménophis.

AMENOPHIS
(*to Moses, aside*)

You are to blame, you must dissuade her!

Tu m'en réponds... veille sur elle.

Ensemble.

MOSES
(*to Anna, Miriam, Eleazor*)

You have Jacob's blood in your veins,
Your resolve and your faith now falter!
You're afraid of chains and of death!
Faith and love shall burn ever brighter!
Hear the voice of God who is calling,
All shall follow in Moses' path.

De Jacob vous êtes les fils,
Votre ardeur, votre foi chancelle!
Vous craignez les fers, le trépas.
Redoublez d'amour et de zèle;
Du Seigneur la voix nous appelle,
De Moïse suivez les pas.

SINAIDA

God, sustain their resolve if it falter,	Dieu, soutiens leur ardeur qui chancelle,
You see their brave hearts facing death.	Toi qui vois leurs cœurs, leurs combats.

ANNA

God, sustain my resolve if it falter,	Dieu, soutiens mon ardeur qui chancelle,
You see our brave hearts facing death.	Toi qui vois mon cœur, mes combats:
Ah, I hear God's voice who is calling,	Ah, j'entends la voix qui m'appelle;
And I soon will follow the faithful,	Et bientôt, du peuple fidèle,
Through the desert that is their path.	Au désert je suivrai les pas.

MOSES, MIRIAM, ELEAZOR

God, sustain my resolve if it falter,	Dieu, soutiens mon ardeur qui chancelle,
As in chains we go to our death.	Sous les fers qui chargent nos bras.
Hear the voice of God who is calling,	Mais de Dieu la voix nous appelle,
He will fill our hearts with his courage	Il remplit nos cœurs de son zèle,
As we go in chains to our death.	Nous bravons les fers, le trépas.

AMENOPHIS, OPHIDIS, PHARAOH, OSIRIDIS, EGYPTIANS

Now destroy this rebellious people!	Détruisons une race rebelle,
Turn these slaves out in chains to their death!	Et livrons nos captifs au trepas.

AMENOPHIS

You intend to leave me, you cruel girl!	Quoi, tu veux me fuir, ô cruelle!
Yet to you I'm ever faithful,	Malgré toi, tendre et fidéle,
I shall follow your steps till death.	Je suivrai pour toujours tes pas.

MOSES, ISRAELITES

The Lord will bless our fetters,	Le ciel bénît ma chaîne,
We will cross the desert sand,	Allons dans les déserts,
And God, despite their hatred,	Et Dieu, malgré leur haine,
Will free us from our chains.	Saura briser nos fers.

PHARAOH, OSIRIDIS, EGYPTIANS

Go, drag them out in fetters!	Allez, marchez, qu'on les entraine
Across the desert sand.	Au loin dans les déserts.
The victims of our hatred,	Objet d'horreur, de haine,
And let them die in chains.	Qu'ils meurent dans les fers.

Ignazio Marini (left) who sang Moses in the first performances of the French version given in Italy, and Ranieri Remorini (right) who sang in the première of 'Mosè in Egitto' at the San Carlo, Naples in 1818 (Opera Rara)

Act Four

Sand-dunes, with a view of a very small part of the Red Sea shore.

Scene One. *Anna and Amenophis enter with Ophidis and some soldiers. Amenophis dismisses them with a sign and remains alone with Anna. / No. 13 Scene and Duet.* [18]

ANNA

Where are we going now? O my lord, I am afraid!	Où me conduisez-vous? Dissipez mon effroi.

AMENOPHIS

What should you fear now here with me,	Que peux-tu craindre près de moi,
Here with the man who adores you?	Près de l'amant qui t'adore?
I was born to command, yet I come as a beggar.	Je pourrais commander, et c'est moi qui t'implore;
I come here to beg for my love,	C'est moi qui ne veux t'obtenir
From the hands of the man whom I might well have punished!	Que les mains de celui que je devrais punir.

ANNA

What! Shall I see again both Moses and my mother?	Quoi! Je pourrais revoir et Moïse et ma mère . . .

AMENOPHIS

The very moment that on this spot	A l'instant même . . . en ce sejour:
They allow you to be my bride,	Qu'ils te rendent à mon amour;
I'll revoke the command of Pharaoh	Et j'enfreins l'ordre de mon père;
And I'll save from the wrath of unforgiving priests	Du courroux immortel des prêtres de Memphis
The Hebrews banished by my father.	Je sauve les Hébreux proscrits.
My love means more to me than my throne and its splendour!	Qu'importe à mon amour l'éclat qui m'environne!
To love you and call you mine, is now my one desire;	T'aimer, te posséder est mon unique loi;
And I vow on this day I shall renounce the throne	Dès ce jour je fais vœu de renoncer au trône,
If you are not there by my side!	Ou de n'y monter qu'avec toi!

No. 13 Duet.

ANNA

O beloved, life together	[19]	Jour funeste, loi cruelle!
From this cruel day is over.		Mon courage, hélas, chancelle . . .

AMENOPHIS

Anna mine, do not forsake me,	Anaî, sois-moi fidèle,
You will find new courage here.	Et partage mon ardeur.

ANNA

Then would you battle against a future	D'une victime infortunée
That was destined for me by Heaven?	Daignez plaindre la destinée!
God has called me, and this very day now	Dieu m'appelle, et cette journée
He will part us, for evermore.	Nous sépare et pour jamais.

AMENOPHIS

All your troubles now are over!	Plus de craintes, plus d'alarmes;
Dry your tears, beloved Anna,	Anaî, sèche tes larmes,
Do not refuse, do not refuse my love.	De ton amant accepte les bienfaits.

ANNA

God of might, O God of mercy,	Dieu puissant, Dieu de clémence,
Keep me steadfast in my duty,	Oh, ranime ma constance.

| Help me now and lend me courage, | Prête-moi ton assistance |
| Keep my faltering faith alive. | Et soutiens mon faible cœur. |

AMENOPHIS

Gods of innocence have mercy,	Dieux vengeurs de l'innocence,
Oh, look down on helpless beauty,	Prêtez-lui votre assistance,
Give her hope, renew her courage,	Ranimez son espérance,
Keep her faltering love alive.	Protégez ma vive ardeur.

The song of the Israelites is heard in the distance.

AMENOPHIS

| Do you hear those sounds of rejoicing? | Entends-tu ces chants d'allégresse? |

ANNA

| It is Moses! | C'est Moïse! |

AMENOPHIS

He believes that he has got his wish,	Il se croit au terme de ses vœux;
But I will show him! Though he refuse my request,	Il va m'entendre: puisse un refus orgueilleux
He cannot spoil this happy day:	Ne pas changer ce jour heureux
For us today there'll be no parting!	En jour de deuil et de tristesse!

Scene Two. *The same, Miriam, Moses, Eleazor, the Israelites. Amenophis and Anna withdraw to the side but remain in view.*

MOSES

My children, this great day will end all your despair,	Ce grand jour, mes enfants, termine vos malheurs.
For I will lead you out of danger,	Sous la conduite de Moïse,
And soon the promised land will lie there before you!	Bientôt vous entrerez dans la terre promise.

MIRIAM

I alone will follow you in tears,	Seule j'y verserai des pleurs,
For she, my dear daughter Anna,	Anaî, ma fille chérie,
Could not be parted from her lover,	Victime d'un amour impie,
And has stayed there in Memphis, instead of joining us.	Hors des murs de Memphis n'a point suivi nos pas.

MOSES

| God will look after Anna. | Dieu veillera sur elle. |

ANNA
(running to Miriam and throwing herself into her arms)

| She is here in your arms! | Elle est entre vos bras! |

MIRIAM

| My daughter, oh, joy beyond belief, | Ma fille! O joie inattendue! |
| She is mine once again! | Anaï m'est rendue. |

MOSES

| Oh, praise be to the Lord. | Béni soit le Seigneur! |

ANNA
(revealing Amenophis)

| See the man who has set me free. | Vous voyez mon libérateur. |

MOSES

| It is the Prince! | Aménophis! |

Now listen, time is pressing;
I have come here myself to explain what has passed.
You see my love for Anna and how deep it is:
Once in my power, the object of my love
Could be easily forced to remain at my side,
But I wanted to receive her from you.
I have come here to pledge in the presence of Miriam,
My betrothal to Anna!

Ecoute: le temps presse.
Et je viens avec toi m'expliquer sans détour:
Tu vois pour Anaï jusqu'où va mon amour;
Je possédais l'objet de ma tendresse;
Je pouvais la forcer à vivre sous ma loi;
J'ai voulu la tenir de toi.
J'ai voulu consacrer sous les yeux de sa mère
Les serments d'un hymen.

MOSES

May your father reprove you!
Anna, now you must choose at this hour, in this place,
Either Sinaïda or your mother,
Our promised land, or life in Memphis.
Choose between your lover and your God!
With a word I could put you to shame;
You alone must decide.

Que réprouve ton père.
Anaï doit choisir en ce jour, en ce lieu,
Entre Sinaïde et Marie,
Entre Memphis et sa patrie,
Entre son amant et son Dieu.
D'un mot je pourrais te confondre,
Anaî seule doit répondre.

No. 14 Air.

ANNA

What a dreadful choice confronts me!
Ah! Whatever shall I say?
I am torn in two already,
What a choice, what can I say!
At my feet a yawning chasm,
And my hope turned to despair.
O God help me choose between them;
Either duty or my love.

Quelle horrible destinée!
Ciel! Que vais-je devenir?
Suis-je assez infortunée!
Quel torment, quel avenir!
[20] Sous mes pas je vois l'abîme,
Tout espoir fuit sans retour!
Grand Dieu! Sauve la victime
Du devoir et de l'amour.

MOSES
(*severely*)

Anna come!

Anaï . . .

AMENOPHIS
(*to Moses*)

Dare you betray me!

Tremble, perfide!

MIRIAM, ELEAZOR

God sustain her in her need!

Dieu clément, sois son appui!

MOSES
(*to Anna*)

Why do you wait? Answer, come choose now!
Is it God, or is it he?

Qu'attends-tu? Parle, décide!
Entre Dieu, ta mère, et lui.

ANNA

Help me, Lord, to find the answer,
Torn between my faith and love.

Dieu! Protège la victime
Du devoir et de l'amour.

MOSES, ELEAZOR, MIRIAM, ISRAELITES

Help her, Lord, help her decide now,
Help her leave without delay!
— Anna, choose —
— Be faithful my daughter —
To the holy law of the Lord!
Think of your faith, and of your country,
Fear the righteous anger of God.

Sous ses pas s'ouvre un abîme;
Qu'elle quitte ce séjour.
— Anaï —, sois fidèle —
— Ma fille chérie, sois fidèle —
Aux lois du Seigneur.
Songe au devoir, á ta patrie,
Crains de Dieu la juste fureur.

ANNA
(inspired)

It is done, for Heaven directs me,	C'en est fait! Le ciel m'inspire,
I shall now obey God's decree!	[21] J'obéis aux lois du Seigneur.

MOSES, ELEAZOR, MIRIAM, ISRAELITES

She obeys Jehovah, who guides her;	Elle cède au Dieu qui l'inspire;
Her duty has won over love.	Elle a triomphé de son cœur!

AMENOPHIS
(aside)

Anna turns down my royal favour;	Anaï brave mon empire,
Then force shall make them all obey.	Que tout succombe à mon fureur!

ANNA

O Lord, I pray to You for mercy,	Grand Dieu, j'implore ta clémence!
And for the prince I pray as well;	J'ose pour lui t'offrir mes vœux:
That he may do as You direct him	Qu'il cède enfin à ta puissance,
Quenching the flame of burning love.	Change son cœur, éteins ses feux.
How I loved! But now I renounce him,	Je l'aimais! . . . Je fuis sa presence;
Deign then, O Lord, to grant my prayer.	Daigne, ô grand Dieu, combler mes vœux.

AMENOPHIS
(aside)

I can no longer restrain my anger,	Mon cœur aspire á la vengeance,
The Gods shall help me to have my way.	O Dieu, daigne combler mes vœux.

MOSES, ELEAZOR, MIRIAM, ISRAELITES

The moment comes of our deliverance,	L'instant de notre délivrance
Soon the day of freedom will shine.	Va bientôt briller à nos yeux.
O day of glory, day we hope for,	O jour de gloire et d'espérance!
Oh, praise and thank the Lord of Heaven.	Hommage, honneur au Roi des cieux!

MOSES
(to Amenophis)

Anna has given her answer.	Vous entendez sa réponse.

AMENOPHIS

Your death has been decreed	C'est votre arrêt de mort
In the words she has spoken!	Que sa bouche prononce:
The fate of all Israel is sealed.	Hébreux, apprenez votre sort,
At the head of a mighty army	Contre vous Pharaon s'avance
The Pharaoh swiftly marches upon you.	Cerné par une armée immense.
To a people who are in chains	De ton peuple chargé de fers
Even courage is useless,	Le courage inutile
And you have now no refuge	N'a désormais d'asile
But the bottomless sea!	Que le goufre des mers.

ISRAELITES

Mighty Pharaoh is marching on us!	Contre nous Pharaon s'avance!

MOSES

We defy all his host,	Nous bravons les pervers;
Our God yet will defend us!	Dieu prend notre defense.

AMENOPHIS
(furiously)

You Jews! You are going to die!	Hébreux, périssez tous!
You will see me again, but armed to take my vengeance!	Vous allez me revoir armé par la vengeance,
[Hebrews, remember,	Hébreux, souvenez-vous,
When my anger avenges this injury,	Alors que ma fureur vengera mon injure,
That a woman forsworn	Qu'une femme parjure
Directed the blows.]	A dirigé mes coups.

Exit.

155

Scene Three. *The same, without Amenophis.*

MOSES

My sons! Upon this earth there is none you need fear!	Hébreux! Ne craignez rien des puissants de la terre;
Come, follow your friend and your shepherd,	Suivez votre ami, votre père,
Having no fear but the fear of the Lord.	Et de Dieu seul redoutez le courroux.

The scene changes to the shores of the Red Sea. March.

Now in this awful moment	Dans ce moment terrible,
An invisible power	Une force invincible
Has raised me above mortal man.	M'élève au-dessus d'un mortel.

ANNA, MIRIAM, ELEAZOR

And in lowly submission	Et d'une âme soumise,
Humbly we call on Moses!	Nous invoquons Moïse.

MOSES

And Moses now calls upon the Lord.	Moïse invoque l'Eternel.

No. 15 Prayer

Look down on us from Heaven,	[22]	Des cieux où tu résides,
Lord God, and guide your children,		Grand Dieu, toi qui nous guides,
Give ear to them and lead them		Comble les vœux timides
That trust in You alone.		D'un peuple obéissant.

ISRAELITES

Give ear to them and lead them,	Comble les vœux timides
Oh, hear Your people groan, Lord God.	D'un peuple gémissant.

ELEAZOR

When storms at last are over,	Aprè un long orage,
Then guide us into harbour;	Conduis-nous au rivage,
From shipwreck and disaster	Et sauve du naufrage
Lead faithful Israel home.	Tes fidèles Hébreux.

ISRAELITES

Then guide us into harbour,	Conduis-nous au rivage,
That land for which we long, Lord God.	Objet de tous nos vœux.

MIRIAM

O You, revered of all men	O toi que tout révère,
On earth and in the Heavens,	Aux cieux et sur la terre,
Oh, hear my humble prayer then,	Ecoute ma prière,
And save us 'ere we die!	Protège tes enfants!

ISRAELITES

O You, revered of all men,	O toi que tout révère,
Oh, hear us when we cry, Lord God.	Ecoute nos accents, Grand Dieu.

ALL

Look down on us from Heaven	Des cieux où tu résides,
Lord God, and guide Your children,	Grand Dieu, toi qui nous guides,
Give ear to them and bring them	De tes enfants timides,
An end to all their pain.	Termine les revers,
O God, behold our chains.	Grand Dieu, tu vois nos fers.

At the last reprise of those verses, the Israelites' chains fall from them. / No. 16 Finale. Scene and Storm.

ELEAZOR

That sound!	Quel bruit!

MIRIAM

Oh heaven!	O ciel!

ANNA

Look there upon the mountain,	Du haut de la montagne,
Where an army prepares to over-run the plain!	D'innombrables soldats inondent la campagne.

MIRIAM

They are advancing!	Ils s'avancent.

ANNA

With all their power...	Que d'ennemis!

ELEAZOR

Death is in their ranks!	La mort les accompagne.

ISRAELITES
(to Moses)

Where, oh where, is the help you promised we should have?	Où sont-ils ces secours que tu nous as promis?

ELEAZOR

How can we fight them?	Comment combattre?

MIRIAM

Or escape?	Où fuir?

MOSES

Trust yourselves to the sea!	Au sein des flots soumis.
Israel, do you forget that it is God who guides me,	Hébreux, oubliez-vous que le Seigneur me guide,
And He will punish them that doubt!	Et qu'il punit les fils ingrats?
Go forth through the midst of the waters,	Marchez sur la plaine liquide,
That He will make firm as the land!	Que Dieu raffermit sous mes pas!

Moses advances into the waves, and the Israelites follow him.

ISRAELITES
(in the sea)

Amazing! The waves are retreating!	Prodige! La vague timide
They rise in a wall on either hand!	S'élance et ne nous couvre pas.
We are walking through where the sea was —	Nous marchons, la plaine liquide
The sea bed is firm as the land!	Partout s'affermit sous nos pas!

Scene Four. *Pharaoh, Amenophis, the Egyptian army.*

PHARAOH

Oh, where have they gone? They surely must have drowned	Que sont-ils devenus? Au sein des mers profondes
In such an angry sea.	Ont-ils trouvé la mort?

AMENOPHIS

No, look across the water	Non, à travers les ondes
Where the waves have left them a path!	Voyez-les s'ouvrir un chemin!
Hurry on! We must catch them, and quickly;	Hâtons-nous et volons sur leur trace,
With the edge of the sword we shall destroy	Et le glaive à la main exterminons une
that wicked tribe of Israel!	coupable race!

Pharaoh and Amenophis advance into the sea; all the Egyptians follow them; a terrible storm blows up; Pharaoh and his men are drowned. During the storm some fragments of verse are heard.

After the storm, the clouds disperse, the heavens calm down, the air clears and the Israelites are seen on a flowery shore, where they sing the following: / No. 17 Canticle 'The Song of Miriam'.

MIRIAM

The Lord is my strength and my song.	Chantons, bénissons le Seigneur!

157

The Lord is my strength and my song!	Chantons, bénissons le Seigneur!
Now is He become our salvation,	Nous avons souffert pour sa gloire;
He has triumphed gloriously over them,	Il nous a donné la victoire;
For He has cast into the sea	Il frappe le persécuteur,
All Pharaoh's chariots and hosts.	Il frappe le persécuteur,
He drowned their army like a stone.	Il frappe le persécuteur.
The Lord is my strength and my song!	Chantons, bénissons le Seigneur!

Towards the end of the canticle a heavenly light shines more and more brightly at the back of the stage, and there is a vision of Jehovah. The Israelites prostrate themselves. The curtain falls.

Bibliography

The most enthusiastic and stimulating account of Rossini's life is Stendhal's (trans. Richard Coe, London, 1970) but there are two other (comparatively) recent biographies by Weinstock (Oxford, 1968) and Francis Toye, *Rossini: A study in tragi-comedy* (London, 1955). Earlier than these two is the amusingly anecdotal *Rossini and Some Forgotten Nightingales* by G.H. Johnstone (Lord Derwent).

There is a wide-ranging study of Rossini's work, as yet untranslated from the Italian, by G. Radiciotti: *G. Rossini, Vita documentata, opera ed influenza sul arte* (3 vols. Tivoli, 1927-29).

The New Grove *Masters of Italian Opera* (London, 1983) has an excellent chapter on Rossini by Philip Gossett and in Volume 1 of Julian Budden's *The Operas of Verdi*, he writes illuminatingly on 19th-century opera and the legacy of Rossini in the opening chapter, 'Verdi and the world of the primo ottocento'. The convoluted workings of the opera industry in Rossini's time are described in *The Opera Industry in Italy from Cimarosa to Verdi: The Role of the Impresario*, by John Rosselli (Cambridge, 1984). Performance style of the time is described in *The Castrati in Opera* by Angus Heriot, (London, 1975).

The full score of the edition of *Il Barbiere di Siviglia* made by Alberto Zedda was published by Ricordi and Co. in 1969, and a facsimile edition of Rossini's original manuscript for *Mosè in Egitto*, edited and with an introduction by Philip Gossett, is published by Garland (1979). An exhaustive and fascinating comparison of the three versions — *Mosè in Egitto, Moïse et Pharaon* and *Mosè* — along with the Italian and French texts, by Paolo Isotta, is published (in Italian) by Unione Tipografico-Editrice Torinese (1974).

The Complete Figaro Plays by Beaumarchais (trans. John Wood), are published by Penguin Classics.

For an extensive bibliography, the reader is referred to the French magazine *L'Avant scène*, issue No. 37, *Le barbier de Seville*.

Selective Discography by *Cathy Peterson*   The Barber of Seville

Conductor	A. Galliera	E. Leinsdorf	V. Gui	S. Varviso	C. Abbado
Orchestra/Opera House	Philharmonia O.	Met. Opera O.	RPO	Rossini di Napoli	LSO
Date	1957	1958	1962	1964	1972
Almaviva	L. Alva	C. Valletti	L. Alva	U. Benelli	L. Alva
Rosina	M. Callas	R. Peters	V. de los Angeles	T. Berganza	T. Berganza
Figaro	T. Gobbi	R. Merrill	S. Bruscantini	M. Ausensi	H. Prey
Basilio	N. Zaccaria	G. Tozzi	C. Cava	N. Ghiaurov	P. Montarsolo
Bartolo	F. Ollendorf	F. Corena	I. Wallace	F. Corena	E. Daro
UK Disc Number	SLS 853	–	SLS 5165	SET 285/7	2720 053
UK Tape Number	TCC SLS 853	–	TC SLS 5165	–	3371 003
US Disc Number	S-3559	LSC 6143	–	–	2709 041
US Tape Number	4X3X-3559	–	–	–	–

On a recording of the opera dating from 1929 (Historical Archives EMI 3C/153–18403/05) Mercedes Capsir performs Variations composed by her to her own verses, 'Un verde praticel', exploiting a theme from Mozart's variations for pianoforte K299a entitled 'Je suis Lindor', which had in turn been taken from an arietta composed by Antoin Lauren Baudron for Beaumarchais' play *Le Barber de Seville*. / *Marco Spada*

The Barber of Seville

Conductor	J. Levine	R. Chailly	N. Marriner
Orchestra/ Opera House Date	LSO	La Scala	St Martin's Academy
Almaviva	N. Gedda	P. Barbacini	R. Araiza
Rosina	B. Sills	M. Horne	A. Baltsa
Figaro	S. Milnes	L. Nucci	T. Allen
Basilio	R. Raimondi	S. Ramey	R. Lloyd
Bartolo	R. Capecchi	E. Dara	D. Trimarchi
UK Disc Number	—	D3 37862	6769 100
UK Tape Number	—	403 37862	7654 100
UK CD Number	—	—	411 058-2
US Disc Number	SX 3761	13M 37862	6769 100
US Tape Number	4X3X 3761	403 37862	7654 100

Moses

Version	1818 — Naples	1827 — Paris
Conductor	*C. Scimone*	*L. Gardelli*
Orchestra/ Opera House	**Philharmonia**	**Hungarian State Opera**
Date	*1982*	*1982*
Mosè/Mosè	R. Raimondi	J. Gregor
Aronne/Elisero	S. Fisichella	A. Molnár
Faraone/Faraone	S. Nimsgern	S.S. Nagy
Osiride/Amenofi	E. Palacio	J.B. Nagy
Mambre/Aufide	K. Lewis	A. Fülop
Amenosi/Maria	S. Browne	E. Póka
Elcia/Anaïde	J. Anderson	M. Kalmár
Amaltea/Sinaïde	Z. Gal	J. Hamari
UK Disc Number	6769 081	SLPX 12290/2
UK Tape Number	7654 081	MK 12290/2
US Disc Number	6769 081	SLPX 12290/2
US Tape Number	7654 081	MK 12290/2